Mark Montano

Vision Box

idea book

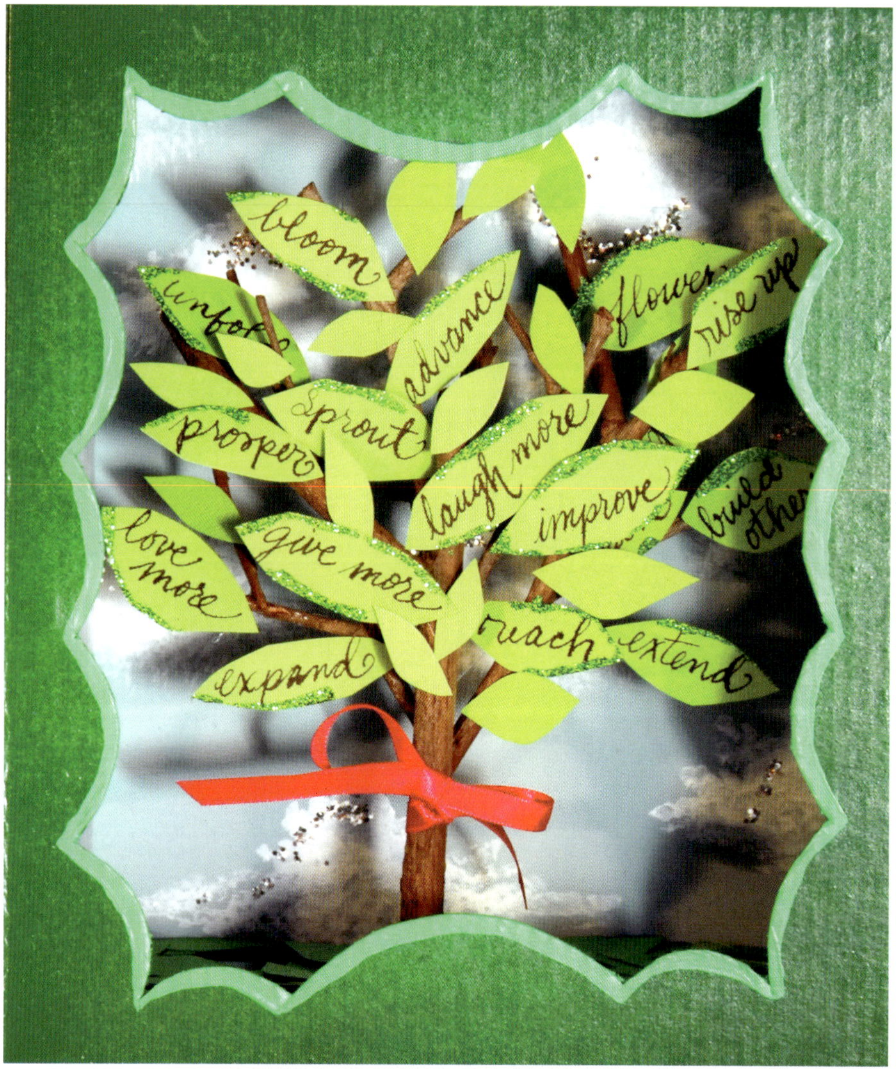
bloom
advance
flower
rise up
sprout
prosper
laugh more
improve
love more
give more
reach
extend
expand

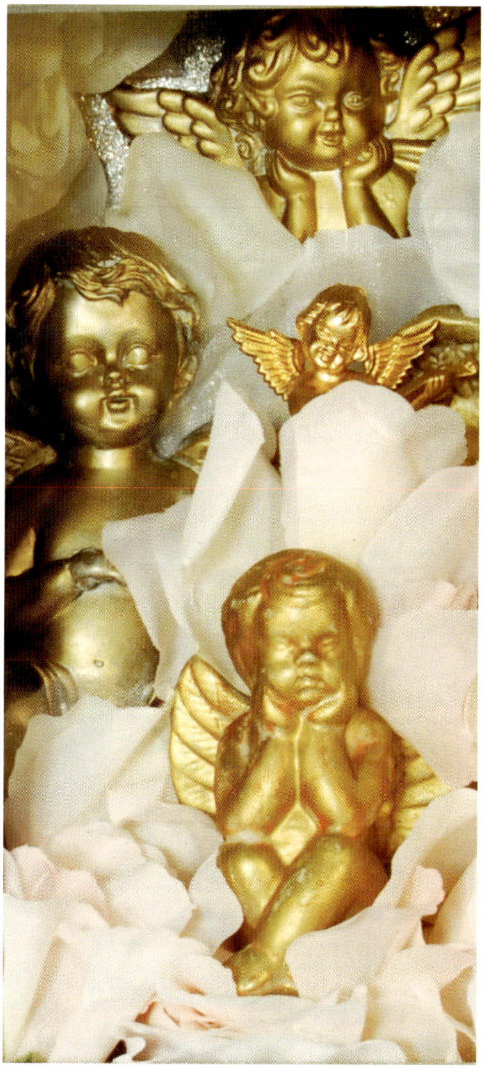

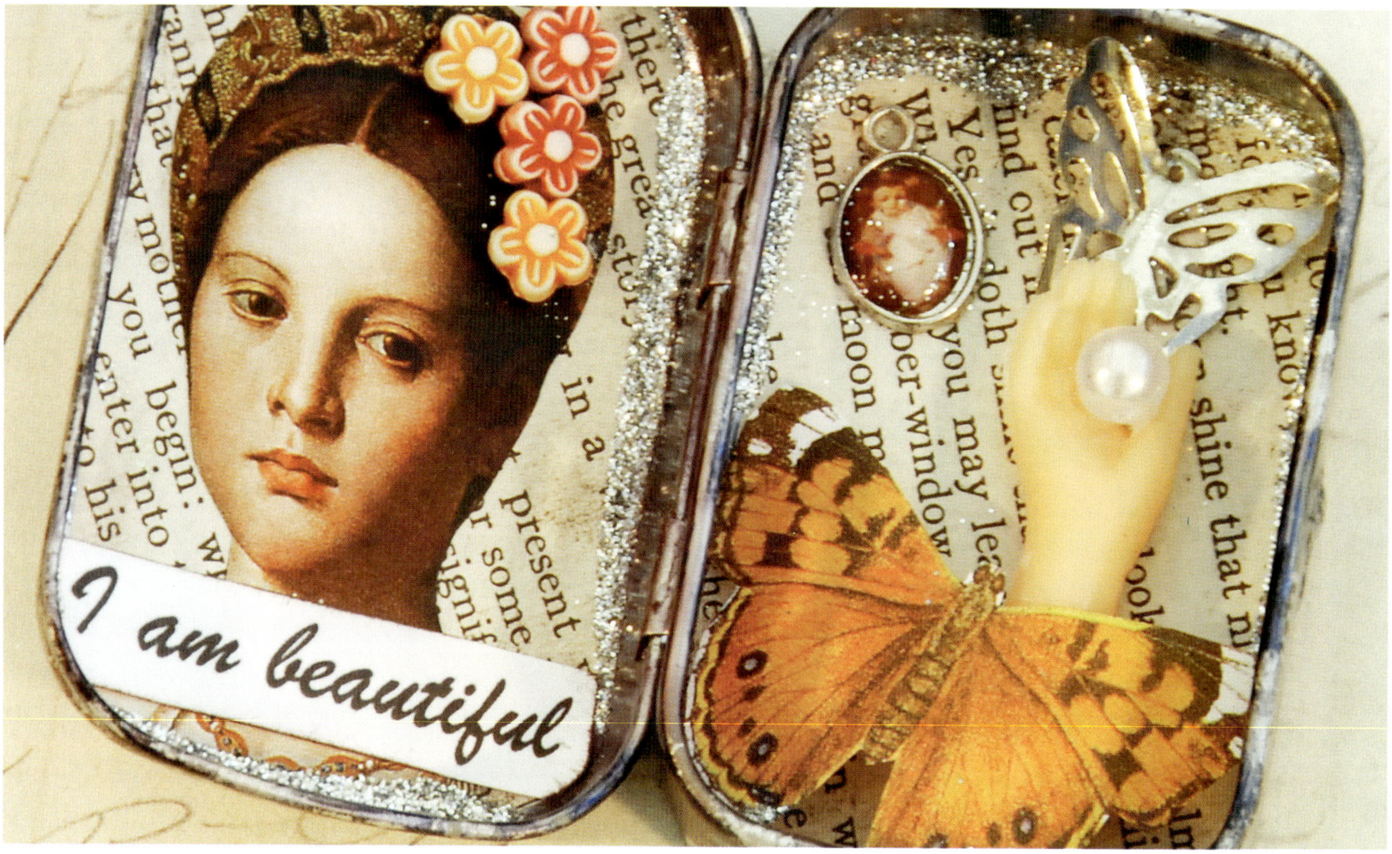
I am beautiful

Mark Montano

Vision Box idea book

Mixed Media Projects for
Crafting the Life of Your Dreams

Design Originals

Photography by Auxy Espinoza.

ISBN 978-1-57421-407-9

Publisher's Cataloging-in-Publication Data

Montano, Mark.
Vision box idea book : mixed media projects for crafting the life of your dreams / Mark Montano.
p. cm.
ISBN: 978-1-57421-407-9
1. Mixed media (Art). 2. Handicraft. I. Title.
TT857 .M66 2012
702.8—dc22

To learn more about the other great books from Design Originals/Fox Chapel Publishing, or to find a retailer near you, call toll-free 800-457-9112 or visit us at *www.FoxChapelPublishing.com.*

Note to Authors: We are always looking for talented authors to write new books in our area of crafts. Please send a brief letterdescribing your idea to Acquisition Editor, 1970 Broad Street, East Petersburg, PA 17520.

Printed in Indonesia
First Printing

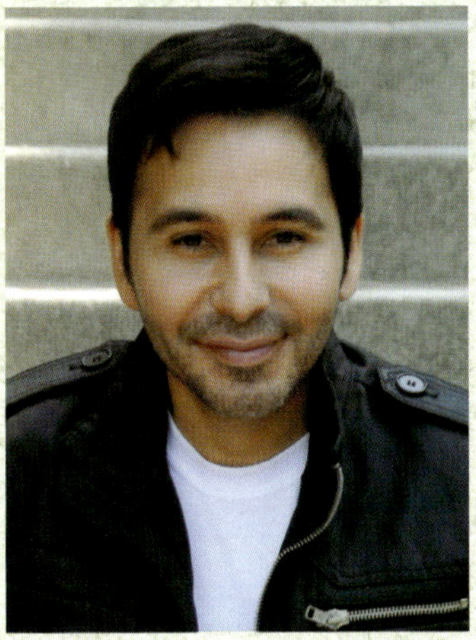

About the Author

Mark Montano is a creative force who has been using his ingenuity to inspire, motivate, and empower people around the world through his work as a designer, author, and television host. Armed with a glue gun and the uncanny ability to transform ordinary objects into imaginative statements about life and love, Montano encourages others to take delight in self-expression through crafting and creativity.

Montano began to explore the world of fashion when he was a teenager in La Junta, Colorado, a journey that eventually led him to New York City, where he earned a master's degree in costume history from the Fashion Institute of Technology and had the opportunity to participate in an internship at Oscar de la Renta. Inspired by New York's vitality and colorful atmosphere, Montano went on to design his own clothing line, establish a boutique in the East Village, and become the youngest inductee into the Council of Fashion Designers of America.

Montano's ideas eventually led him to *CosmoGirl!* Magazine, where he became the author of a monthly room makeover column titled "Cool Room." Beyond *CosmoGirl!*, Montano also produced the column "Make Your Mark," which appeared in newspapers throughout the United States. Montano later combined several of his "Cool Room" columns, resulting in the book *Super Suite*. He has gone on to author such works as *The Big-Ass Book of Crafts*, *Dollar Store Décor*, and *Pulp Fiction*.

Appreciation for Montano's fun and exhilarating style and philosophy grew, and he was offered a role as a designer on TLC's *While You Were Out*. Later Montano became the host of *10 Years Younger* on the same network. Montano also appeared on Style Network's *My Celebrity Home*, We TV's *She's Moving In*, Fox's *My Home 2.0*, and *The Tony Danza Show*.

Montano is based out of Los Angeles and New York, where he continues to write, create, and inspire. Learn more by visiting *www.markmontano.com*.

Table of Contents

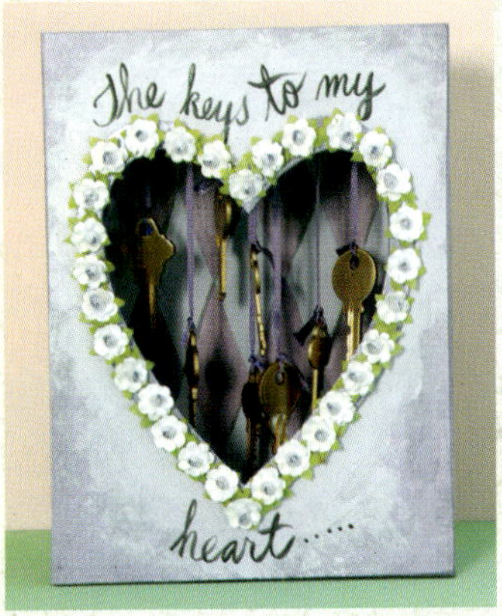
The keys to my
heart.....

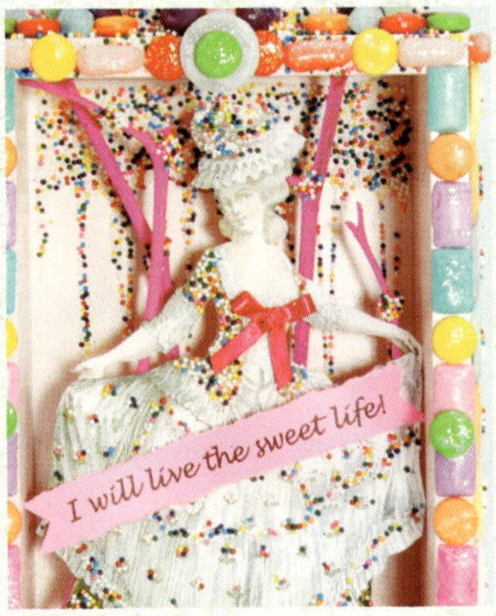
I will live the sweet life!

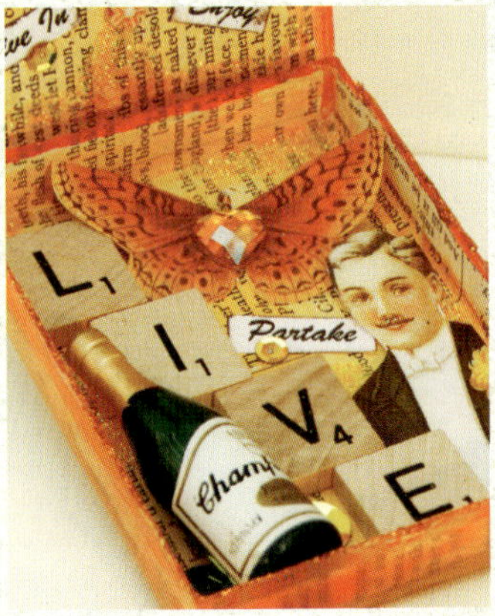
Partake

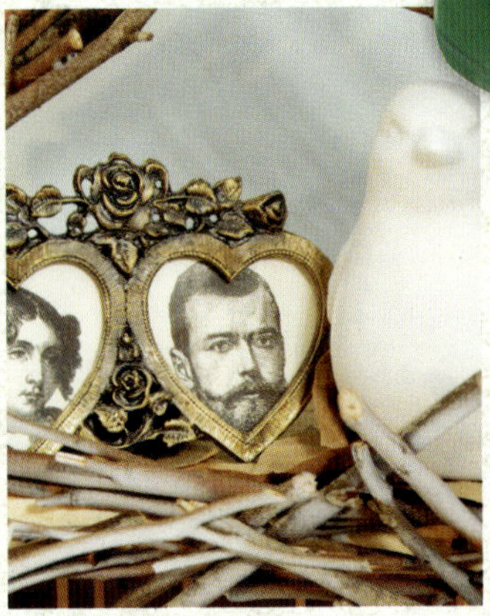

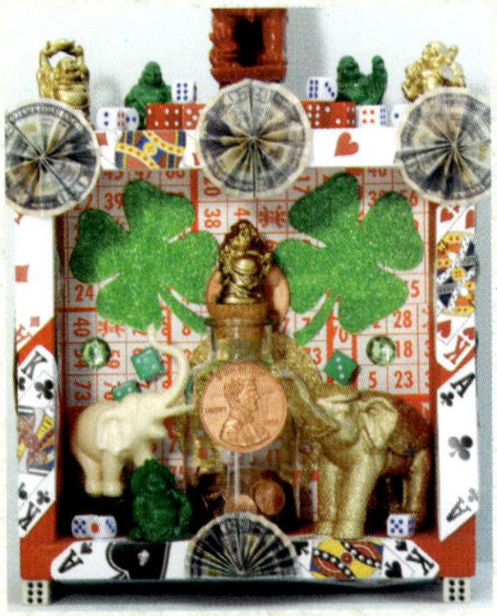

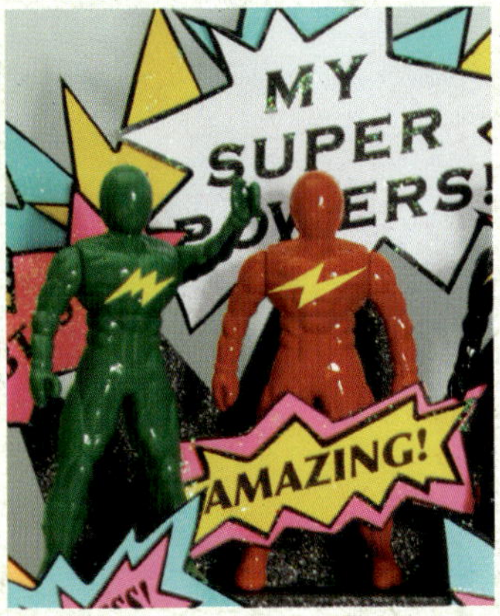
MY
SUPER
AMAZING!

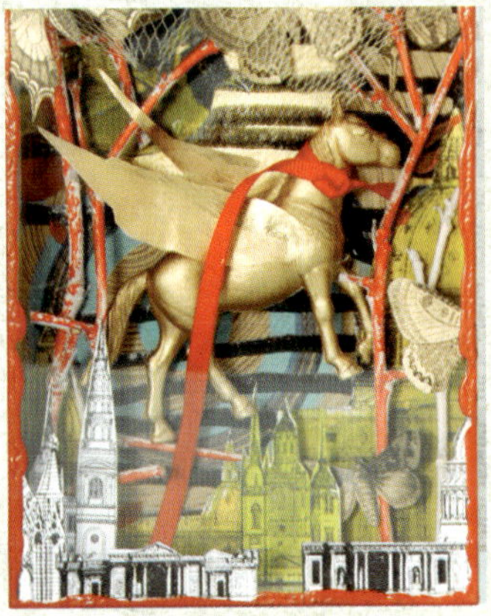

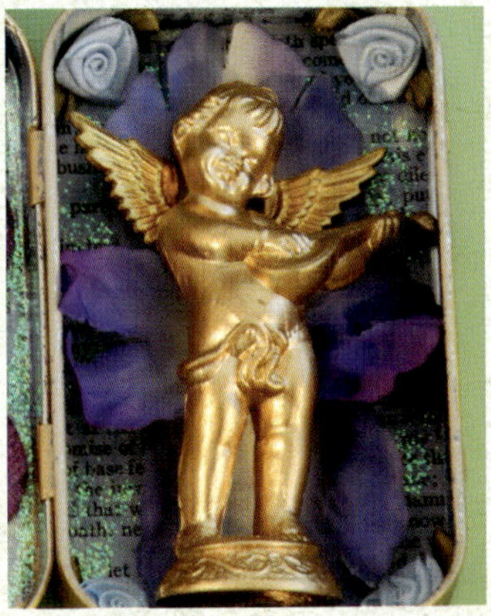

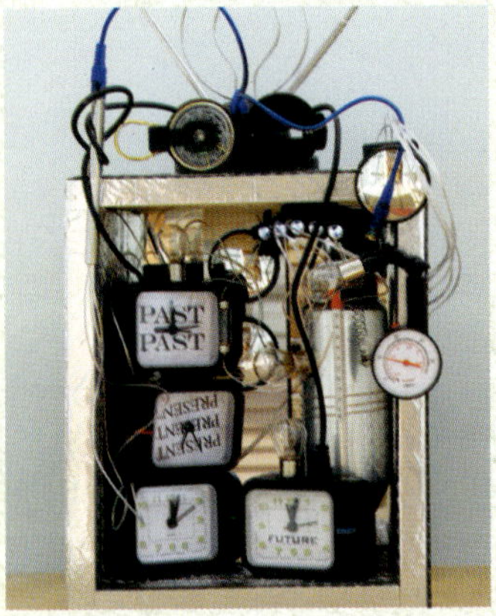

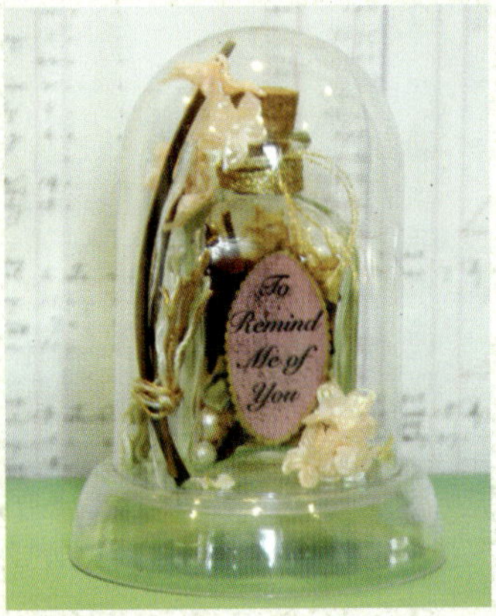
To Remind Me of You

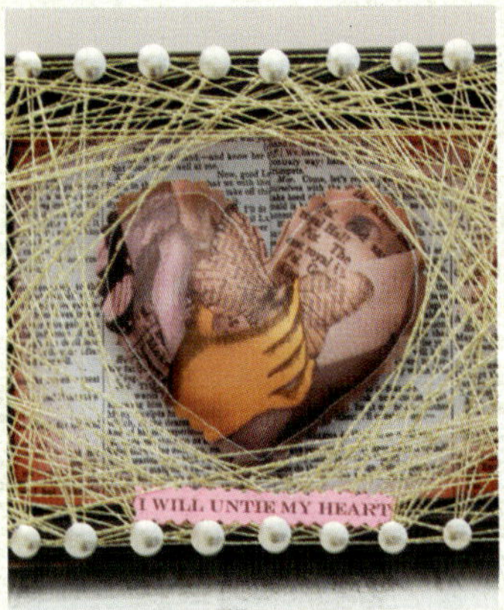
I WILL UNTIE MY HEART

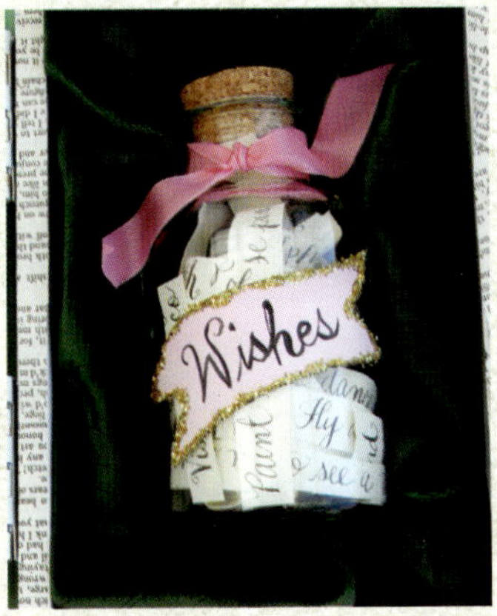
Wishes

What Mark's Readers are Saying

Mark inspires me to be a better person and to express myself through art and being creative. It's my honor to know this wonderful, creative, and inspiring person. He's made my life richer and more colorful just by being my friend.

—SHEILA JEAUX GOLDSBERRY

Mark shows you how to turn objects others overlook into pieces of wonder and art that profess love, dreams, self-realization, and adventure. Creating a Vision Box is a labor of love; to give one is a blessing.

—ROSALIE M. D'ANGELO

The most perfect craft is one made out of love (and a glue gun), or as Mark says, "Perfectly imperfect." Vision Box Idea Book is another awesome book by an awesome and crafty man. Be inspired or inspire others with Vision Box gifts, or dare to expand your horizons by creating a Vision Box design on your own. Your friends and family will love them.

—DAVE CAPPER

All of Mark's ideas make you think about using what you already have lying around to create in new, innovating, and exciting ways. Vision Box Idea Book is truly a vision for any crafter!

—AMY MITCHELL TEETS

What a fantastic way to create a keepsake worth keeping! Inspiration, imagination and a little sass—and all Mark!

—KELLI BARKEMA

No one can do a crafting book like Mark Montano. Mark shares his ideas with all of us in a format that any craft novice can understand! Bravo to you, Mark, for bringing crafting back to a level we can all enjoy and afford!

—GENELLE VOSS

MARK MONTANO HAS TO BE THE MOST STIMULATING AND INSPIRING CRAFT AUTHOR AROUND. HE TAKES EVERYDAY, ORDINARY OBJECTS AND CREATIVELY TURNS THEM INTO ART. AFTER READING THIS, YOU'LL NEVER WANT TO THROW ANYTHING AWAY, BECAUSE YOU WILL SEE "ORDINARY" IN A WHOLE DIFFERENT LIGHT.

—ERICA KELINSKE

MARK MONTANO IS ONE OF THE MOST INNOVATIVE AND EXCITING CRAFT DESIGNERS IN THE WORLD TODAY. HIS ENTHUSIASM FOR CREATIVITY AND HIS ENCOURAGING, HUMOROUS STYLE MAKE HIS BOOKS MUST-READS FOR ANYONE WHO ASPIRES TO GET CRAFTY. HIS DESIGNS ARE UNEXPECTED AND FUN, AND HE USES EVERYDAY MATERIALS AND DOWN-TO-EARTH TECHNIQUES THAT MAKE CRAFT SUCCESS ACHIEVABLE FOR EVERYONE.

—HEATHER MANN

In Vision Box Idea Book, Mark touches the lives of his readers by offering personal stories about each project, inviting readers to share his experiences while building their own meaningful representations of realities, goals, and dreams. By making art and DIY accessible to everyone through the use of available materials and tools, he encourages artists, crafters, designers, do-it-yourselfers, and dabblers to enrich their own lives through artistic expression.

—SHANNON GANSHORN

Mark has once again made a book that is whimsical and creative. I love his easy-to-follow instructions and little personal tips and tricks.

—AMY HARPER

What an awesome book! With each page, the reader can see the time and effort Mark put into each project and feel the love and passion he has for what he does. Thanks, Mark, for inspiring me with your talent!

—VICKIE WILLIAMS

Thanks for sharing this book of wonderful ideas, crafts, and memories. You inspire me to be more creative and have helped me realize we can all have luxury for less.

—JALESA MORA-SCOTT

Mark Montano has rummaged through our emotional junk drawers and creatively fashioned our wishes, hopes, dreams, and fears into a visual feast. He validates our collections and shows how to fashion them into exciting works of art that are easy to make, colorful, and meaningful.

—JAN CANYON

MARK MONTANO, THE ROCK STAR OF THE CRAFTY WORLD, HAS DONE IT AGAIN. HE'S MADE US AVERAGE CRAFTERS FEEL LIKE SMOKIN' HOT CREATIVE GENIUSES! IN VISION BOX IDEA BOOK, MARK GENEROUSLY OPENS A PORTAL TO HIS AUDIENCE SO THEY MAY PARTICIPATE IN THE MANIFESTATION OF THEIR OWN VISIONS. FROM DEEP AND MEANINGFUL TO FUN AND WHIMSICAL, VISION BOX IDEA BOOK PUTS THE POWER OF MAKER MAGIC INTO OUR HANDS.

—CHRISSY KRAIS

Mark's creativity, passion, heart, and vision pour out into every project he does. This book is no exception. The projects featured demonstrate a fun and unique way to help yourself through tough times or remind yourself of what is important in life. Take Mark's great ideas and run with them. You will love what you discover!

—EMILY GALL

Mark Montano is an amazingly creative man and that is apparent in this book. Such fun creative ideas! Just when you think he couldn't come up with more he does. Pure creative genius!

—KIMBERLY FUSCO

Mark's talent for crafting is inspiring, but his generosity in sharing years of experience, wisdom, and resources is rare. It's this gift that truly sets him apart—a true visionary who creates to express who he is, inject beauty into this world, and encourage others to be their very best.

—COURTNEY BARTON

The only thing better than a Mark Montano book is the great fun you'll have while creating the designs inside of it. Mark is an artist and author who will take care of you from the start with great instructions and inspiration while never leaving your side on the creative adventure. You'll find yourself using this book as a reference many, many times over.

—MARIA NERIUS

Visions Box Idea Book isn't just another beautiful craft book showcasing the work of a talented artist. Mark has a gift for generously, sharing real and attainable techniques that make me want to dive right in and create my very own, unique Vision Box.

—ANGELA DANIELS

Introduction

What is a Vision Box?

That's a good question!

A Vision Box is a 3-D mixed media art project that helps you focus on something important to you—very much like a Focus Board.

I'll say it before you do: some look like shrines, but you'll notice they're also very different from the beautiful religious shrines we often see. These help you focus on all kinds of things from finding love to living a sweeter life. Whatever you put into them I'm hoping you get back. My mom told me once that in order for you to get to your destination, you first have to figure out where you're going. The process of making a Vision Box is just like figuring out where you're going and what you want. You can put into it whatever you want. All of your hopes, desires, plans, lucky coins, charms, photos, whatever! I hope you enjoy making these as much as I did making them for you.

If I've said it once I've said it a thousand times: PERFECTION IS OVERRATED! I strive to be perfectly imperfect. I don't want anything I make to look like it came off of a production line in a factory. I want it to look like I made it! When you're making a Vision Box, make it your own, change the colors, the objects, change everything! It's all up to you and your own journey.

Remember, I'm always here to help at *MarkMontanoNYC@aol.com*.

Mark

Box Basics

BASIC VISION BOX #1

Basic Vision Box #1 is built with ⅜" (10mm)-thick basic square floorboard molding. Most hardware stores and home centers sell it and many will cut it for you. It comes in 8′ (244cm) lengths so you can make three boxes out of one strip.

For each box, you will have two pieces cut 8" (203mm) in length and two pieces cut 6" (152mm) in length.

You can make two different size options when gluing these four pieces together. The first size option is made by sandwiching the 8" (203mm) pieces between the 6" (152mm) pieces, which makes it exactly 6" (152mm) wide and 8¾" (222mm) tall. The second size option is made by sandwiching the 6" (152mm) pieces in between the 8" pieces, which makes it exactly 8" (203mm) tall and 6¾" (171mm) wide.

ALSO: If you are getting an entire length of 8′ (244cm) molding cut to make Vision Boxes, you could make them different sizes by using four 8" (203mm) pieces together and four 6" (152mm) pieces together. It really depends on the size of Vision Box you want to make.

Have fun and experiment!

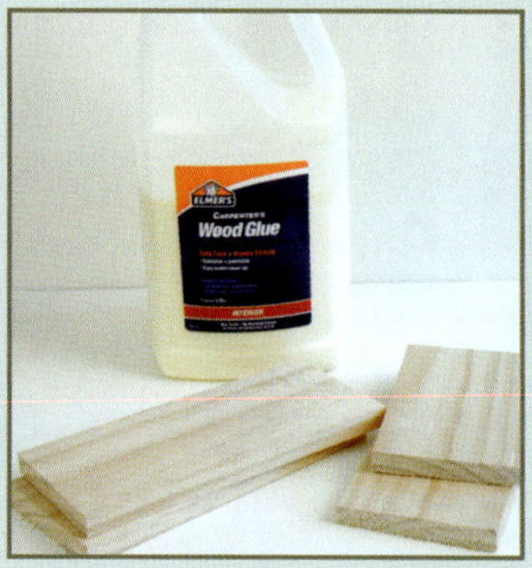

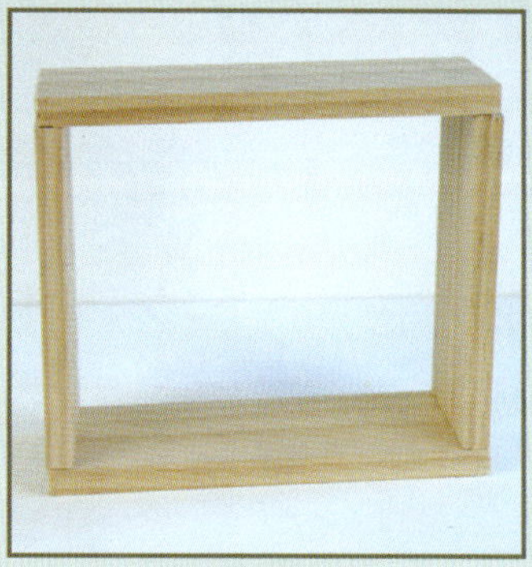

BASIC VISION BOX #2

For Basic Vision Box #2, you will be using 1x4 (19 x 89mm) pine planks, which generally come in 8′ (244cm)-long pieces. You can have them cut to size at your local hardware store or home center. Look for pieces that are in good condition because there are different grades of wood.

For each box, you will need two 8" (203mm)-long pieces and two 10" (254mm)-long pieces. You will glue them together using Elmer's wood glue. For this box, you have two size options when gluing them together. The first size option is sandwiching the two 8" (203mm)-long pieces in between the two 10" (254mm)-long pieces. This would make your box exactly 10" x 9½" (254 x 241mm). Your second option is to sandwich the two 10" (254mm) pieces in between the two 8" (203mm) pieces, making your box exactly 8" x 11½" (203 x 292mm) in size.

If you choose to get a full 8′ (244cm)-long piece you can get two full #2 Vision Boxes from the wood and have approximately 24" (610mm) left over, which you could have cut into four equal pieces for a smaller Vision Box.

Waste not, want not, right?

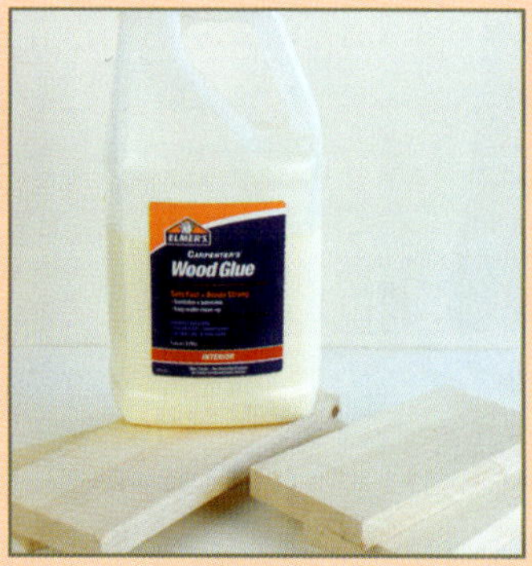

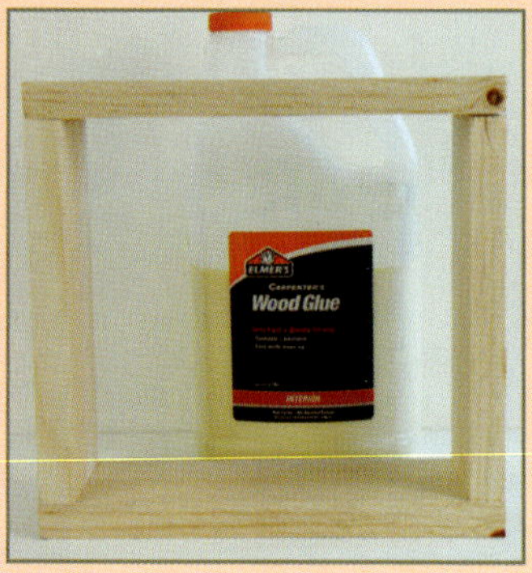

BASIC VISION BOXES #3 AND #4

Basic Vision Box #3 is plain. Basic Vision Box #4 has a gable (pointed roof).

For Basic Vision Box #3, you need two pieces of 16" (406mm)-long 1x6 (19 x 140mm) pine plank and two pieces of 8" (203mm)-long 1x6 (19 x 140mm) pine plank.

Sandwich the two 8" (203mm)-long pieces in between the two 16" (406mm)-long pieces 3½" (89mm) in from the edge of the 16" (406mm)-long pieces. Glue them together and let dry.

For Basic Vision Box #4, you will need two pieces of 16" (406mm)-long 1x6 (19 x 140mm) pine plank and four pieces of 8" (203mm)-long 1x6 (19 x 140mm) pine plank.

Sandwich the two 8" (203mm)-long pieces in between the two 16" (406mm)-long pieces 3½" (89mm) in from the edge of the 16" (406mm)-long pieces. Glue them together and let dry. Glue the other two 8" (203mm)-long pieces together to form an "L" shape and let dry and then glue on top of your Vision Box #3 structure.

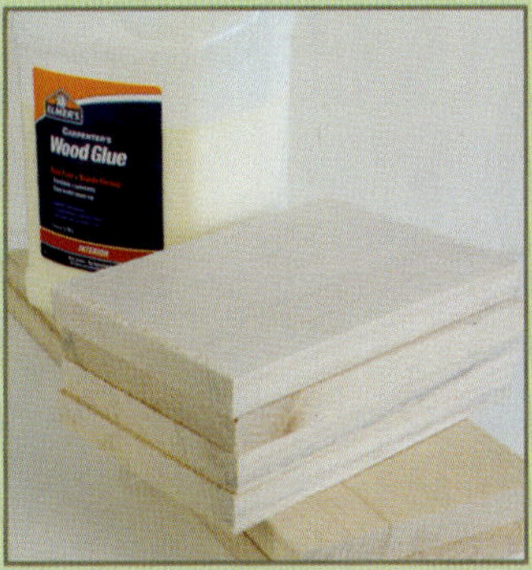

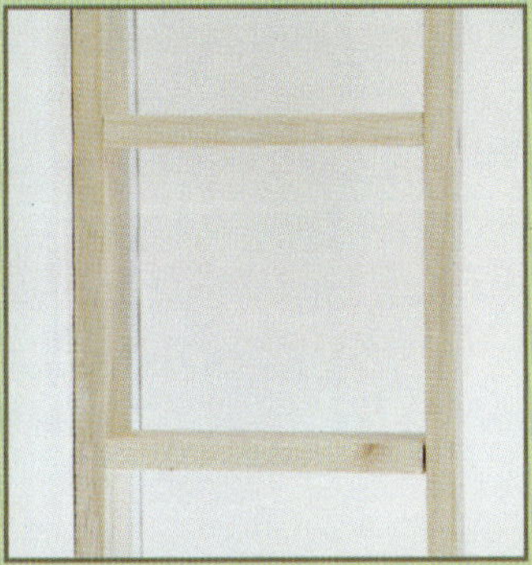

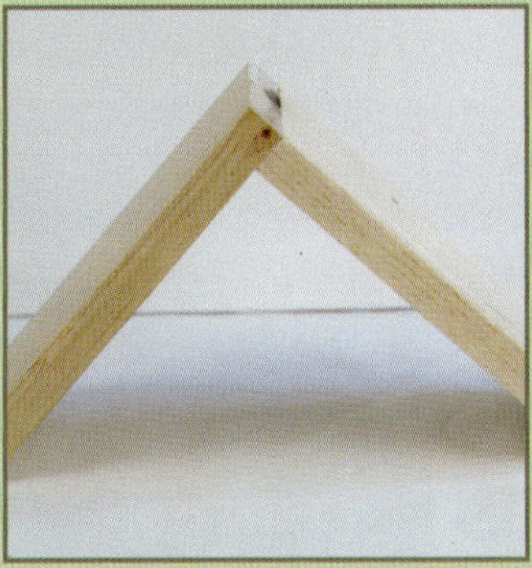

BASIC VISION BOX #5

Basic Vision Box #5 is totally up to you, but I wanted to share the secret with you about making it. Many times you can find inexpensive deep frames. I get mine at the 99 Cent store because it doesn't matter how they look since I'll be altering them. If you find a frame that is pretty deep but you need one that's deeper, purchase two of the frames, remove the glass and cardboard backing, and use E-6000 to glue them together front to back. Cut a piece of cardboard for the back and if you want, you can glue the glass on the front.

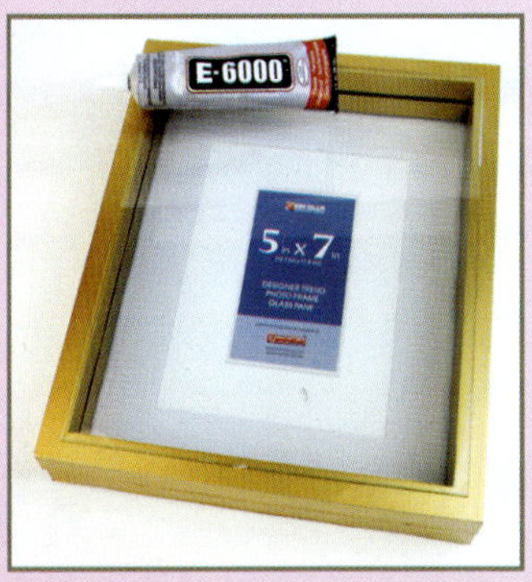

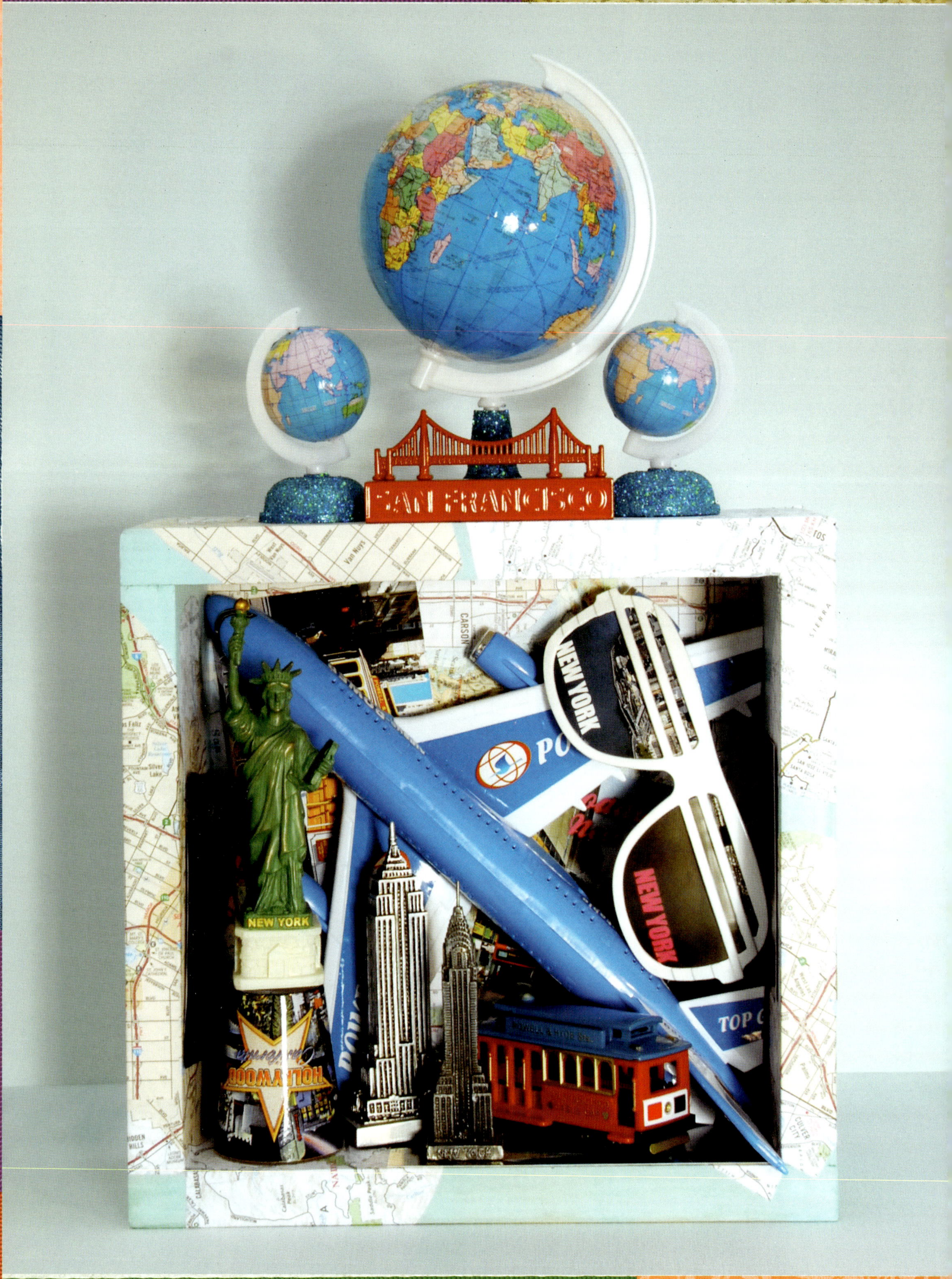
SAN FRANCISCO
NEW YORK
NEW YORK
NEW YORK

Bon Voyage!

When I was 13, I made a decision: I was going to move to New York City, live in a penthouse with a swimming pool, work at Macy's, and then become a famous fashion designer. I'm not sure where those ideas came from, but somehow they popped into my head. At that age, I had never been on a plane or even been to a town that was bigger than 10,000 people, but somehow, I knew my destiny.

Guess what? Most of that stuff happened. I never worked at Macy's or lived in a penthouse, but I did move to New York City at 19 and became a successful fashion designer. At 13, I would post photos of New York City all over my bedroom and whenever I met someone who had visited there, I would pick their brain mercilessly to learn all I could. I spent my youth focusing on my future and it happened.

The magic of this *Bon Voyage! Vision Box* is that you can fill it with any place you dream of going and then work to make it happen.

Have a good trip!

The magic of this Bon Voyage! Vision Box is that you can fill it with any place you dream of going and then make it happen.

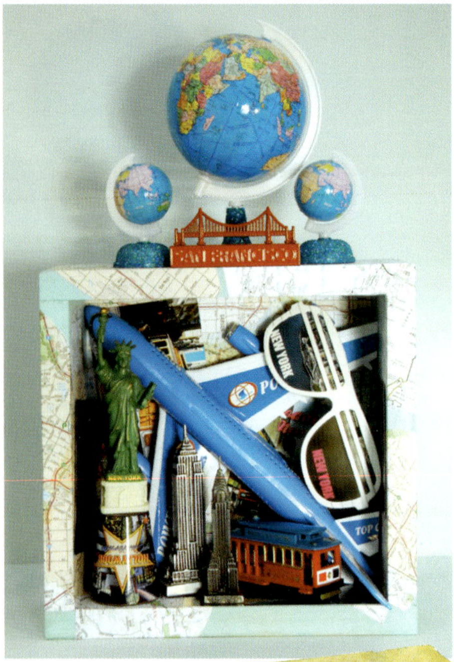

You'll need:

(Most of this I picked up at a 99 Cent store!)

- Vision Box #2 on page 12
- Light blue Krylon spray paint
- Cardboard to fit the back of the box
- Maps
- Old cheap sunglasses
- Toy plane
- Souvenirs from various places
- Postcards from various places
- Small globes (the ones in the photo are pencil sharpeners)
- Blue glitter
- Scissors
- Craft Knife
- Paintbrushes
- Elmer's glue
- E-6000 Craft Adhesive

The author used these products for the project. Substitute your choice of brands, tools, and materials as desired.

1. Cut your cardboard to fit on the back of the box.
2. Spray paint the box and the cardboard light blue all over.
3. Cut out your maps and with very slightly watered down Elmer's glue, cover the box and the back piece of cardboard with maps and let dry. Be creative!
4. Cut your post cards to different sizes and glue them to the cardboard and sides of the box.
5. Punch out the lenses from the cheapy sunglasses and use the lens as a stencil to make a postcard lens and pop in.
6. If your plane is too big, cut the wings down so it fits inside the box.
7. Add some blue glitter to the bases of your tiny globes so they sparkle. These are your toppers.
8. Glue the back cardboard to the box with some Elmer's glue and let dry.
9. Glue the airplane in first using E-6000 and let dry.
10. Fill with your souvenirs by first arranging them where you want them and then gluing them in with the E-6000 so they don't move.*
11. Glue on your toppers and you're done.

I didn't glue in my Statue of Liberty on the shot glass because I'm tucking money under the shot glass for my next trip!

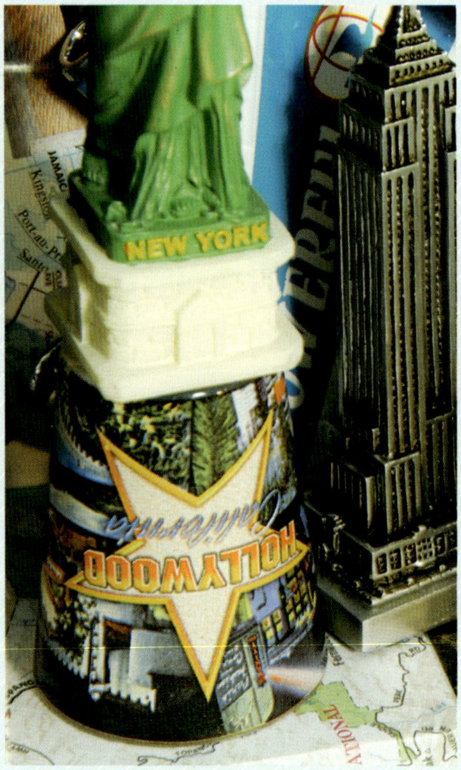

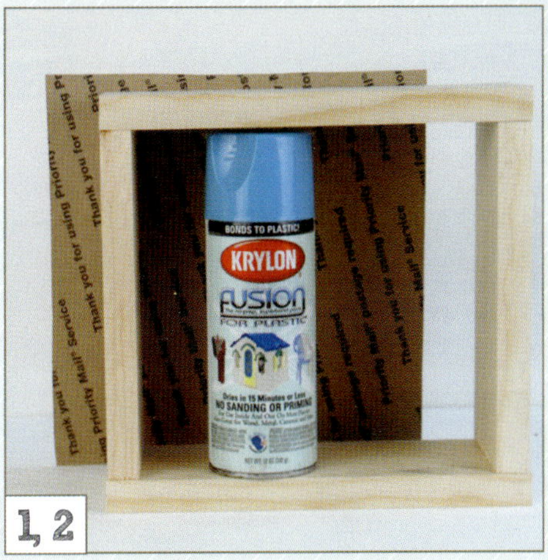
KRYLON
FUSION
FOR PLASTIC
1, 2

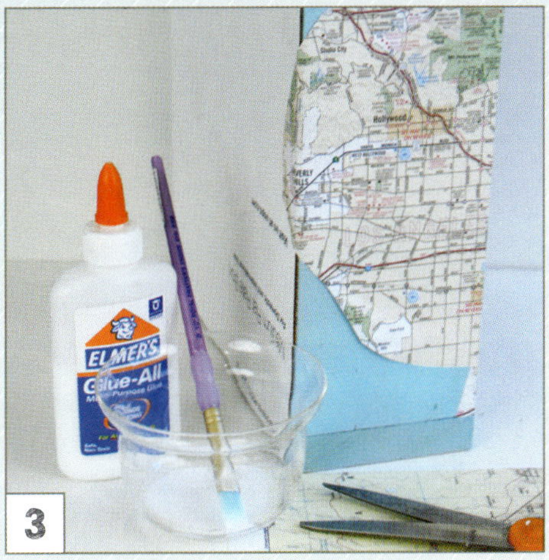
ELMER'S
Glue-All
3

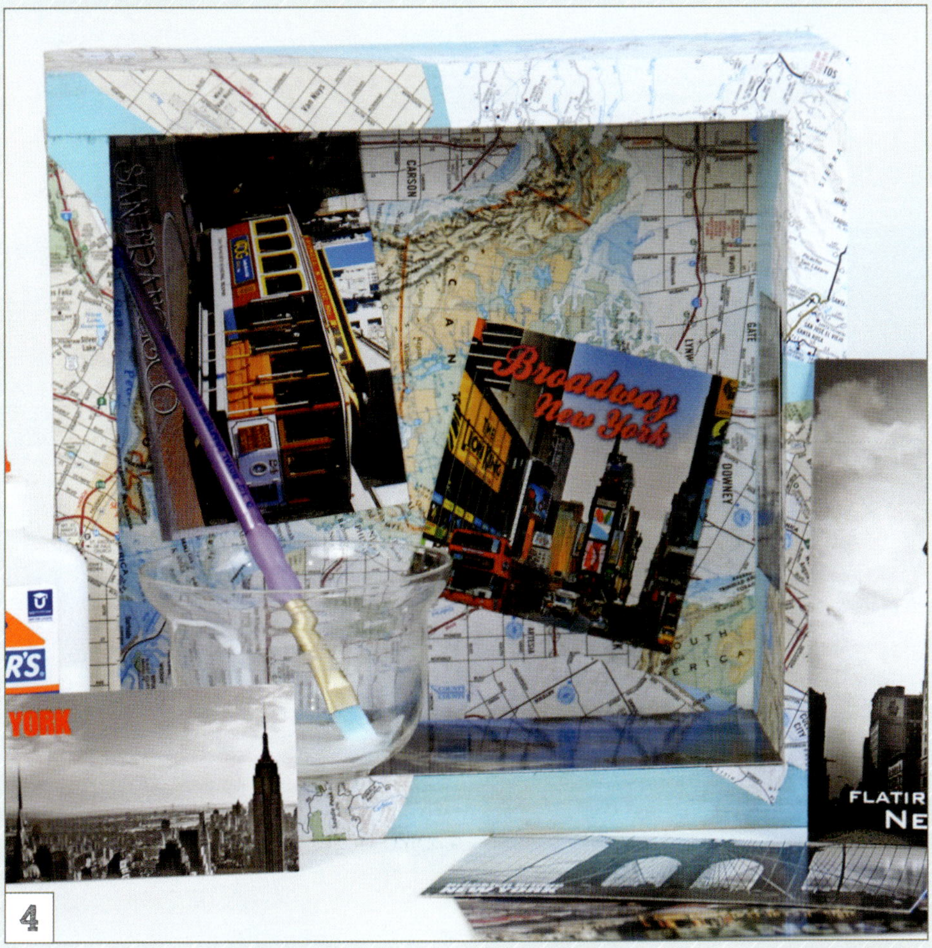
Broadway
New York
YORK
FLATIR
NE
4

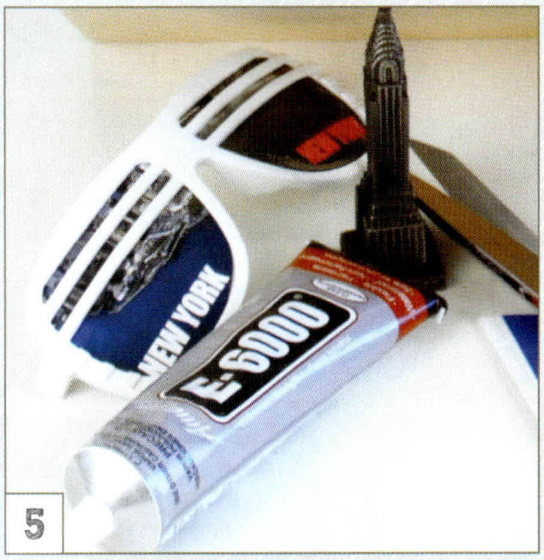
NEW YORK
E-6000
5

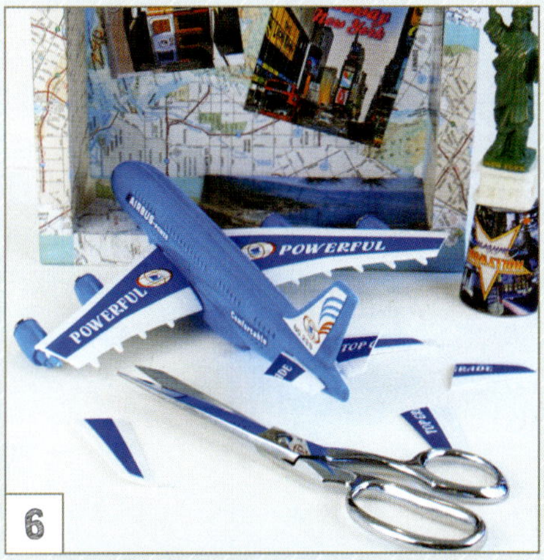
POWERFUL
POWERFUL
6

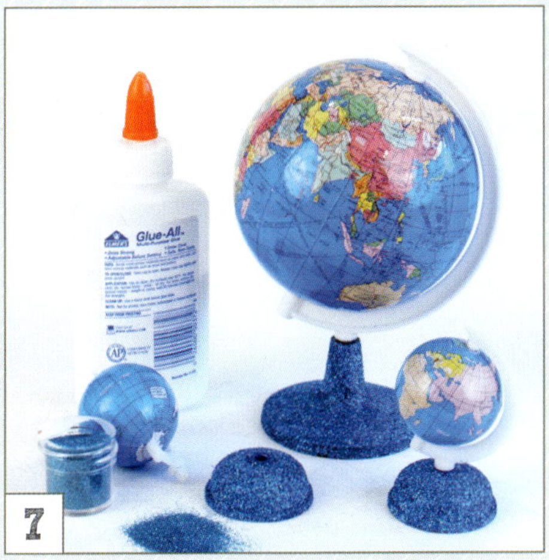
Glue-All
7

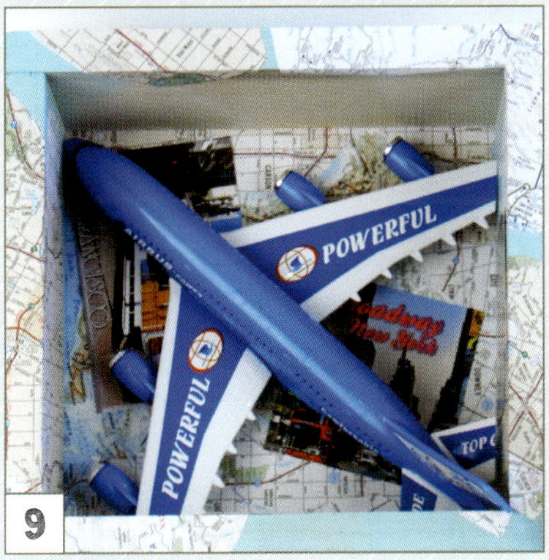
POWERFUL
POWERFUL
9

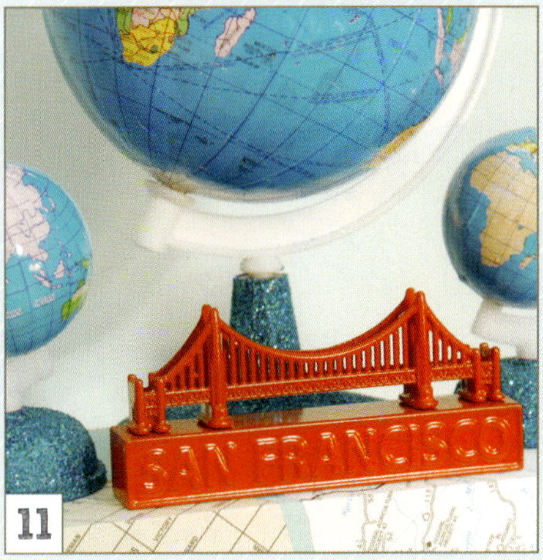
SAN FRANCISCO
11

Box of Angels

Even if you don't believe in traditional angels, isn't it nice to think that they are flying around us keeping us safe? My Gram always told me I had guardian angels and I never questioned it,

NEVER.

There have been too many times that I "almost" had something terrible happen and the only thing I can think of is that my guardian angels were keeping me out of danger.

Over the years, I've been given angel figurines and I finally found a way to harness their power! I put them all together in a Vision Box so I can talk to them all at once.

Yes, I talk to my angels.

Don't you?

My Gram always told me I had guardian angels and I never questioned it. NEVER! Yes, I talk to my angels. Don't you?

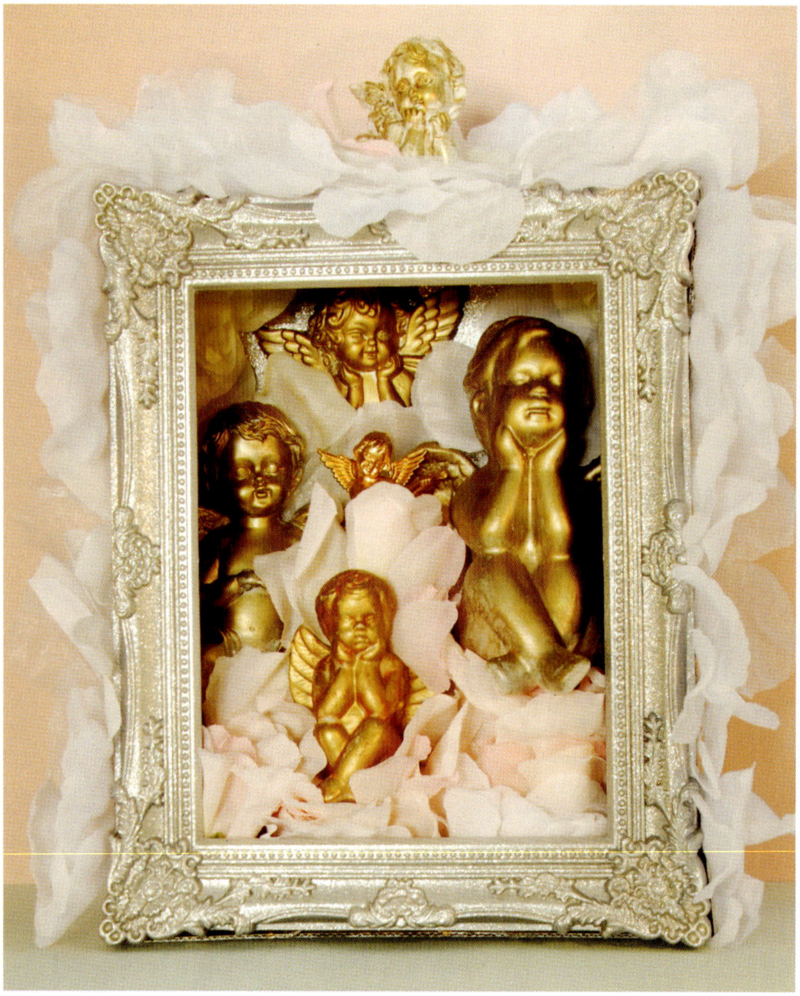

You'll need:

- Large fancy frame (from a 99 Cent store)
- Krylon Silver Flash Glitter Blast
- Flat molding wood pieces to make a box that fits behind your frame
- Cardboard to fit the back of your box
- Angel figurines
- Elmer's wood glue
- Gold acrylic paint
- Gold Krylon metallic paint
- White latex spray paint
- E-6000 Craft Adhesive
- Hot glue gun
- Scissors
- Craft knife
- Lids and plastic shot glasses
- Faux flowers in white and light pink

The author used these products for the project. Substitute your choice of brands, tools, and materials as desired.

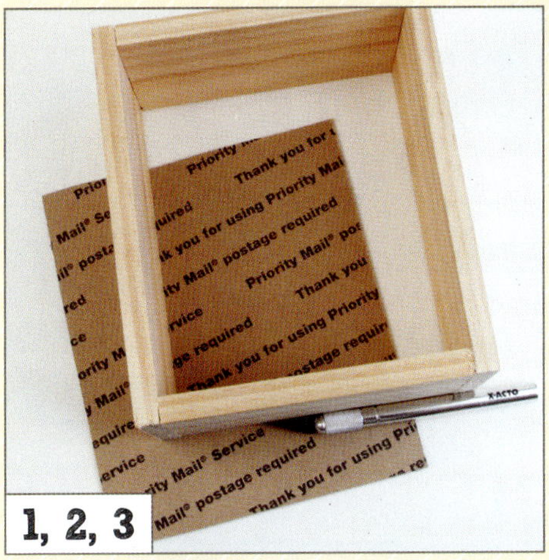
1, 2, 3

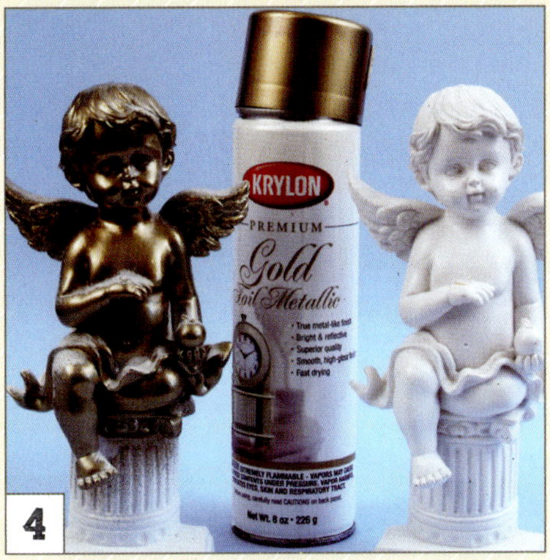

4

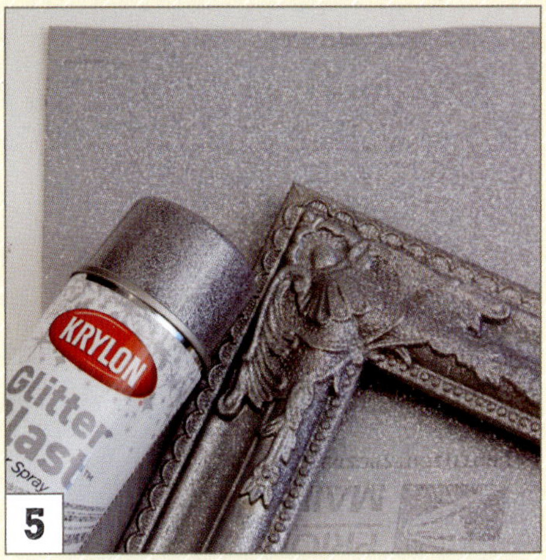

5

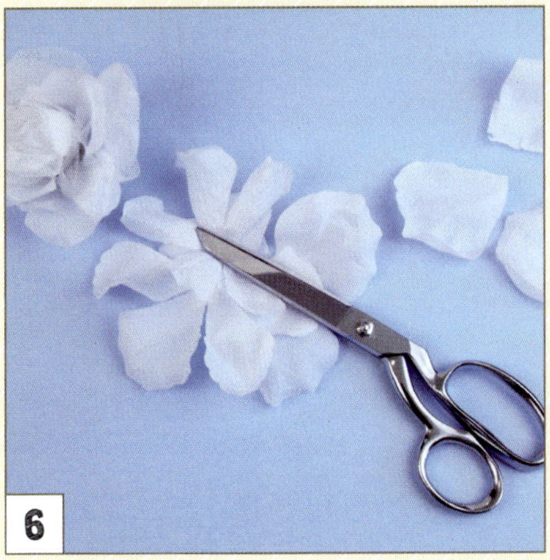
6

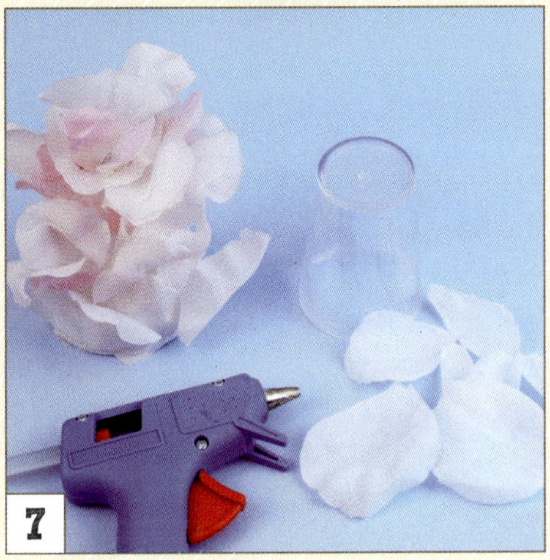
7

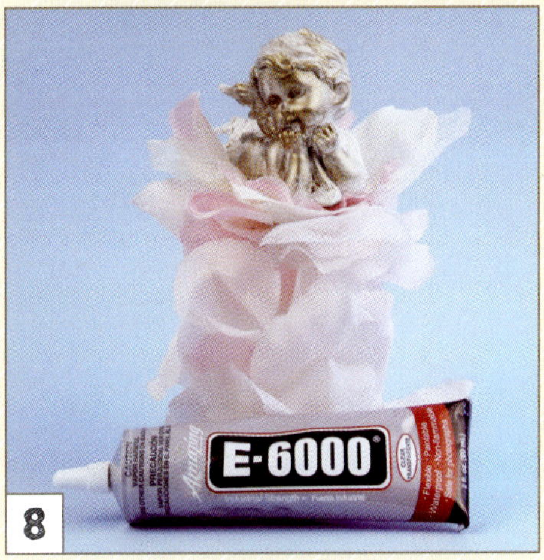

8

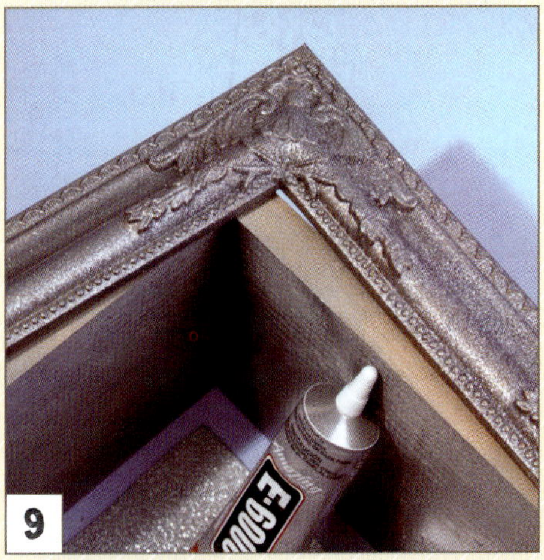
9

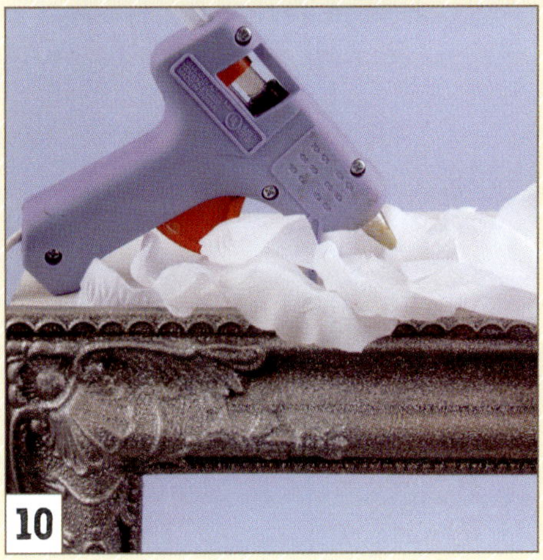
10

1. Have basic flat wood molding cut to make a box that will fit behind your frame. Any home center or hardware store can do this. Just measure the width and height of the box and make sure to subtract the thickness of the wood from your measurements.

2. Wood glue your box together and let dry.

3. Cut a piece of cardboard to fit the back of the box.

4. Paint all of your angels in different gold paints so they match. Use latex spray paint, dab them with white, and give them texture. Play around until you get the looks you want.

5. Glitter Blast your frame and the back piece of cardboard with the Silver Flash and let dry.

6. Take apart your faux flowers and cut the petals apart.

7. Glue them to the shot glasses and lids so you have flower covered pedestals for your angels. This will give them different heights in the box.

8. E-6000 your angels to their pedestals.

9. With the E-6000, glue the frame to the box and let dry.

10. Hot glue the faux flower petals all over the outside and top of the box.

11. Hot glue the glitter covered cardboard back to the back of the box.

12. Arrange your angels inside and glue in place with the E-6000.

13. Hot glue more flower petals around them and inside the frame until you're satisfied.

14. Glue an angel on top of the box.

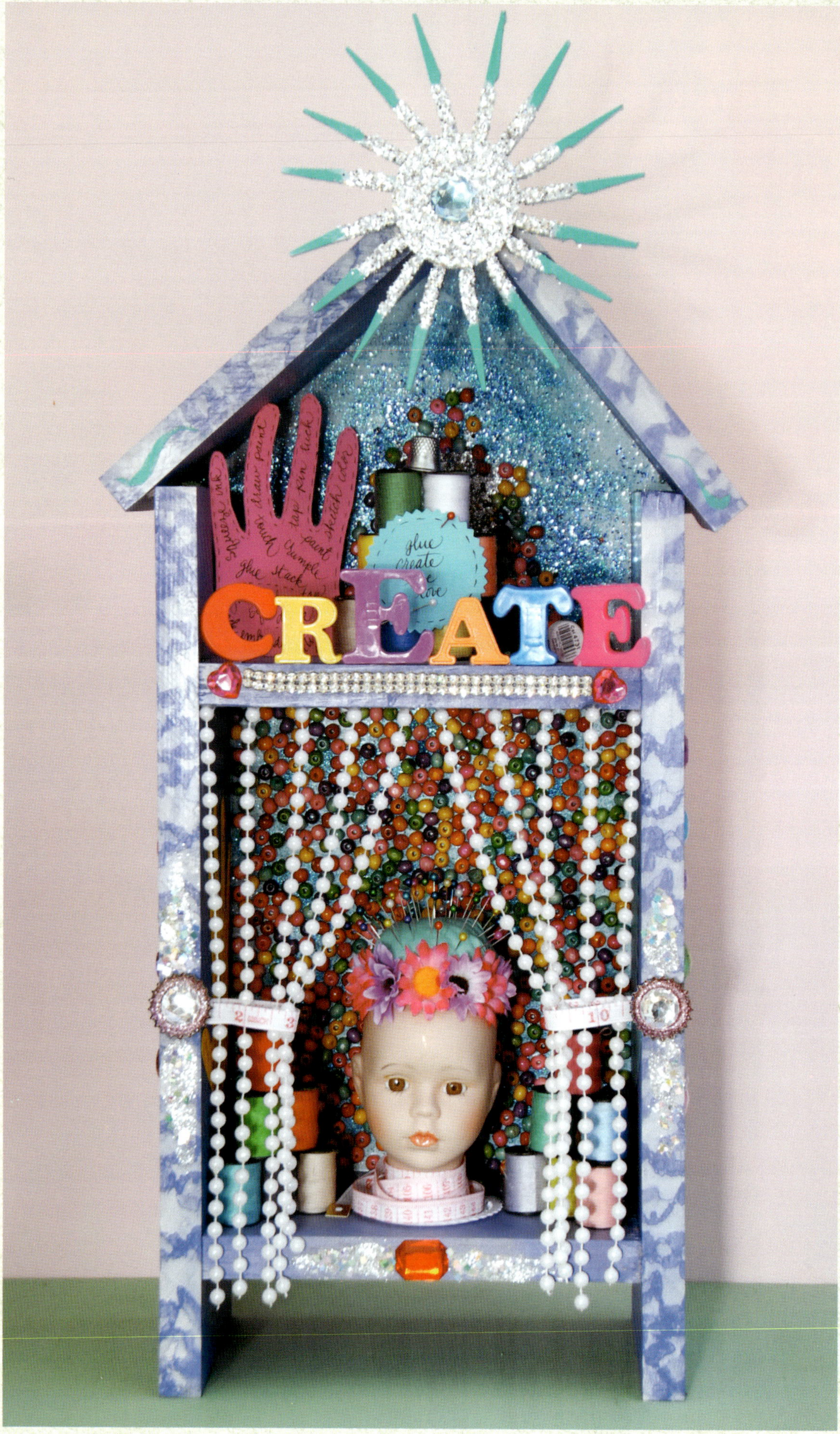
CREATE

Create!

Sometimes I can't jump off the crafty cliff. I stand at the edge and wait in fear that my attempt to be creative might fail. It's not a good feeling.

The magic of the CREATE! Vision Box is that it reminds me it doesn't matter where you land, it just matters that you take the leap. I have filled this box with several tracings of my hand and written on those hands all of the things I like to do. Because sewing is one of my favorite activities, I used lots of inexpensive 99 Cent store sewing supplies to decorate this box.

I think the best part of it is my porcelain doll head pin cushion, which stares at me and says, *"GET BUSY, MISTER!"*

Sometimes I can't jump off the crafty cliff. I stand at the edge fearing I can't be creative. It's not a good feeling.

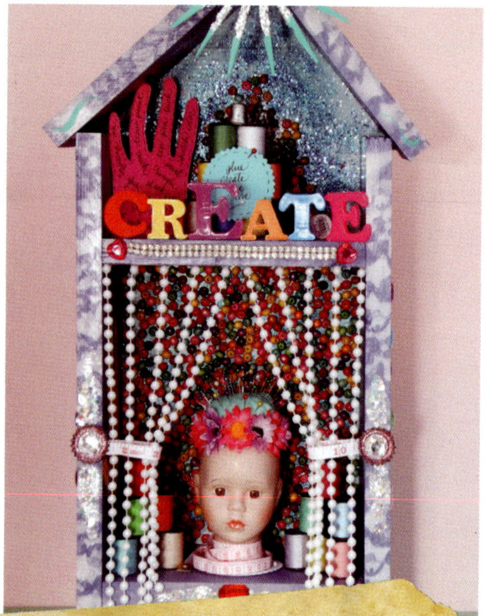

You'll need:

- ✦ Box #4 on page 13
- ✦ Cardboard to cover the back
- ✦ Krylon Fusion spray paint (purple, light blue, and pink)
- ✦ Green acrylic paint
- ✦ Lace
- ✦ Gems
- ✦ Faux flowers
- ✦ 8 wooden clothes pins
- ✦ Plastic magnet letters
- ✦ Strands of fake pearls or Mardi Gras beads
- ✦ Box of cheap beads
- ✦ Glitter
- ✦ Sewing kit from 99 Cent store
- ✦ Porcelain doll head
- ✦ Small amount of pillow stuffing
- ✦ 8" (203mm)-square piece of cotton fabric
- ✦ Cardstock in bright colors
- ✦ 2 bottle caps
- ✦ Sparkly trim or rhinestone trim
- ✦ Glitter glue
- ✦ Elmer's glue
- ✦ E-6000 Craft Adhesive
- ✦ Hot glue gun
- ✦ Craft knife

The author used these products for the project. Substitute your choice of brands, tools, and materials as desired.

1. Cut cardboard to fit on the upper and lower part of the back of your box.
2. Spray paint the entire box purple.
3. Spray paint the cardboard backing either purple or light blue. It's up to you.
4. Lay lace over the entire box and spray it pink. The lace will be like a stencil and give a lace relief.
5. Cover the entire back cardboard pieces in glue and then sprinkle with beads. While the glue is still wet, sprinkle with glitter to get in between the beads and let dry.
6. Build small pyramids with your spools of thread and glue together with E-6000 Craft Adhesive.
7. Create your porcelain doll head pin cushion by wrapping the pillow stuffing in the small piece of fabric and stuffing it inside the doll head and securing it in place with some hot glue.
8. Hot glue the flowers around the head, hiding the spot where the cushion meets the head.
9. Wrap the neck with the tape measure.
10. Glue the word CREATE in plastic letters on the upper part of your Vision Box.
11. Trace your hand and write down all the things you like to do when you create on the tracing and glue those hands on the inside and outside of the box using the Elmer's glue.
12. Fill 2 bottle caps with glitter glue and a gem and let dry.
13. Hot glue strands of pearls from the underside of the upper level of your Vision Box.
14. Loop a piece of the measuring tape around half of the strands (like a curtain tie back) and glue to the edge of the box. Do this on each side.
15. Hot glue the bottle caps on top of each end of the measuring tape.
16. Glue gems and trim around the box and sprinkle glitter on the sides and on the face of the box. Go crazy here!
17. Glue on the cardboard back to your box with hot glue.
18. Fill the box with your porcelain head, the thread pyramids, and more paper hands.
19. To create the starburst on top of this Vision Box, glue a circle of cardboard on top of a circle of clothes pins that have been taken apart and let the glue dry. Spray paint the entire starburst light blue and let dry. Coat the center and part of each clothespin with glue and add glitter. Add a gem to the center of the cardboard circle, and paint the tips of the clothespins green, or any color you like.
20. Glue the starburst to the top of the Vision Box.

Keep adding more and more to this CREATE! Vision Box and you'll see how amazing it will be. You may never finish it!

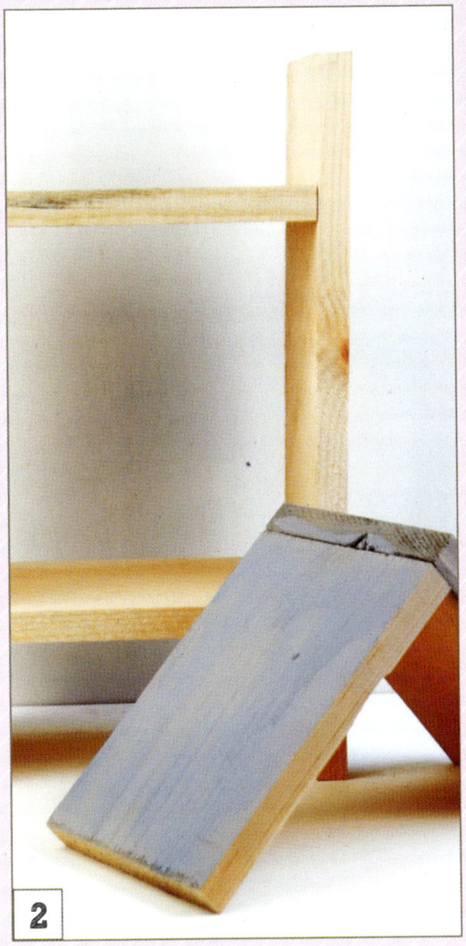
2

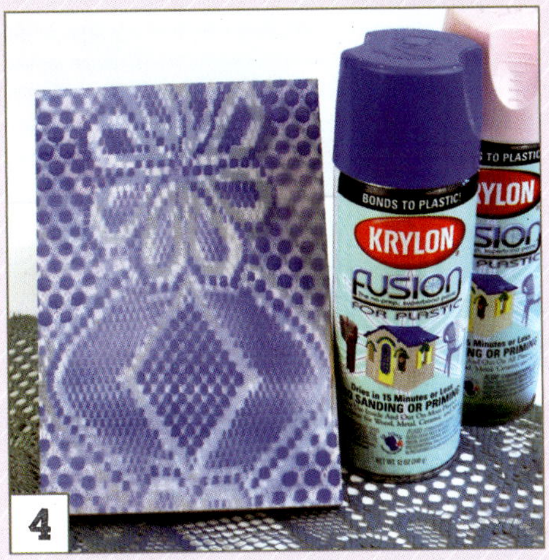
BONDS TO PLASTIC
KRYLON
FUSION
FOR PLASTIC
4

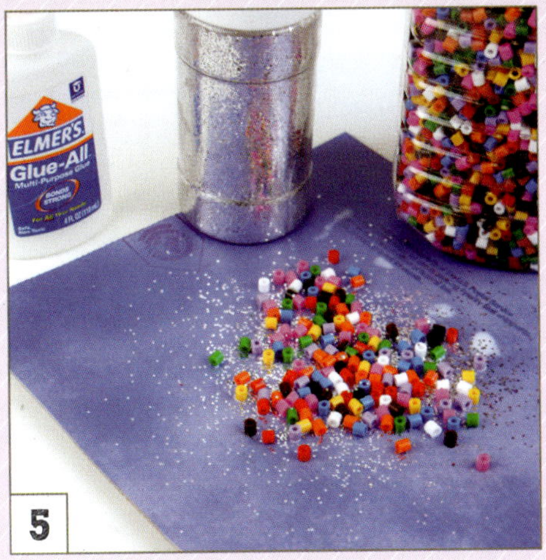
ELMER'S
Glue-All
5

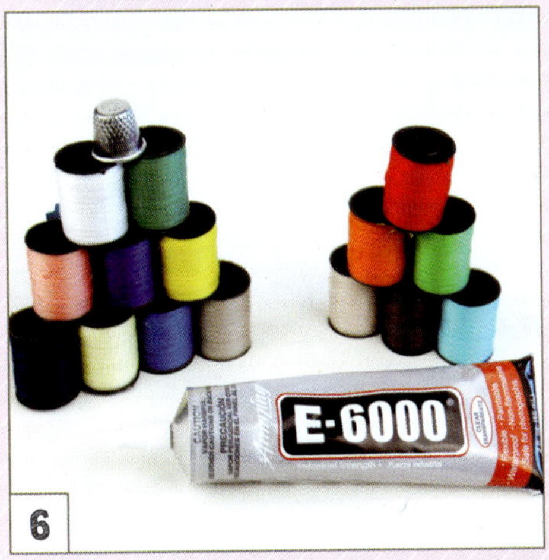
E-6000
6

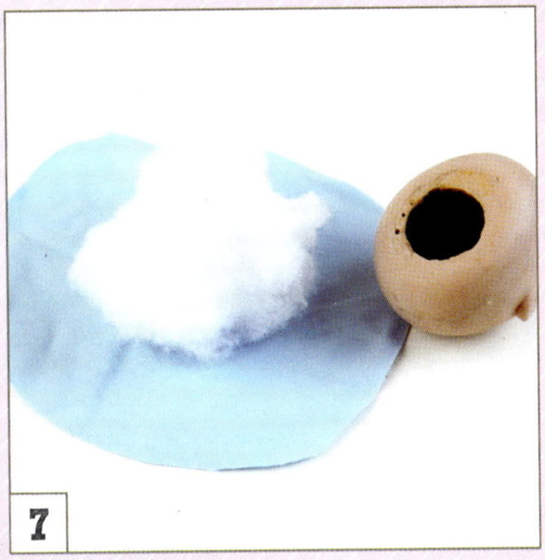
7

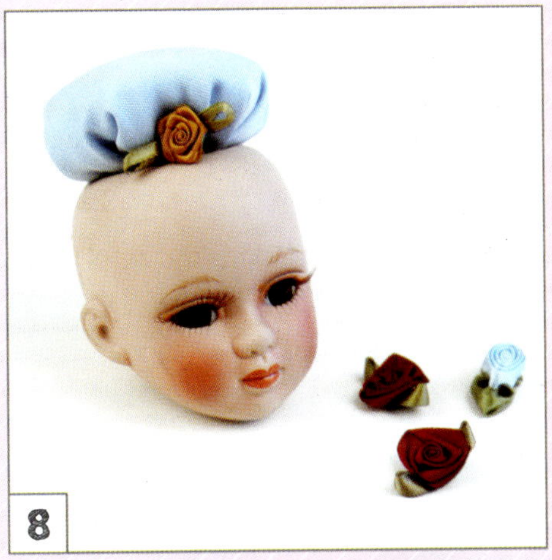
8

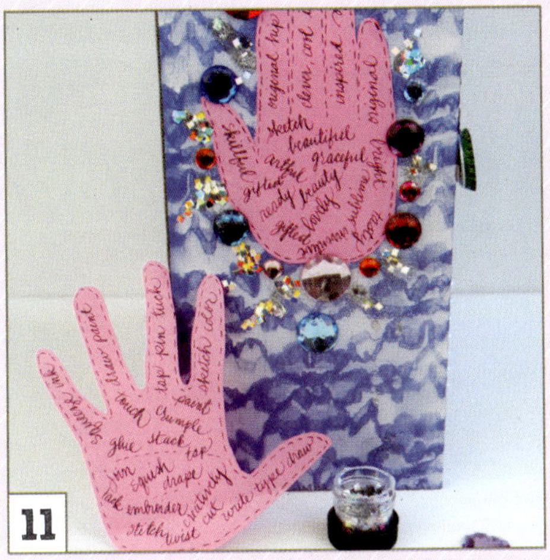
11

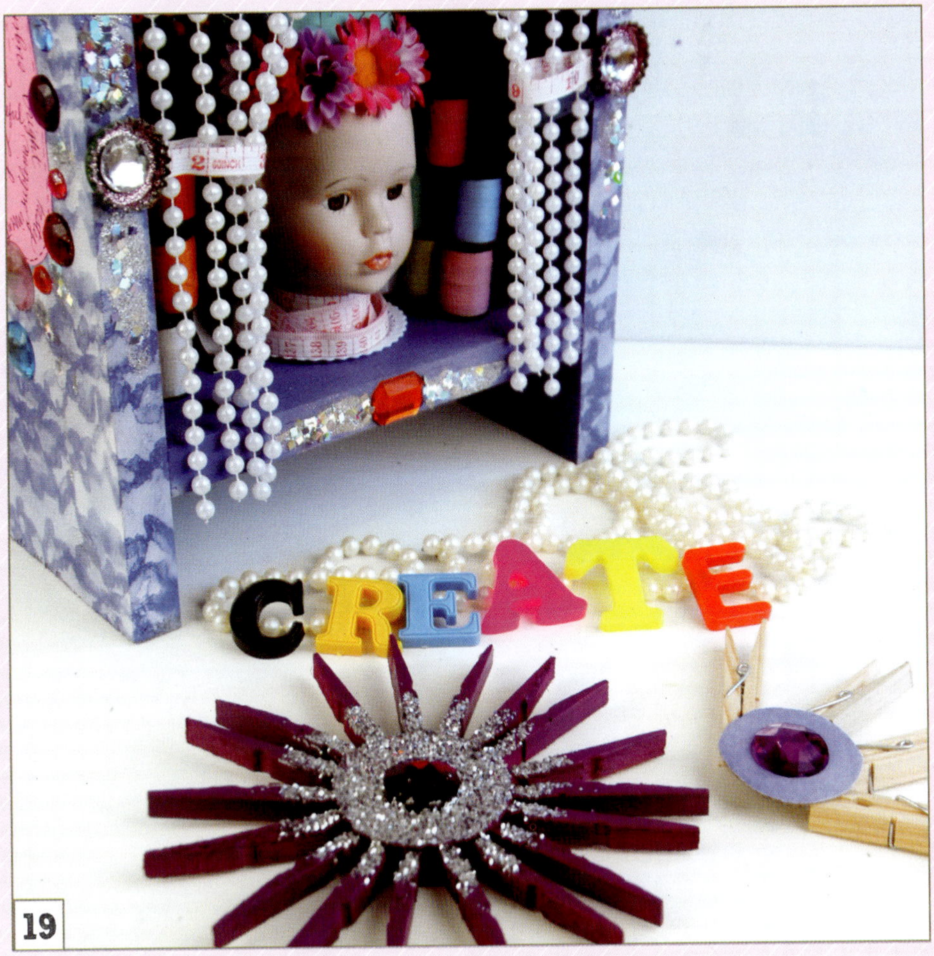
CREATE
19

Flights of Fancy

When I was about 10 years old, I used to have this recurring dream that I could fly. I remember this dream so clearly that at times I can still feel myself up in the air soaring. I can also remember very clearly the feeling of disappointment I had in the morning when I realized it wasn't real.

Lately I've been thinking about the many meanings of flight and that we all have the ability to soar if we really want to. We can reach as high as we want in every area of our lives and we can choose to rise above all the little things that ultimately don't mean anything at the end of the day. The magic of the Flights of Fancy Vision Box is simply that we all have the ability to fly in many ways—not just active flight as do our lucky birds and butterflies.

Perhaps, if I'm lucky, I'll have that dream again.

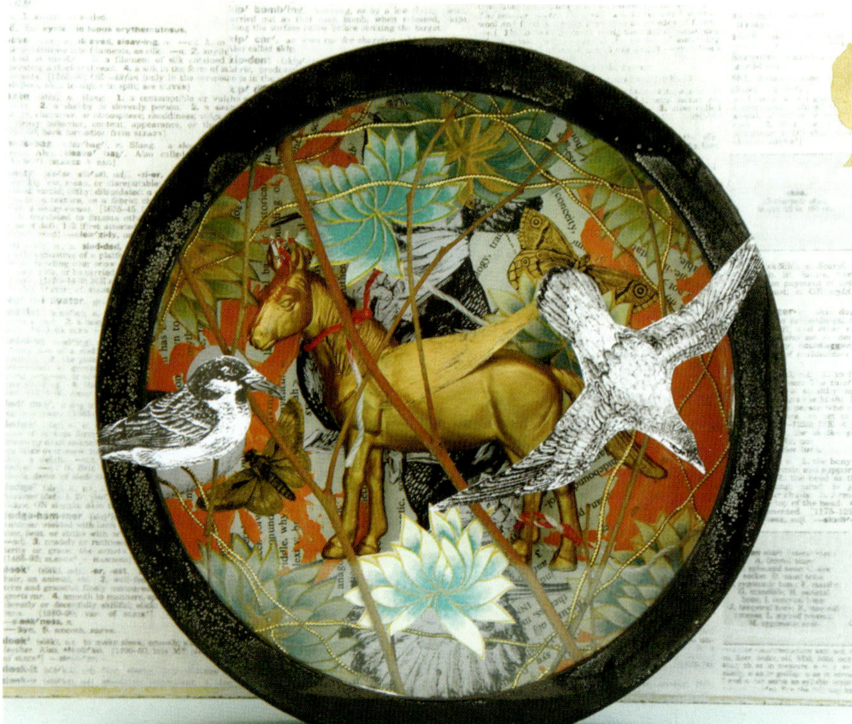

You'll need:

- 1 clock that is at least 6" (152mm) in diameter
- Enough cardboard to wrap around the clock
- Book pages
- Orange acrylic paint (or any color you like)
- 1 toy horse
- Krylon spray paint (metallic gold and black colors)
- Images of flowers, birds, butterflies (page 64–67)
- Gold thread
- Twigs
- Elmer's glue
- Hot glue gun
- Craft knife
- Paintbrushes

The author used these products for the project. Substitute your choice of brands, tools, and materials as desired.

We can reach as high as we want in our lives and rise above the things that at the end of the day don't mean anything.

1. Take the clock apart.
2. Cut a piece of cardboard that is about 1½" (38mm) wide and the circumference of the clock plus 1" (25mm).
3. Curl the cardboard by rubbing it on the edge of a counter or table and hot glue it around the face of the clock. The top of the clock will be put on later, like a lid.
4. Glue some book pages to the cardboard in different places.
5. Working on the face of the clock, add some orange acrylic paint and then collage images using the Elmer's glue.
6. Cut out and glue images on the glass cover of the clock.
7. Cut out a wing of one of the bird images provided and glue it on the horse to make a Pegasus and then spray paint the horse gold and let dry.
8. Hot glue the horse to face of the clock over the collage you just made.
9. Hot glue in some twigs, drape some gold thread, and keep adding until you're satisfied with your box.
10. Glue in some flower images on the twigs to give a 3-D effect.
11. Paint the cardboard sides black and then glue on the face of the clock with E-6000 and let dry.

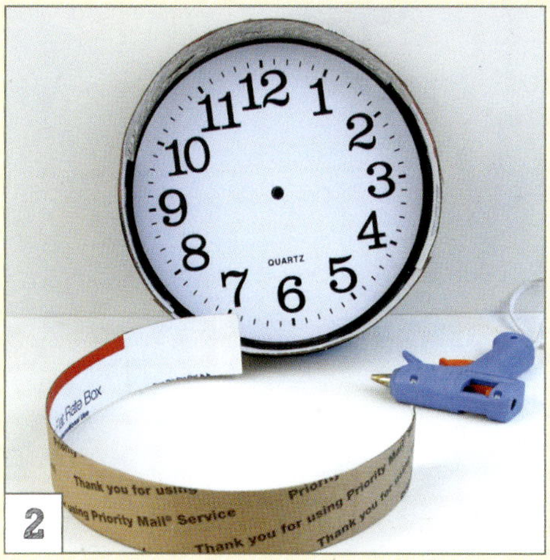

2

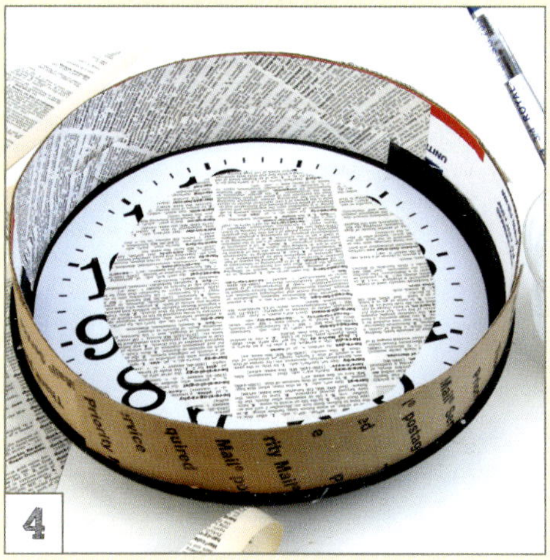
4

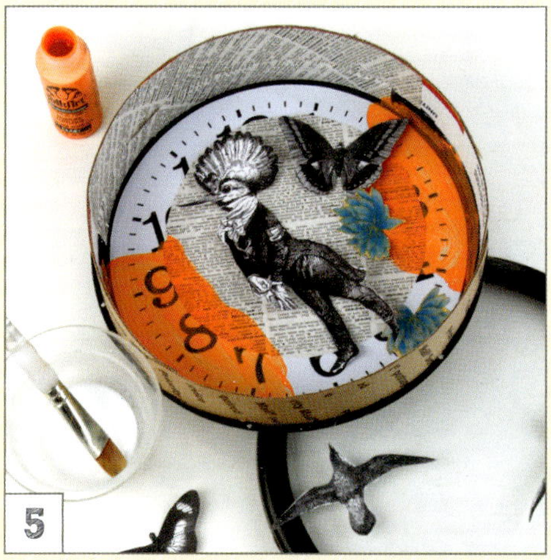
5

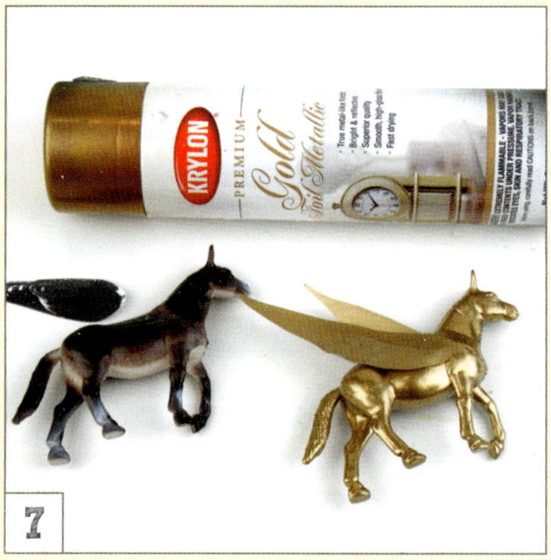

7

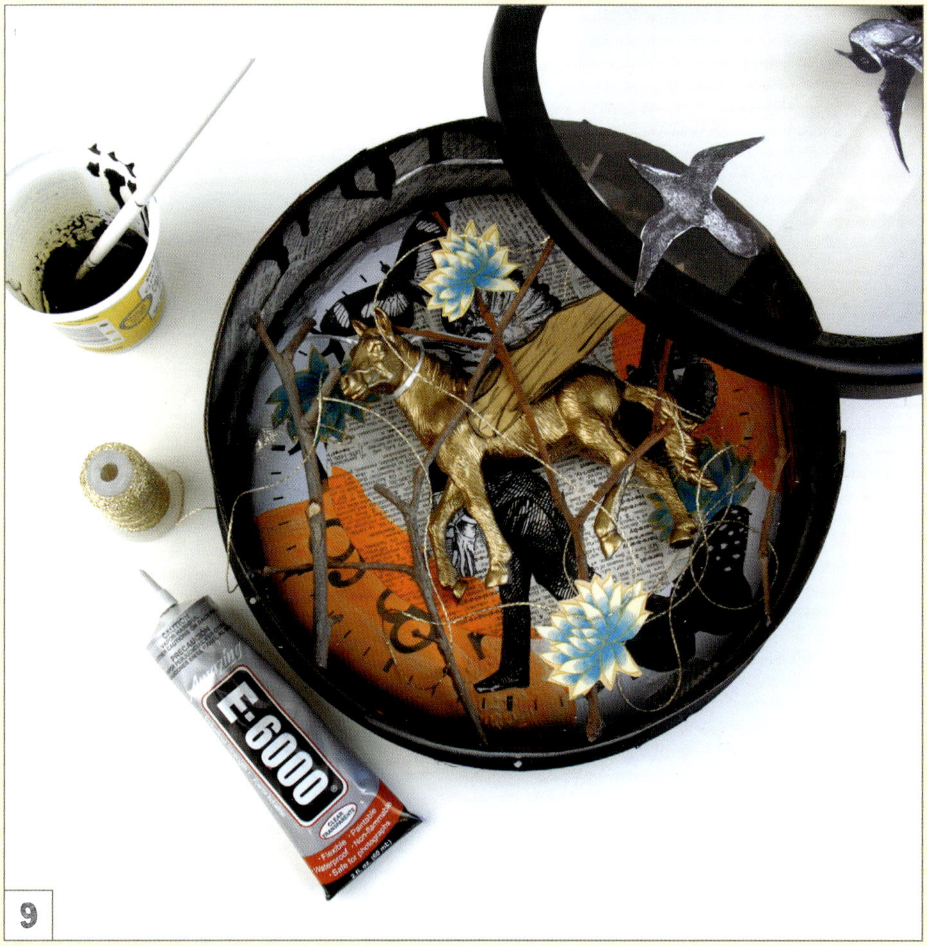

9

Growing Tree

I don't live near my family, and every time I visit, my nieces and nephews are bigger, smarter, and more developed. It's amazing to me.

I have always thought people are very much like trees. We grow, have roots, experience the years, and become heartier as each day passes. We may not always see the growth immediately, but it's happening all the time, and sometimes absence is the only thing that allows us to notice it in others.

The magic of the Growing Tree Vision Box is that we can add things to it that will help with our own personal growth. Each leaf is a different reminder of what we can do that will ultimately make us the people we want to become.

It may not happen right away, but I assure you, it's happening.

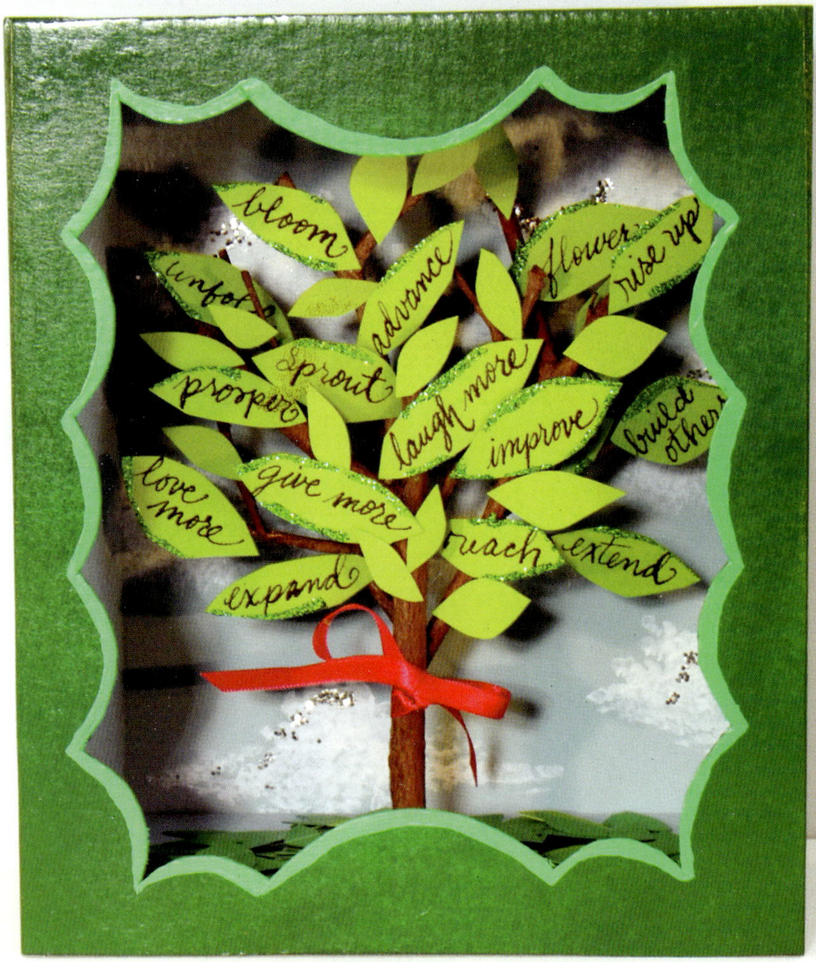

You'll need:

- Vision Box #1 on page 12
- 2 pieces of cardboard the size of your box
- Krylon spray paint (green)
- Light blue, light green, and white acrylic paint
- Paintbrushes
- Several twigs
- Silver and green glitter
- Elmer's glue
- Hot glue gun
- E-6000 Craft Adhesive
- 8" (203mm) of pink ribbon
- Green paper
- Scissors
- Craft knife

The author used these products for the project. Substitute your choice of brands, tools, and materials as desired.

Each leaf is a different reminder of what we can do that will ultimately make us the people we want to become.

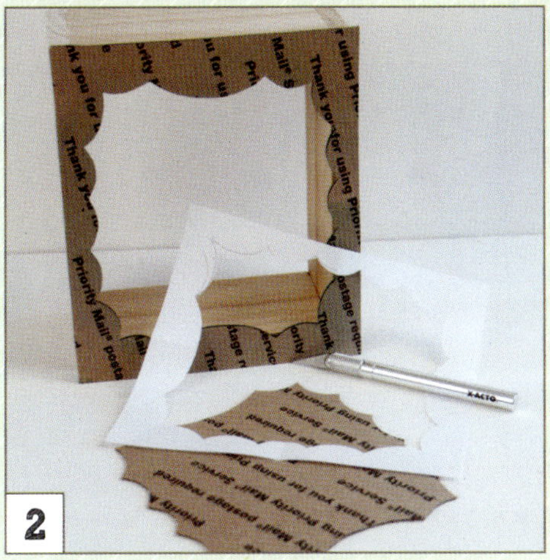

2

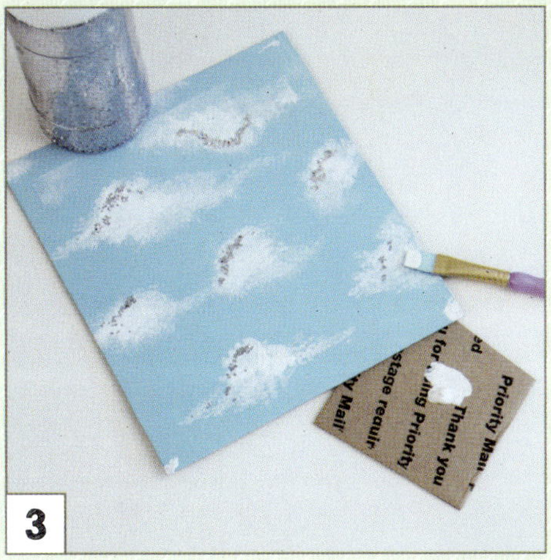

3

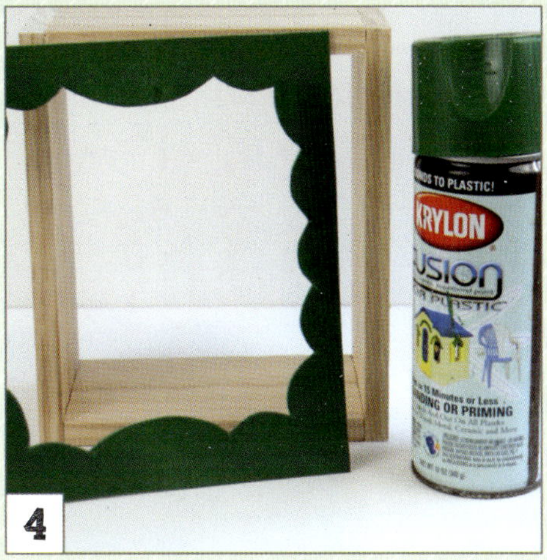

4

1. Cut the cardboard pieces to the exact size of your box.
2. Cut out the center of one of the pieces using a scalloped pattern like the one shown.
3. Paint the other piece of cardboard light blue, add white clouds, and accent it with silver glitter by dabbing on a little Elmer's glue.
4. Paint the scalloped face and the outsides of the box with the green spray paint.
5. Using a small brush, paint the edge of the scallop with a light green acrylic paint.
6. Paint the inside of the box light blue.
7. Glue your twigs together to form a tree with branches. Keep the tree flat.
8. Write your growth words on the green paper and cut them out in leaf shapes.
9. Add some glue and green glitter to the edge of each leaf.
10. Hot glue them on the tree.
11. Tie your ribbon around the trunk of the tree.
12. Hot glue the base of the tree to the bottom of the box
13. Sprinkle more leaves in the bottom of the box.
14. Glue the back and front on the box.

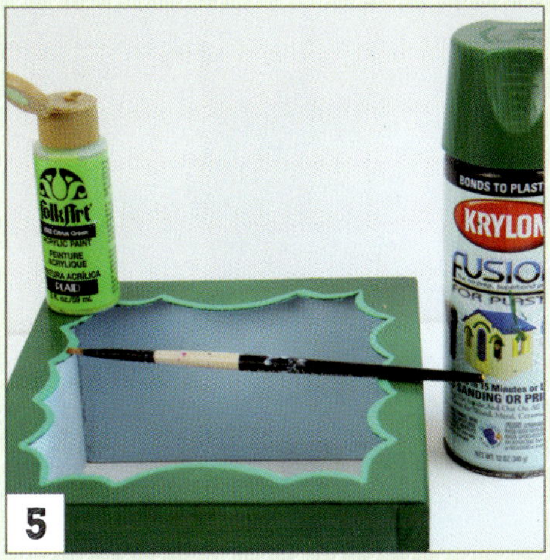

5

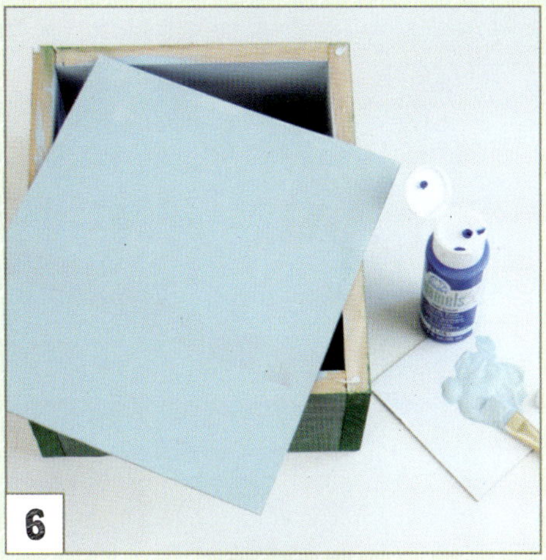
6

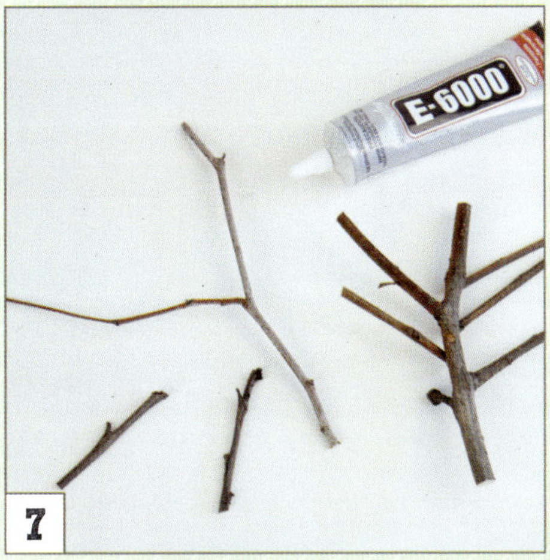

7

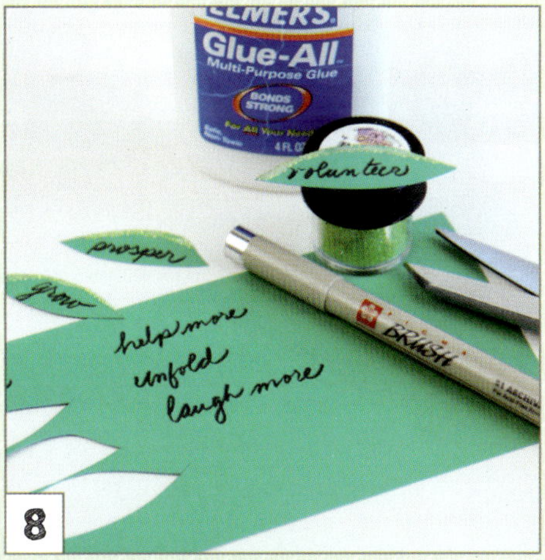

8

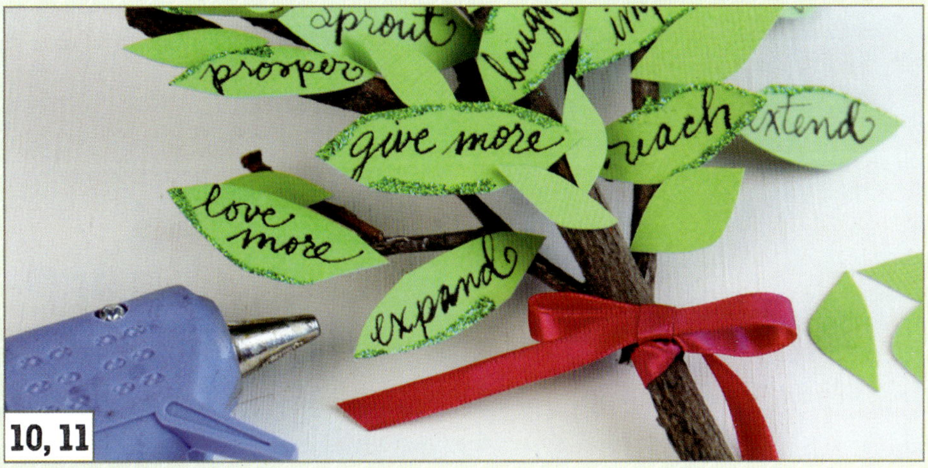

10, 11

Heart on My Sleeve

This Vision Box is for everyone who wants love and isn't afraid to look for it. My mom used to say, "The best way to reach a goal is to be clear about what it is you're reaching for." I agree. So wear your heart on your sleeve and reach out, people!

Make sure the universe knows what you want, and I have a feeling you just might get it.

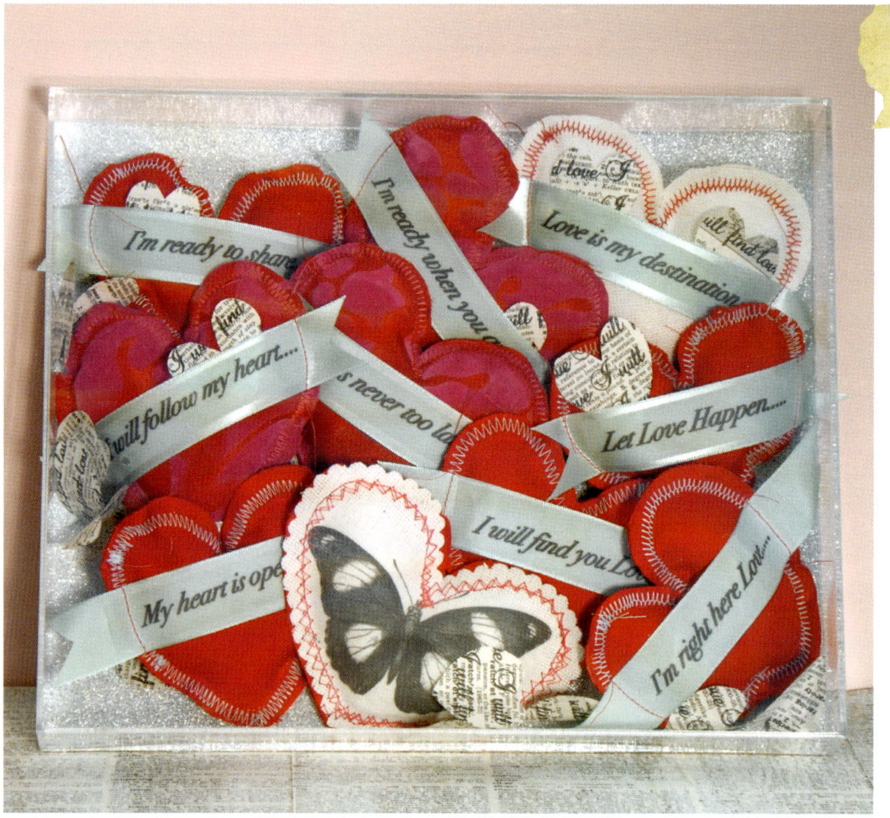

You'll need:

- 8" x 10" (203 x 254mm) clear plastic box frame
- 8" x 10" (203 x 254mm) piece of cardboard for the back
- Krylon Glitter Blast (Silver Flash color)
- ¼ yard (229mm) of red cotton fabric
- Small scraps of white fabric
- 1½ yards (137cm) of 1" (25mm)-wide satin ribbon in light color
- Sewing machine
- Small bag of pillow stuffing
- 1 sheet of Transfer Artist Paper (TAP)
- Butterfly image (page 66)
- 2 large book pages
- Hot glue gun
- Scissors
- Copy machine

The author used these products for the project. Substitute your choice of brands, tools, and materials as desired.

Make sure the universe knows what you want, and I have a feeling you just might get it.

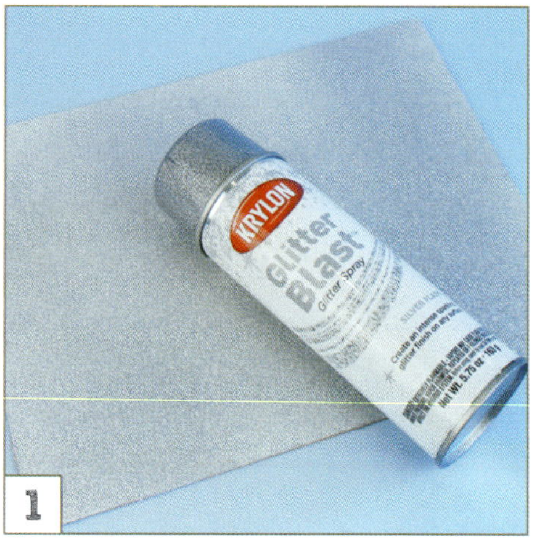

1

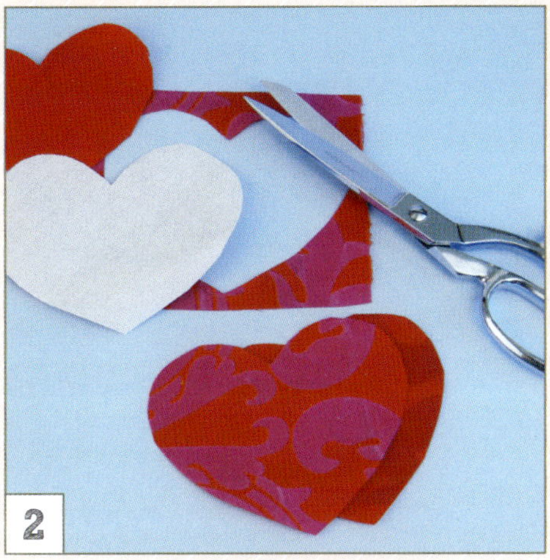

2

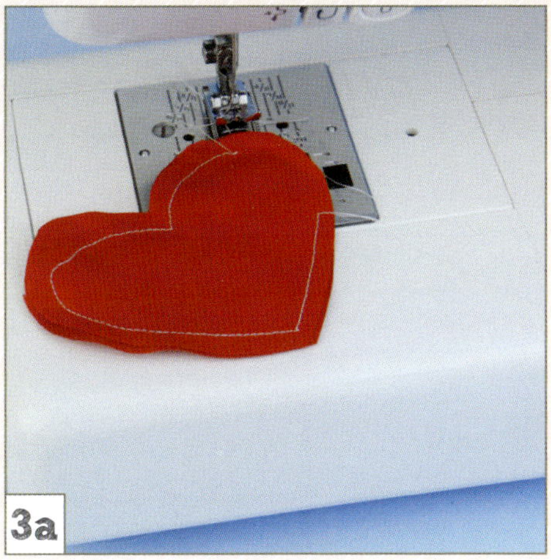

3a

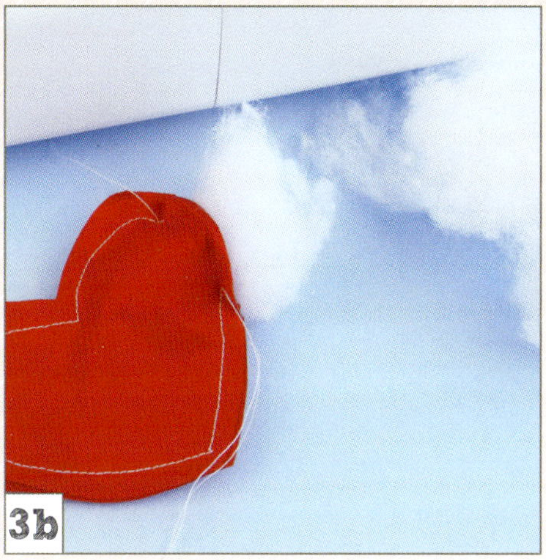

3b

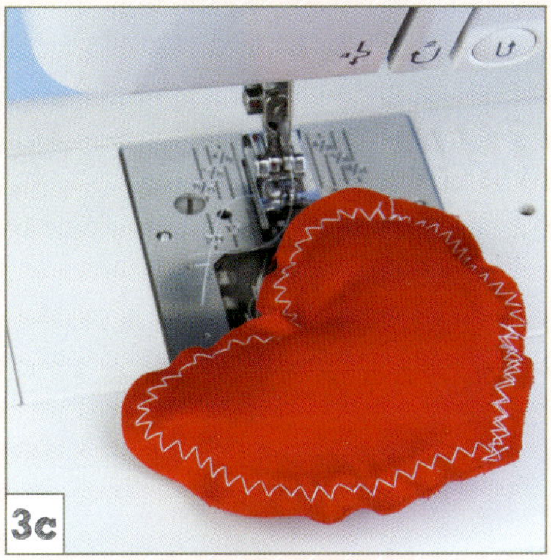

3c

1. Spray your 8" x 10" (203 x 254mm) cardboard with the Silver Flash Glitter Blast and let dry.

2. Cut your hearts out of the red fabric. They should be 3" to 4" (76mm to 102mm) wide at most.

3. Stitch around them with a zigzag or straight stitch, leaving a small 1" (25mm) hole. Fill with stuffing and sew the hole closed.

4. Print out your love words on your TAP paper, making sure to reverse the letters in your printer setting. Because they are being printed on a heat transfer, they must be printed using the mirror setting so they iron on properly. Copy a butterfly on your TAP paper by running it through the copy machine, making sure the butterfly is placed where it won't print on top of your words.

5. Cut out the words from your TAP paper and iron on your ribbons. Cut out the butterfly and iron on a piece of the white scrap fabric.

6. Cut and stitch your white butterfly heart like you did the red hearts.

7. Cut and stitch the ribbons to the hearts as seen in the photo.

8. Print your love words on book pages by simply running the book page through your copy machine like you would normal paper.

9. Cut small hearts out of the paper.

10. Hot glue your stuffed hearts into place on the Glitter Blasted cardboard backing.

11. Sprinkle the paper hearts over the stuffed hearts.

12. Hot glue the clear plastic box frame over the top.

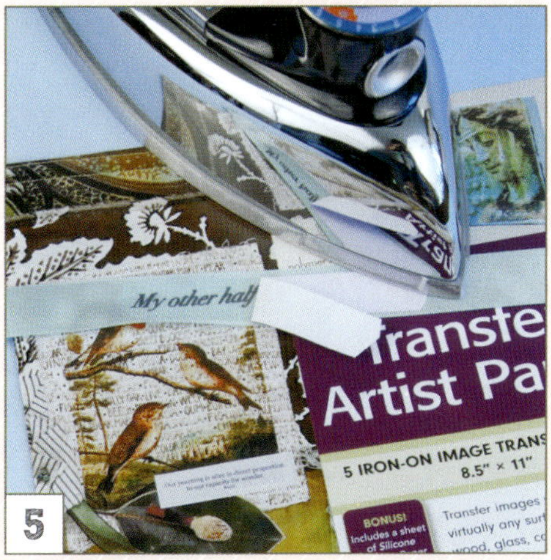

5

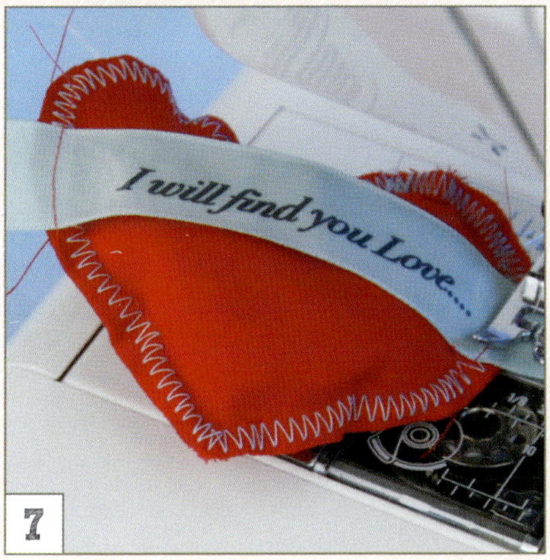

7

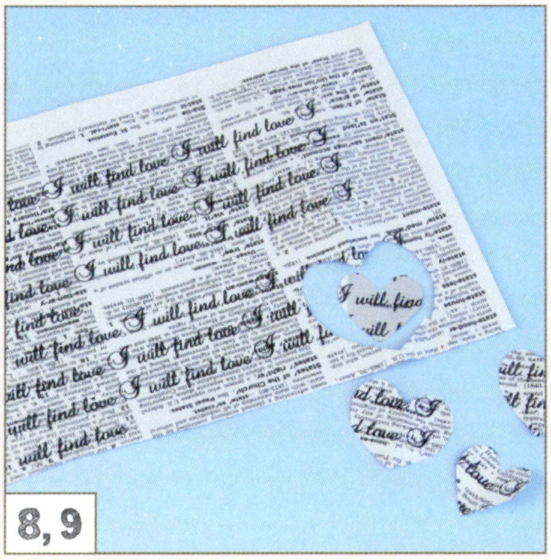

8, 9

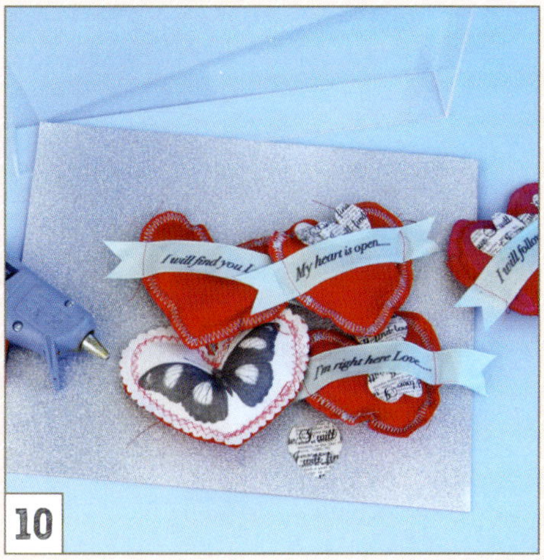

10

Finding the Hidden Magic

As you may have guessed, I'm a professional uncle. Five younger brothers and kids running around like ants when I visit. I LOVE IT. I'm also great at keeping them occupied with craft projects, much to the amazement of everyone.

Creativity is like hidden magic. It's magic that allows you to turn something mundane into something fantastic. Every day I look at ordinary things and try to find the hidden magic in them, and this project helps me do just that.

My niece informed me as I was making it that she was taking this Vision Box home with her when I was done and not to argue with her at all!

Of course I gave in.

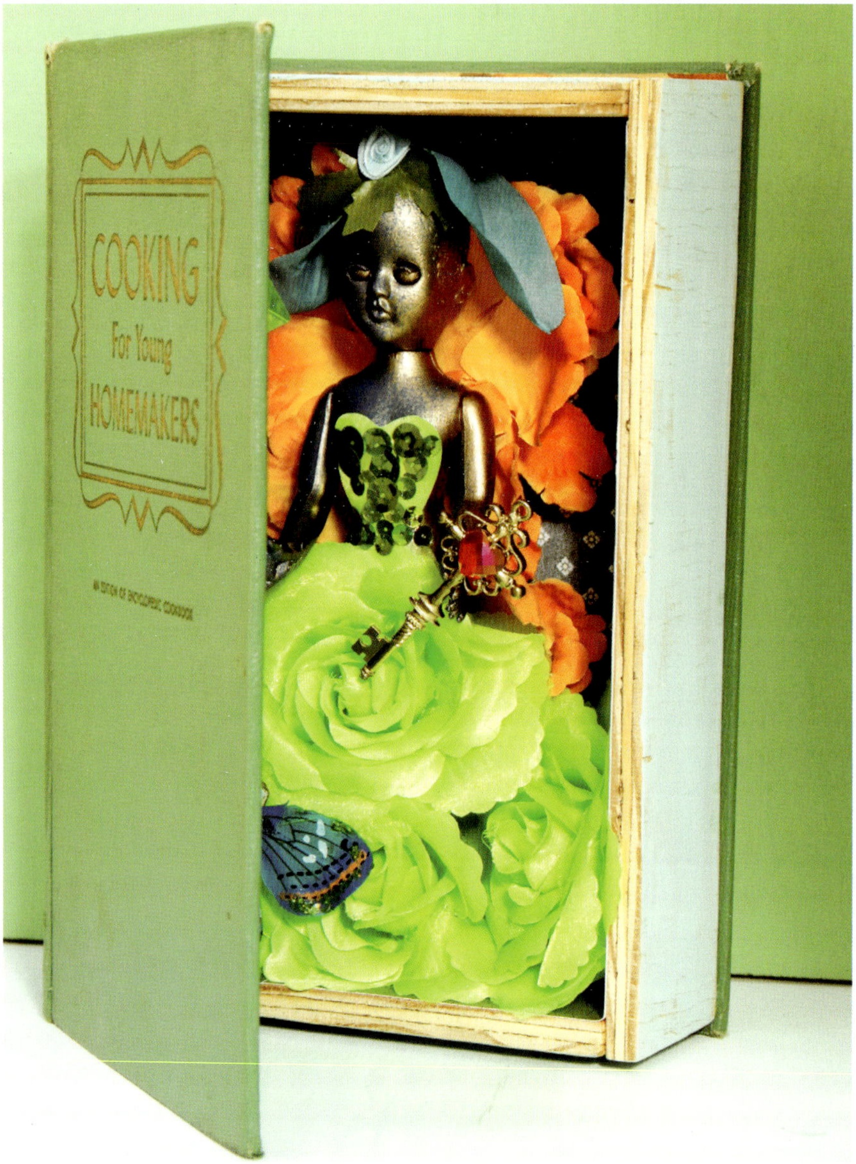

You'll need:

- 1 old hardcover book from the Salvation Army or other thrift store that is at least 2" (51mm) thick (You will be removing the book's pages to make a box out of the cover.)
- Scrap ½" (13mm)-thick plywood (or several layers of cardboard)
- Jig saw
- Elmer's wood glue
- Elmer's glue
- Hot glue gun
- Scrapbook paper
- 1 old doll
- Faux flowers
- Krylon spray paint (gold and blue metallic colors)
- Spray bottle with water
- Purple and light blue acrylic paint
- Faux butterflies
- 1 old key
- Gems and sequins
- Craft knife
- Paintbrushes
- E-6000 Craft Adhesive
- Scissors
- Printout of your Vision Box saying
- Twig
- Gold thread

The author used these products for the project. Substitute your choice of brands, tools, and materials as desired.

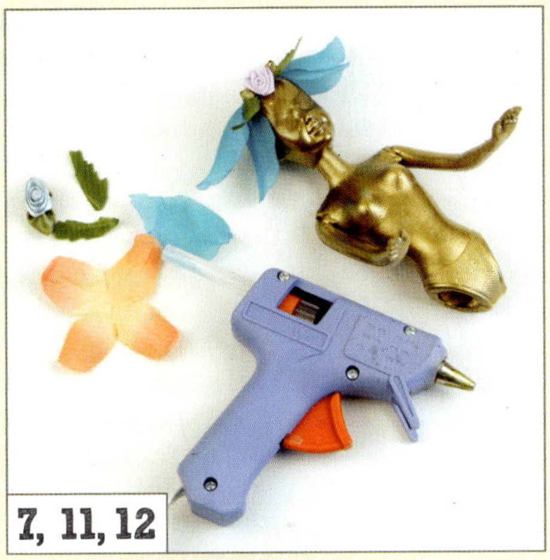

7, 11, 12

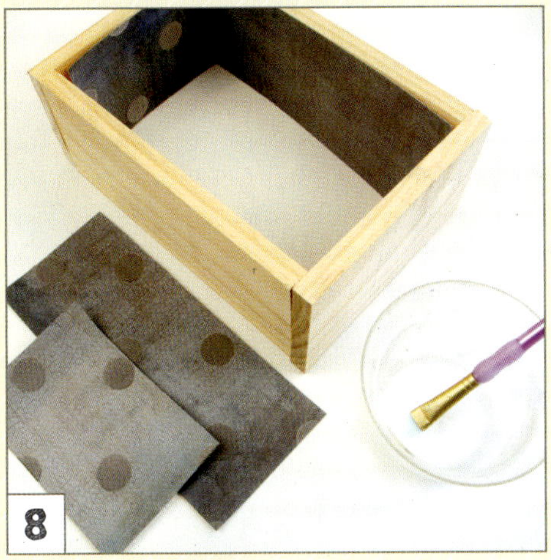

8

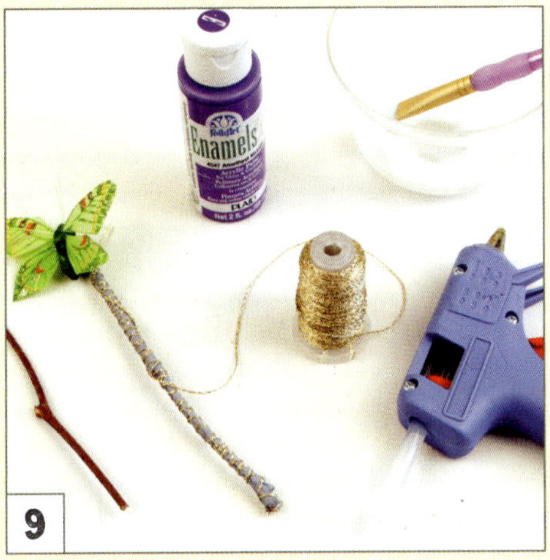

9

1. Cut out the pages of the book with your craft knife on both sides of the binding. The meat of the book will come out easily. Be careful not to slice into the book's cover.

2. Carefully measure the width, height, and thickness of the book.

3. Make your pattern for the walls of the box. The top of your box will be the front cover and the bottom of the box will be the back cover.

4. Use wood glue and the plywood to assemble the box and allow it to dry.

5. Glue one side of the box to the binding of the book and the bottom of the box to the back cover. Make sure the cover of the book can open easily.

6. Paint the sides of the wood box a light blue (or color of your choice).

7. Take the legs and hair off of your doll and spray it gold. Immediately mist it with the water bottle, and then spray it blue and repeat until you get a cool effect and let dry.

8. Cover the inside of your book box with scrapbook papers and slightly watered down Elmer's glue.

9. Paint your twig purple and when it's dry, wrap it with gold thread and hot glue a faux butterfly on top of it.

10. Take some faux flowers apart and hot glue them to the bottom of the box.

11. Glue some faux flower petals on to the head of the doll.

12. Glue a flower petal on the doll to create the top of her dress and then add some sequins.

13. Use E-6000 to glue the doll in place and allow it to dry.

14. Add faux flowers with the hot glue gun to create the bottom of the dress.

15. Glue your butterfly wand to the inside cover and then add your saying with the Elmer's glue over the wand and let dry.

16. Hot glue on more butterflies, the key, and gem.

Creativity is like hidden magic that allows you to turn something mundane into something fantastic.

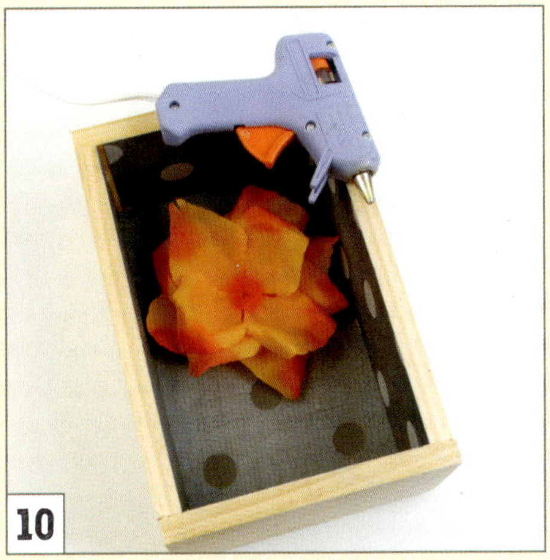

10

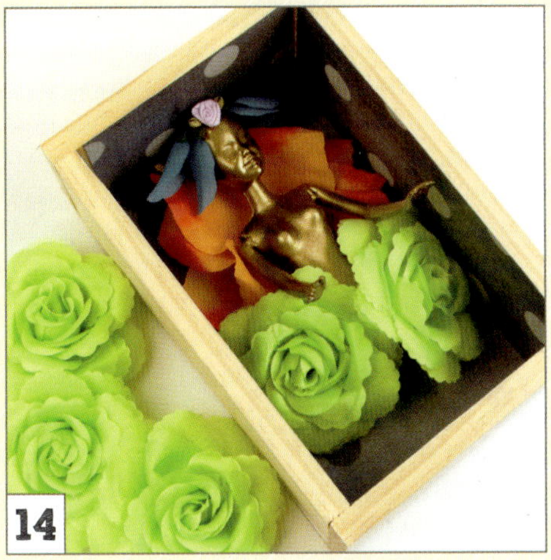

14

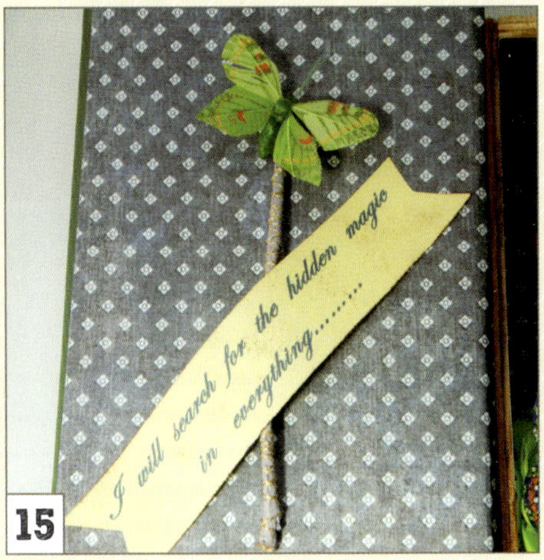

15

I AM Beautiful

Beauty is made up of many things, but I think the most important ingredient is confidence. I made this for a friend and told her to open it right before she went in to a party. She had always felt like a wallflower at parties, and I had a feeling this little magic box might help give her some confidence. It did.

The magic of this *I AM Beautiful Vision Box* is that it's small enough to keep in your purse and you can use it as a reminder to yourself that indeed, you are beautiful.

You'll need:

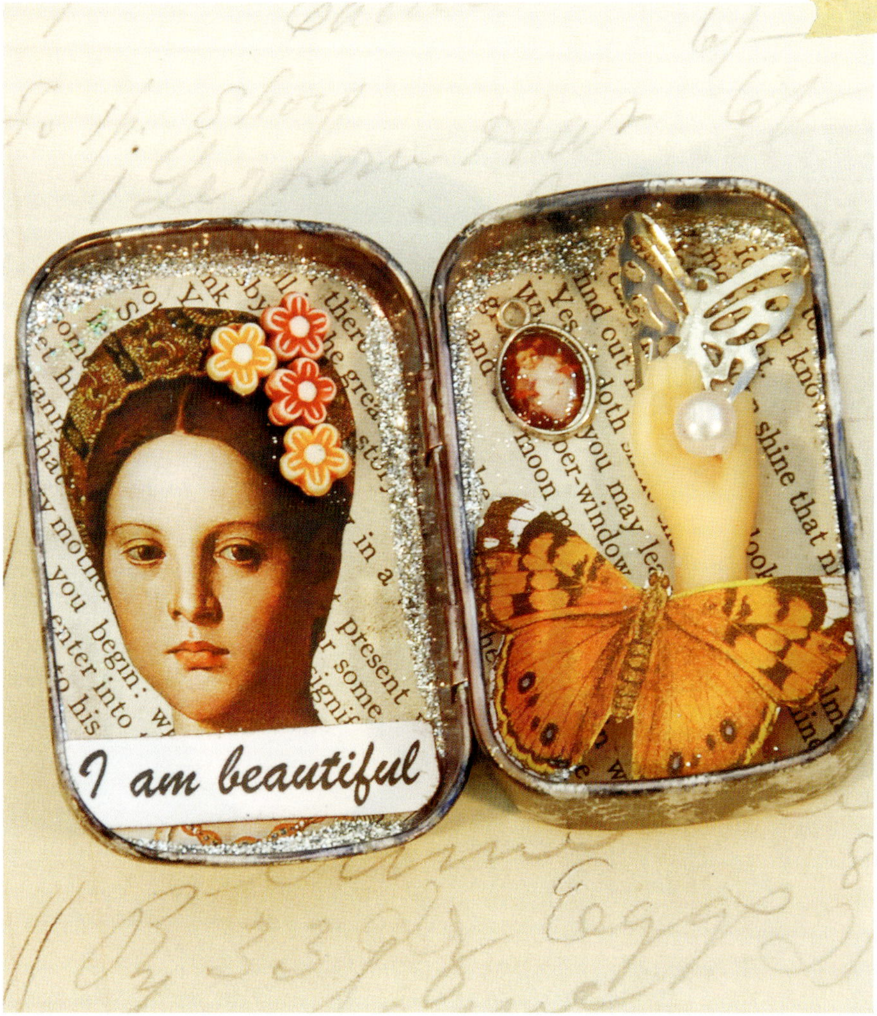

- Small Altoids Minis box
- Doll's hand
- Pearl
- Charms and beads from some junk jewelry
- Any image you like
- Book pages
- Elmer's glue
- E-6000 Craft Adhesive
- Butterfly image
- Printout of your Vision Box saying
- Black spray paint
- Silver acrylic paint
- Rag
- Scissors
- Paintbrushes
- Silver glitter

The author used these products for the project. Substitute your choice of brands, tools, and materials as desired.

This Vision Box is small enough to keep in your purse as a reminder that you yourself are indeed beautiful.

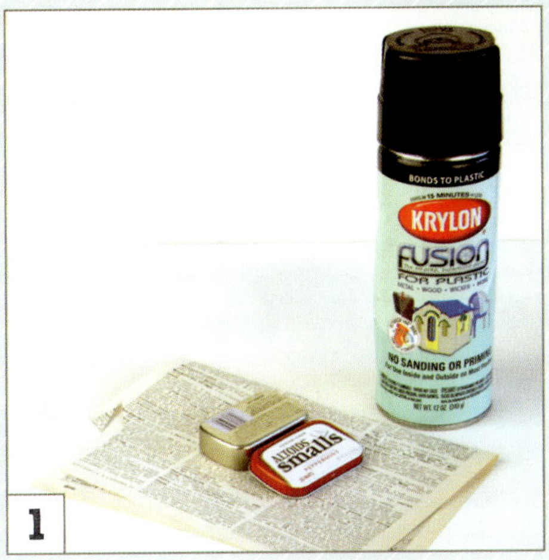

1

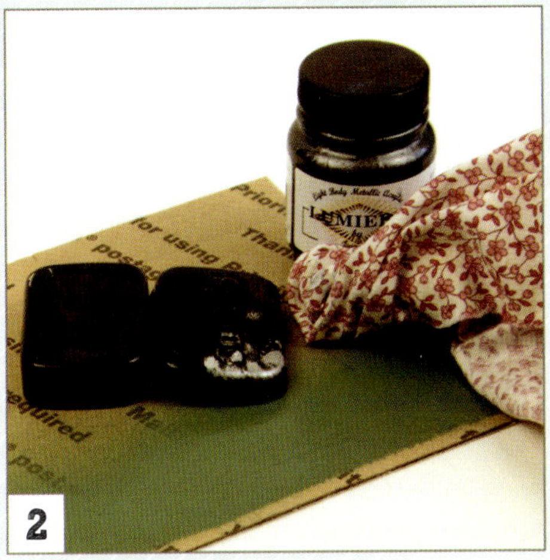
2

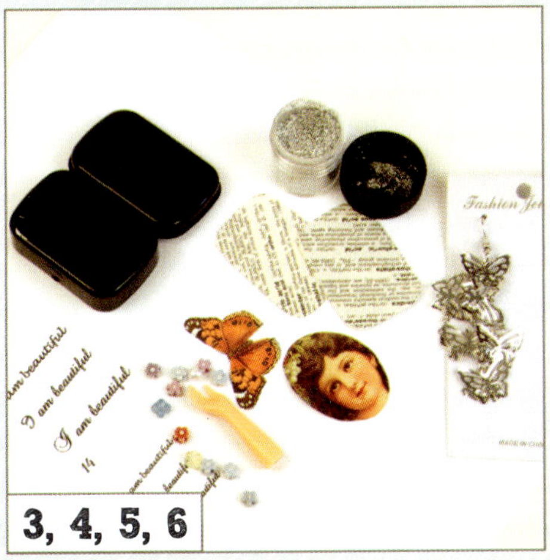

3, 4, 5, 6

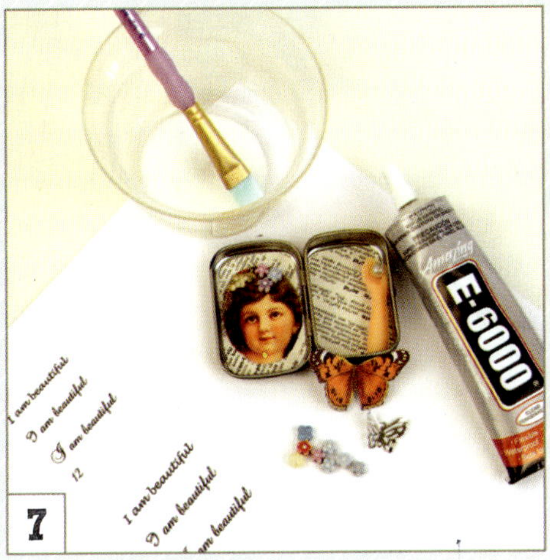

7

1. Spray paint your mini Altoid box black and let dry.

2. Dab with some silver acrylic paint to give it a nice effect.

3. Cut your book pages to fit inside the lid and base of the box and glue them in with Elmer's.

4. Add extra glue around the edges and sprinkle with the silver glitter.

5. Glue in your image. I think it should be a photo of you.

6. Glue on your magic mojo saying.

7. With tiny dabs of E-6000, add your hand, pearl, charms, and beads, and allow them to dry.

8. Glue on your butterfly image over the bottom of the hand.

9. Using E-6000, glue a charm, cameo, or piece of jewelry to the lid of the box and let dry.

10. Stash in your purse or backpack.

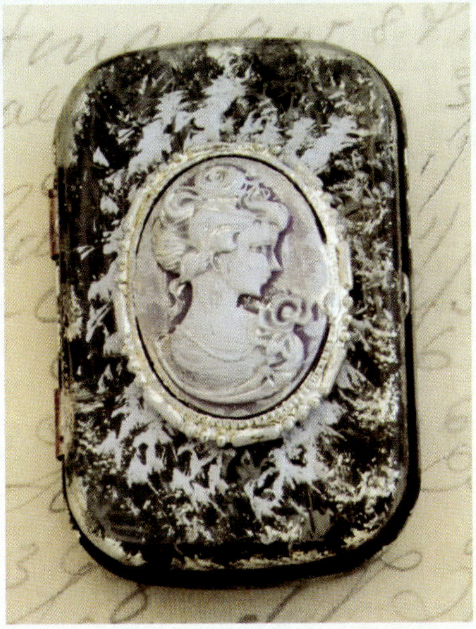

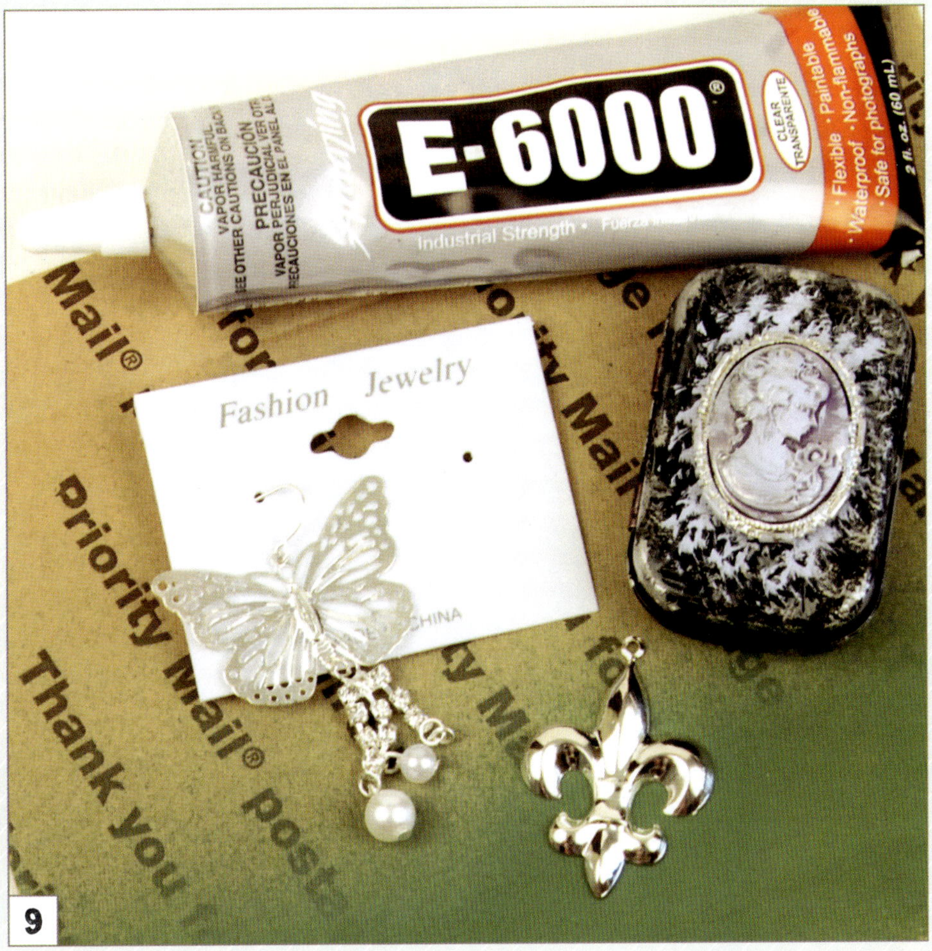

9

I WILL Stand Out

Nelson Mandela said, "It is our responsibility to stand out and share our gifts with the world." and that makes sense. If we all put our best foot forward and shared our gifts, this world would be an even more amazing place in which to live. What good is it if you're an amazing musician and no one gets to listen to you play? Or a fantastic artist and people don't get to see your work?

Share your gifts with the world and DO YOUR BEST TO STAND OUT.

There is magic in sharing your gifts.

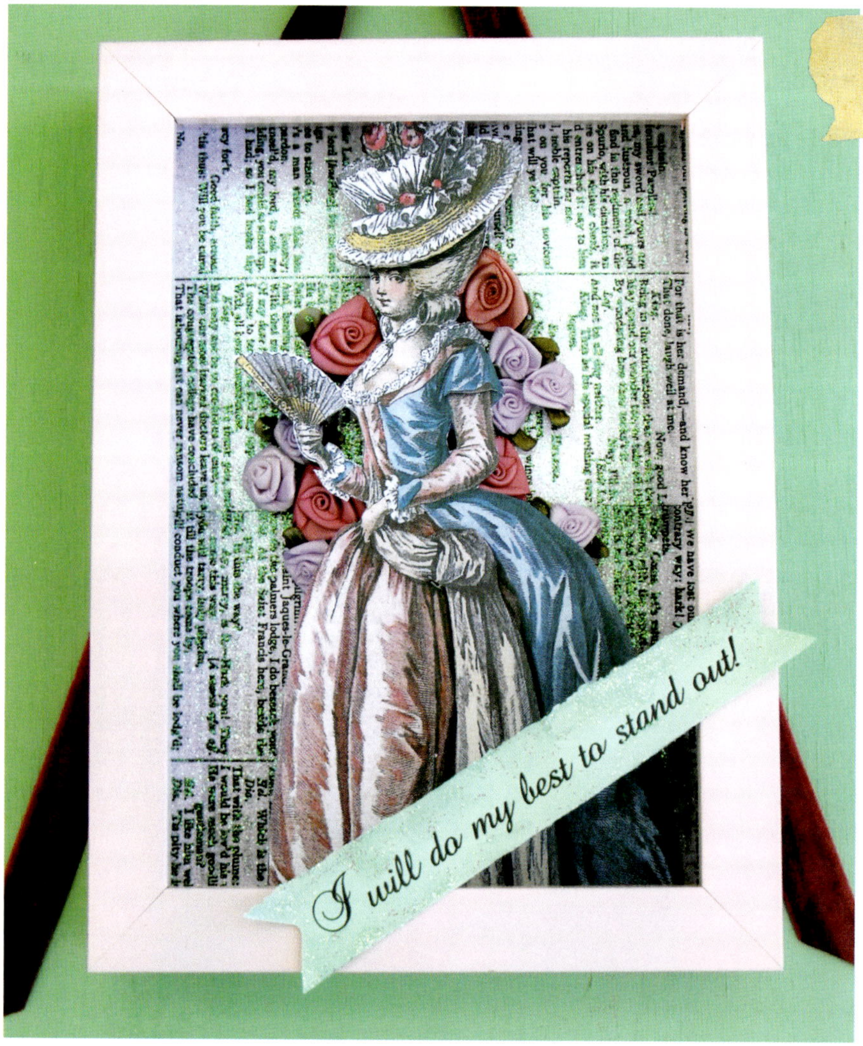

You'll need:

- 1 deep 5" x 7" (127 x 178mm) frame
- Krylon spray paint (pink)
- Cardboard
- Book pages
- Cardstock
- Glitter glue
- 1 copy of an eighteenth century woman (page 72)
- Ribbon roses
- Craft knife
- Scissors
- Elmer's glue
- 1" (25mm)-wide paintbrush
- Hot glue gun
- E-6000 Craft Adhesive
- Printout of your Vision Box words
- 1 yard (91cm) of ½" (13mm)-wide ribbon

The author used these products for the project. Substitute your choice of brands, tools, and materials as desired.

Share your gifts with the world and do your best to stand out! There is magic in sharing your gifts!

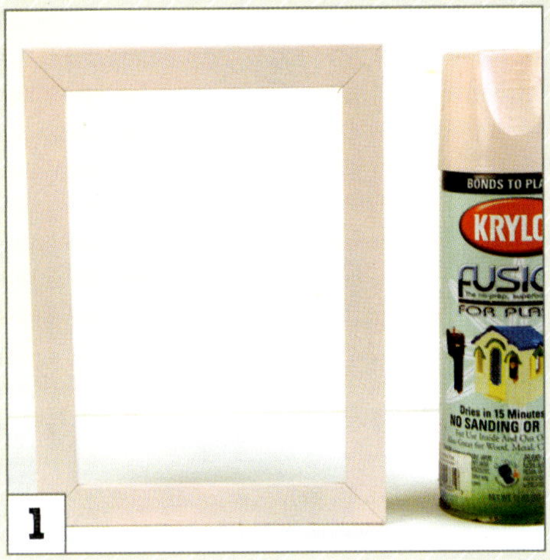
1

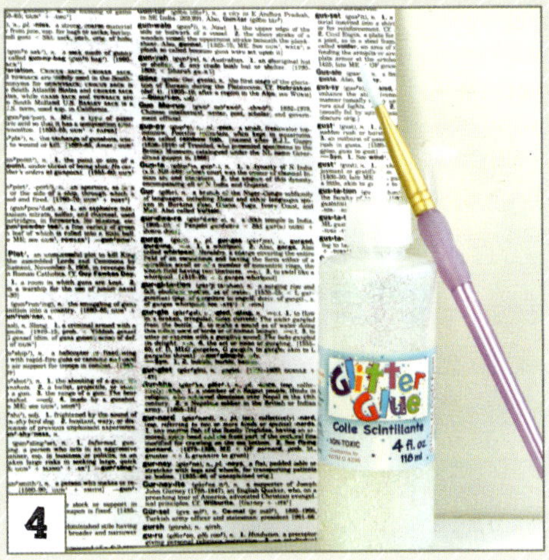
4

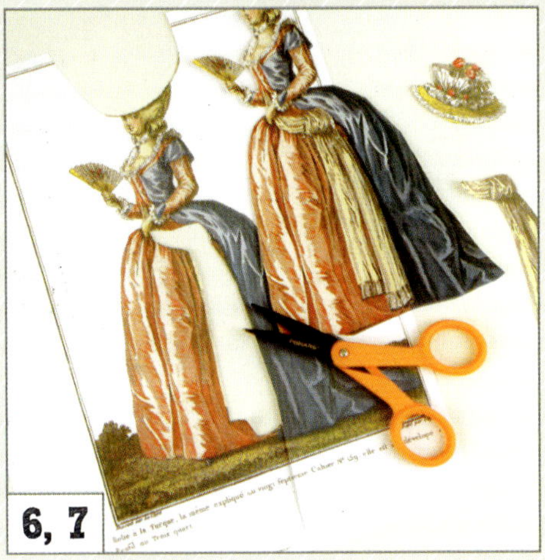
6, 7

1. Spray paint your frame pink.
2. Cut your cardboard the size of the frame. This will be the back of your Vision Box.
3. Cover it with book pages using very slightly watered down Elmer's glue and a 1" (25mm)-wide paintbrush and let dry.
4. Coat the entire book page covered cardboard backing with glitter glue and let dry.
5. Make 3 copies of your eighteenth century lady (or another image if you like) on cardstock.
6. Carefully cut out one entire lady from one copy.
7. From another copy, cut out different elements like her hat, sash, arm, etc.
8. Cut out 25 tiny squares of cardboard and with the Elmer's, glue stacks of 5 underneath the lady in several places. We are creating a 3-D art piece that is raised above the book page backing.
9. Cut out more small squares of cardboard and layer them under the hat, sleeve, and sash, and glue them on top of the full cutout of the lady. This will help it look even more 3-D.
10. Glue the entire lady to the book page covered cardboard backing with the Elmer's.
11. Using the E-6000, glue on several ribbon roses under and around the lady.
12. Print and cut out your Vision Box saying and lightly coat it with more glitter glue and then glue in place when dry.
13. Hot glue a bow on the back of the frame so that you can hang it.

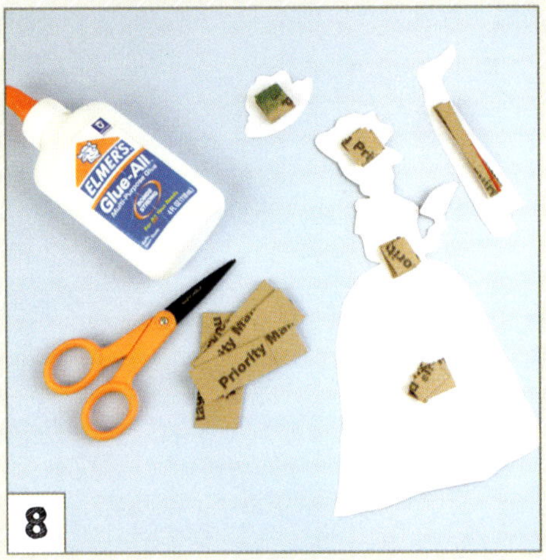
8

9

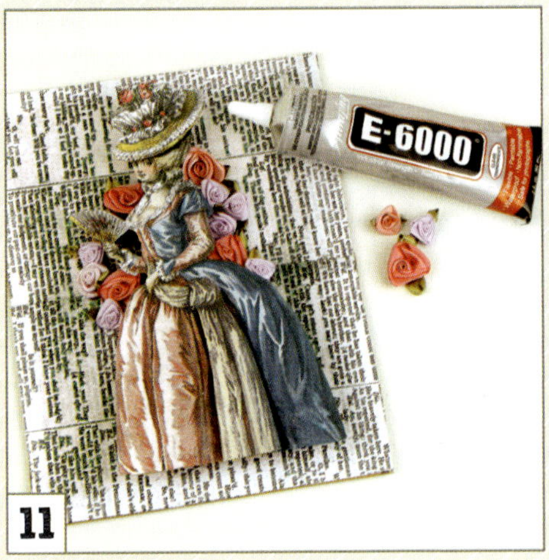

11

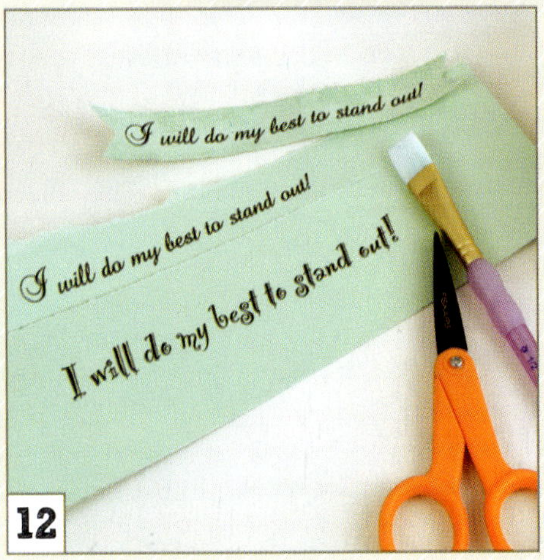

12

Inspiration

Do you have a favorite artist or person who inspires you? Someone you admire and want to be like? I have several, but top on my list is the artist Frida Khalo. She was an amazing person who used her creativity to work through her hardships. When I look at her and her work, I feel something inside that makes me want to be like her, approach life like her, and work to be as talented as her. Magical is the only way I can describe the feeling of inspiration I get from her and her work. It's what I felt when making this Vision Box as an ode to her and how I feel when I look at it.

You can use anyone in your Inspiration Vision Box as long as they make you feel the way Frida makes me feel.

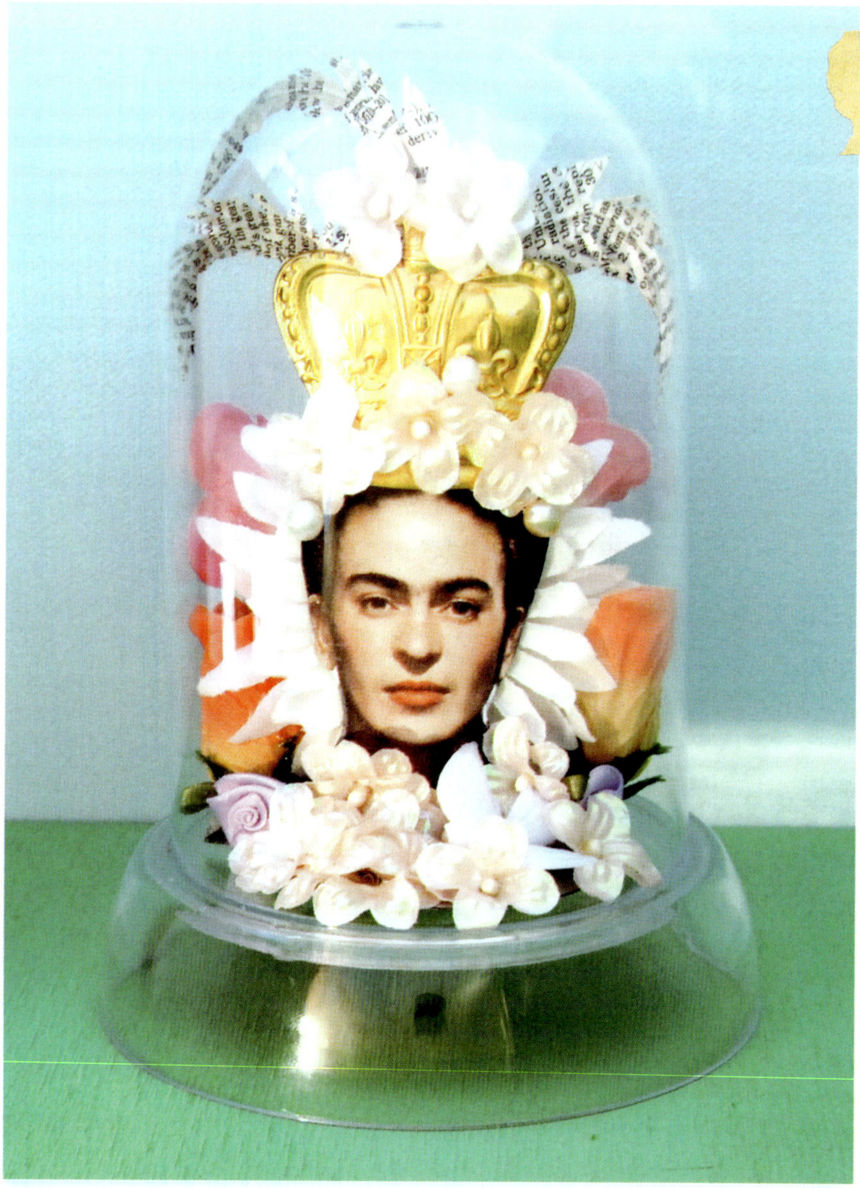

You'll need:

- 7" (178mm)-tall plastic cake topper dome
- Cereal box cardboard
- Color copy of your inspirational person
- Small faux flowers
- Ribbon flowers
- Pearls
- Small plastic bird
- Brass crown
- Book pages
- Small gauge wire and wire cutters
- Elmer's glue
- Scissors
- Hot glue gun
- E-6000 Craft Adhesive

The author used these products for the project. Substitute your choice of brands, tools, and materials as desired.

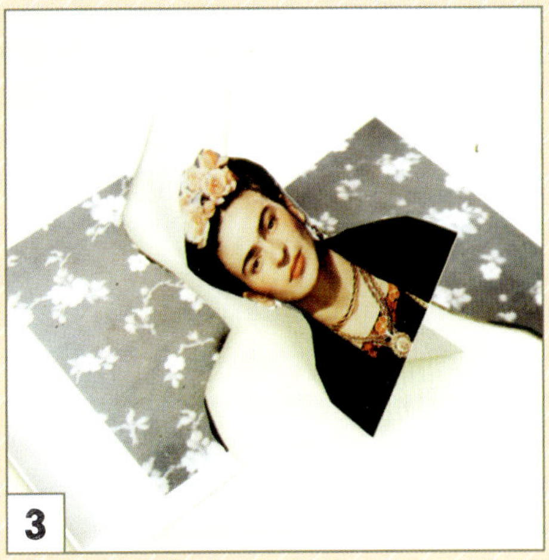

3

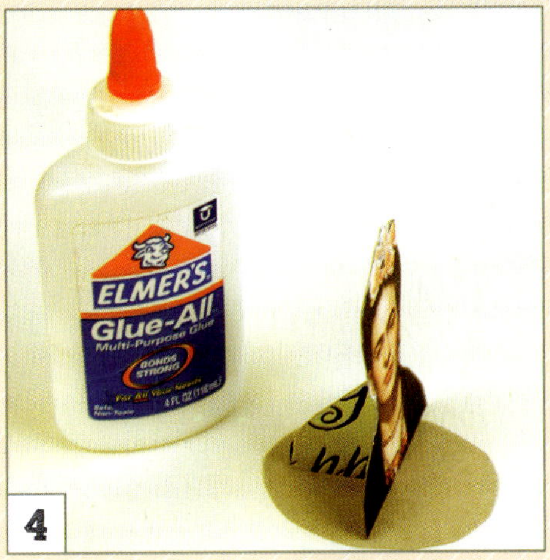

4

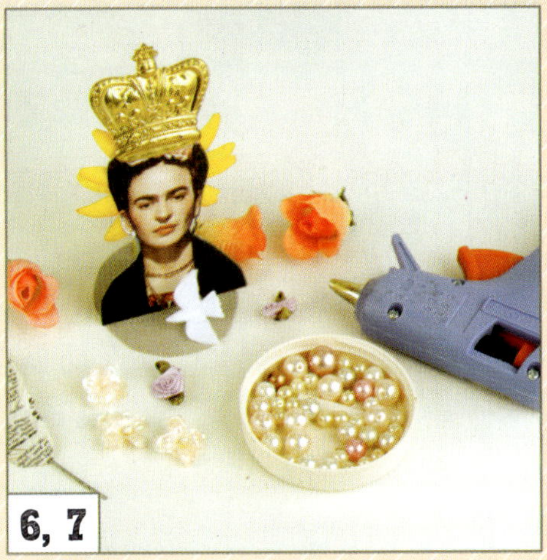

6, 7

1. Measure the height and circumference of your dome. You want to make sure that what you're creating fits inside.
2. Copy your image and with the Elmer's, glue it on some cereal box cardboard to make it sturdy.
3. Cut out your image.
4. Glue a triangle to the back of your image to make a stand (like shown) and glue the standing image on a circle of cardboard.
5. E-6000 your crown on the top of your image and let dry.
6. Hot glue flowers behind your image and around the top.
7. E-6000 the pearls, bird, and ribbon flowers on your image and around your base.
8. Take two small pieces of book page and glue a small piece of wire in between to create your feather. Let it dry and then cut out your feather shape and fringe with your scissors.
9. Hot glue on the back of the crown.
10. Place your flower-covered image on the base of the dome and cover.

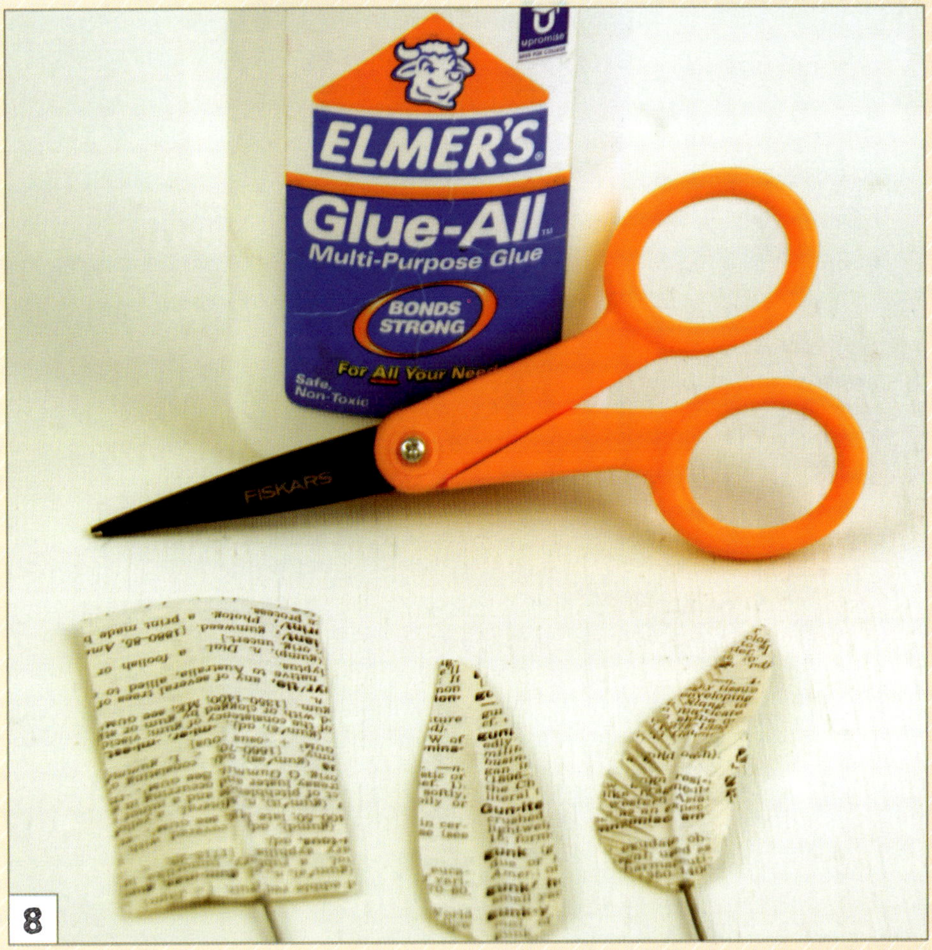

8

Magical is the only way I can describe the feeling of inspiration I get from her and her work.

Keys to My Heart

I love to see groups of people having fun together or couples in love at a restaurant. It just makes me happy. I got to thinking about how these relationships develop and it popped in to my head that we have to let people in. The only way to do this is to give out keys to your heart—not just one key, because we're more complicated than that, but many keys.

The magic of this box is that it shows people that we're open and willing.

What could be better than that?

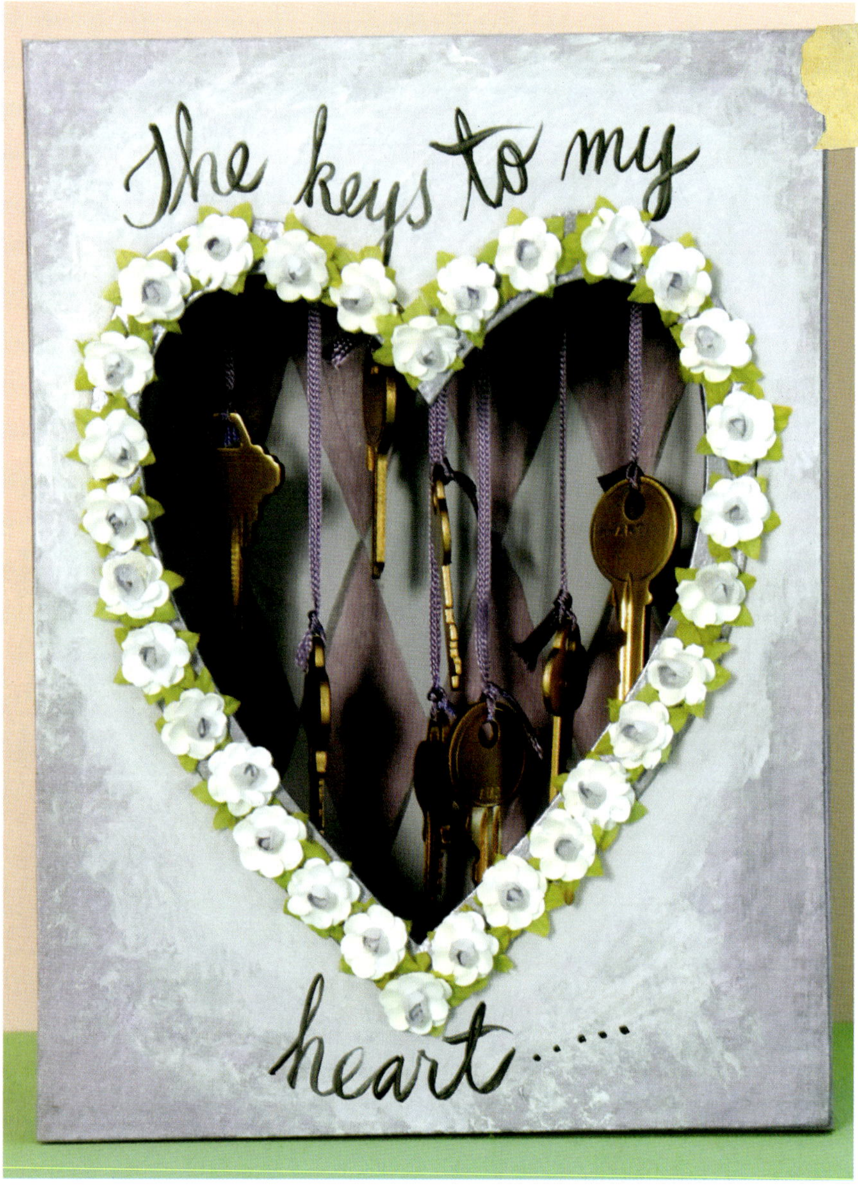

You'll need:

- Vision Box #1 on page 12
- Cardboard to fit over the front and back
- Krylon spray paint (light purple and metallic gold colors)
- Purple, black, and white acrylic paint
- Paintbrushes
- Rag
- Keys
- 1 yard (91cm) of ¼"(6mm)-wide ribbon
- Hot glue gun
- Elmer's glue
- Small flowers
- Craft knife

The author used these products for the project. Substitute your choice of brands, tools, and materials as desired.

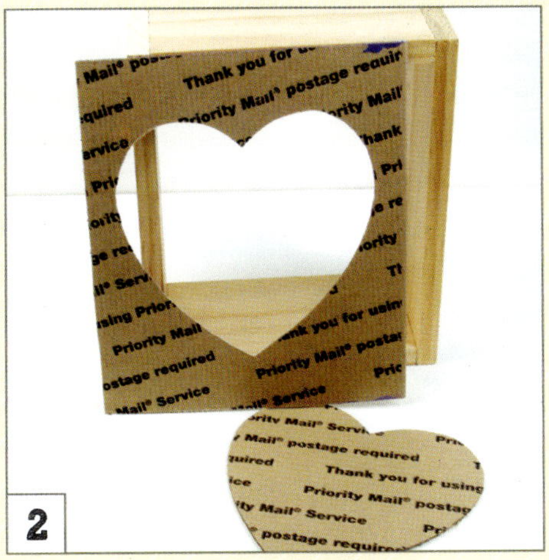

2

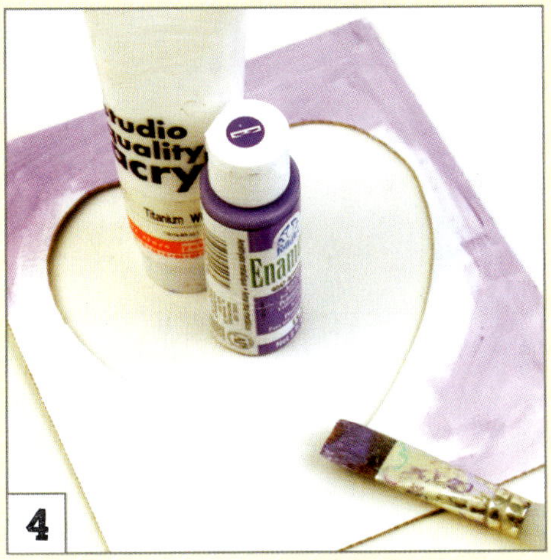

4

1. Cut your cardboard to fit the front and back of the box.
2. Cut out a heart on one of the pieces of cardboard.
3. Spray paint your keys gold
4. Spray paint the cardboard pieces and the box the light purple.
5. Paint your harlequin design on the back cardboard piece, mixing your acrylic paints to get your different colors.
6. Dab different colors of purple on your box and heart cover to get texture and let dry.
7. Paint your Vision Box saying on the heart cover with your black paint using a thin paintbrush.
8. Hot glue on the flowers around the heart.
9. Tie ribbon around your keys and hot glue them from the top of the inside of your box.
10. With Elmer's glue, attach the front and back cardboard covers to your box and let dry.

You have to let people in. The only way to do that is to give out keys—many keys—to your heart.

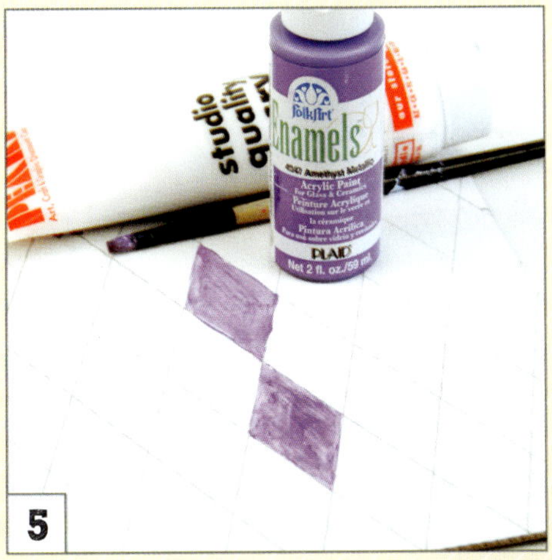

5

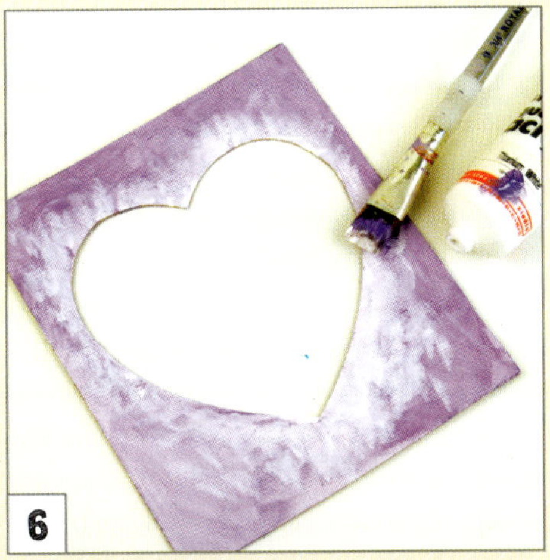

6

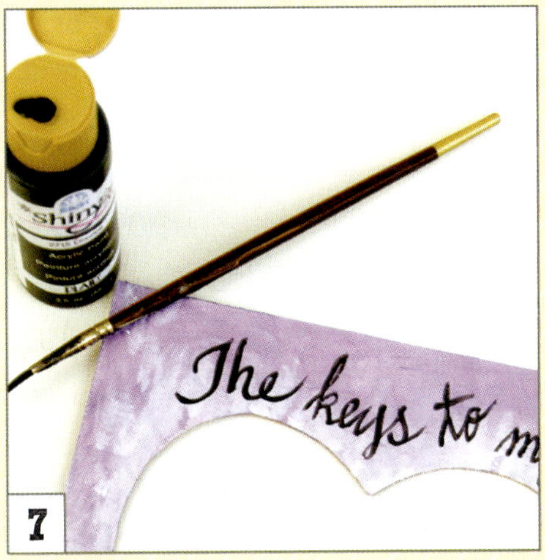

7

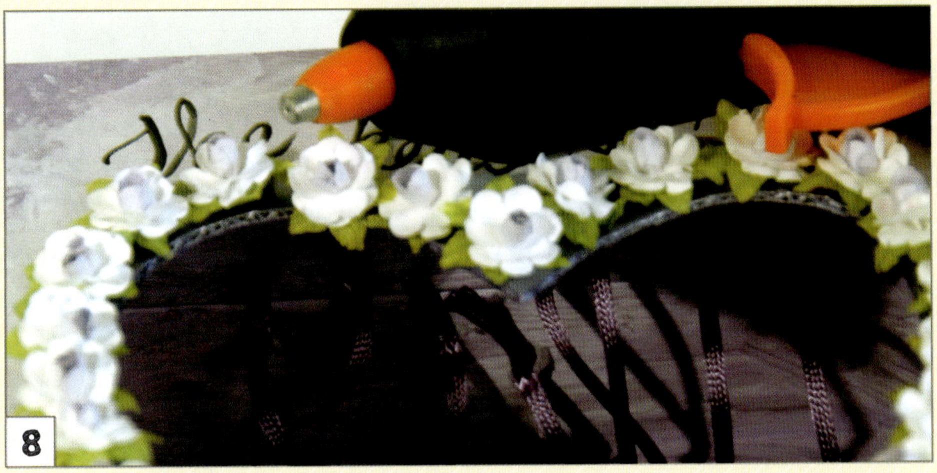

8

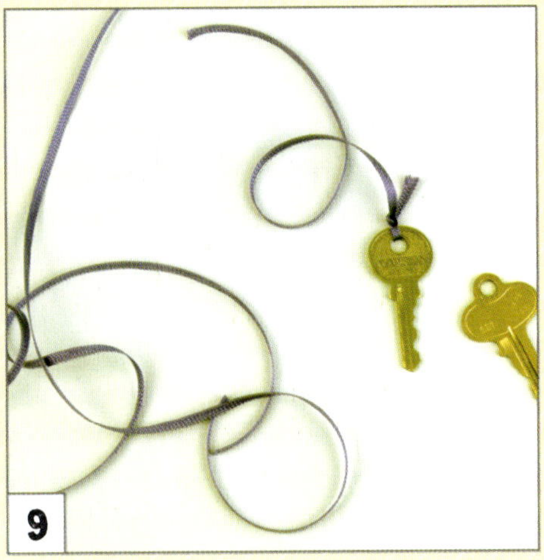

9

Live the Sweet Life!

I gained five pounds making this Vision Box, and oddly, I'm not that upset about it! I realized the magic of this box was about our ability to make ourselves happy. It's a constant reminder that we have to make our lives enjoyable. That means not feeling guilty for having a cookie or for buying a terrific pair of shoes.

If we don't treat ourselves well, then who will?

That's what living the sweet life is about.

It may not happen right away, but I assure you, it's happening.

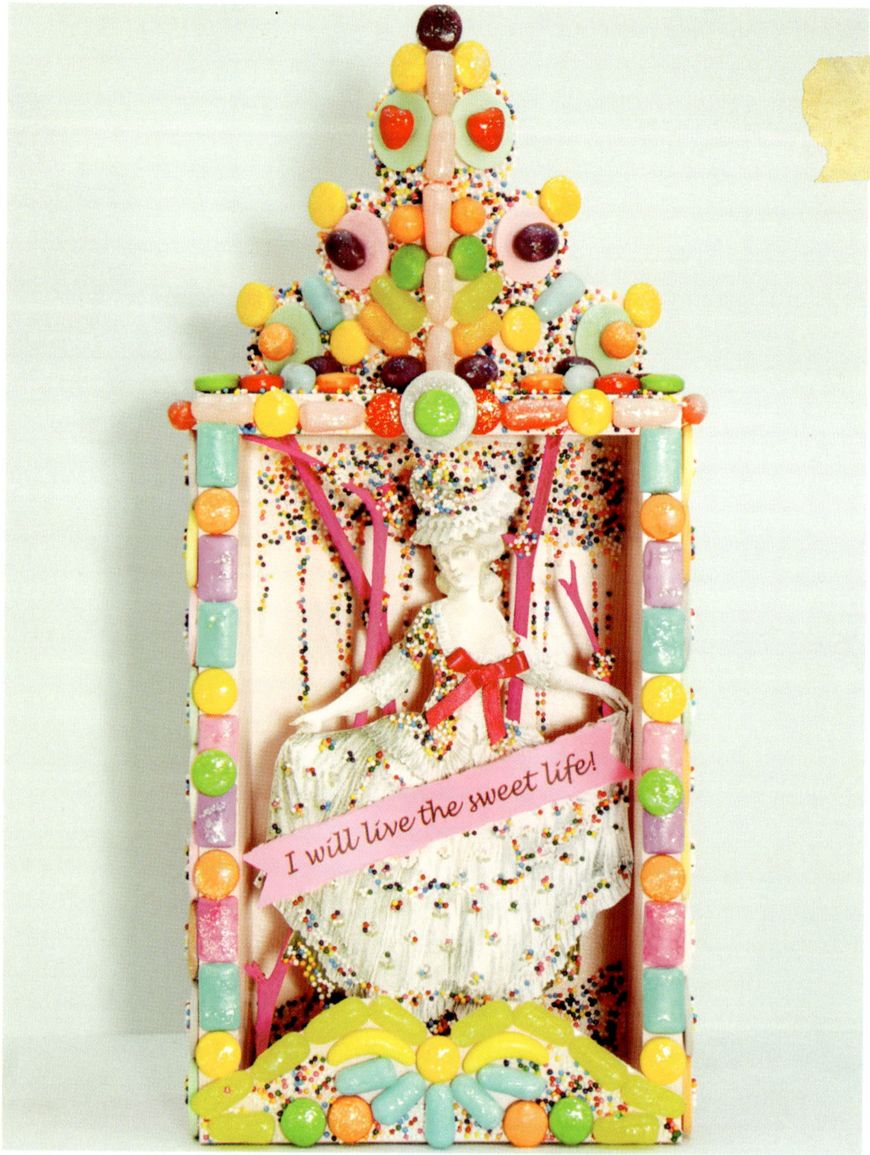

You'll need:

- Vision Box #2 on page 12
- Krylon spray paint (pink)
- Cardboard for the topper and back of the box
- Various colorful hard candies (Spree, Mike and Ikes, Nerds, Jelly beans, Chicklets)
- Hot glue gun
- Colorful sprinkles
- Elmer's glue
- Color copy of eighteenth century woman on cardstock
- Copy of Sweet Life slogan on pink cardstock
- Twigs
- Florescent pink paint
- Craft knife
- Paintbrushes
- Scissors
- Glitter glue

The author used these products for the project. Substitute your choice of brands, tools, and materials as desired.

If we don't treat ourselves well, then who will? That's what living the sweet life is all about.

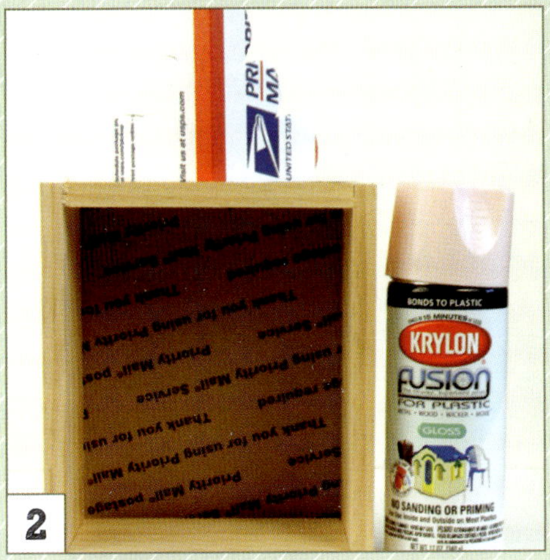

2

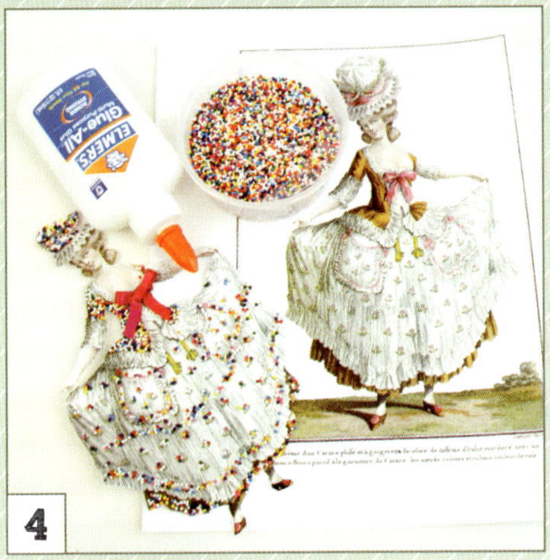

4

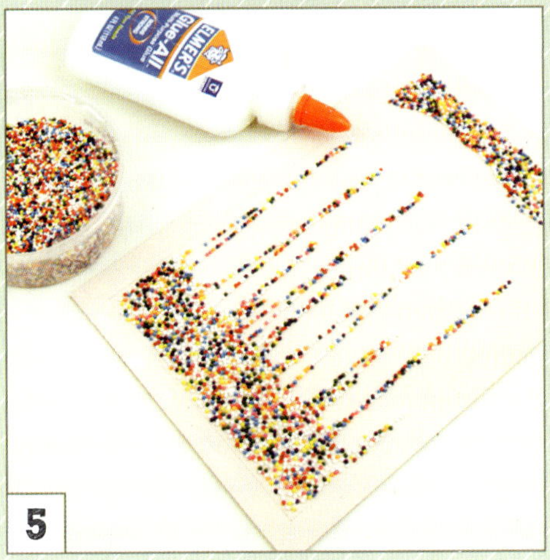

5

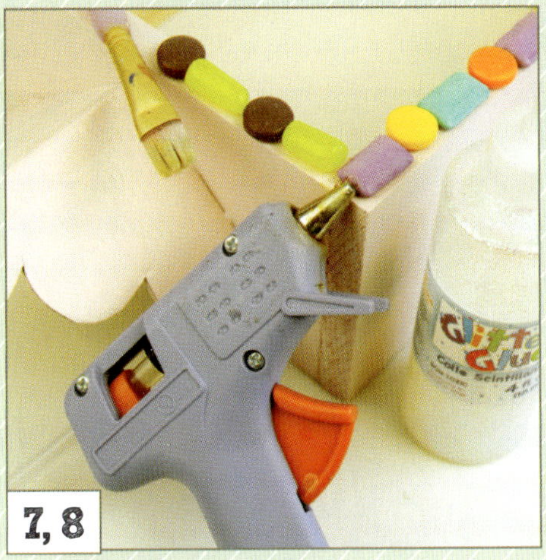

7, 8

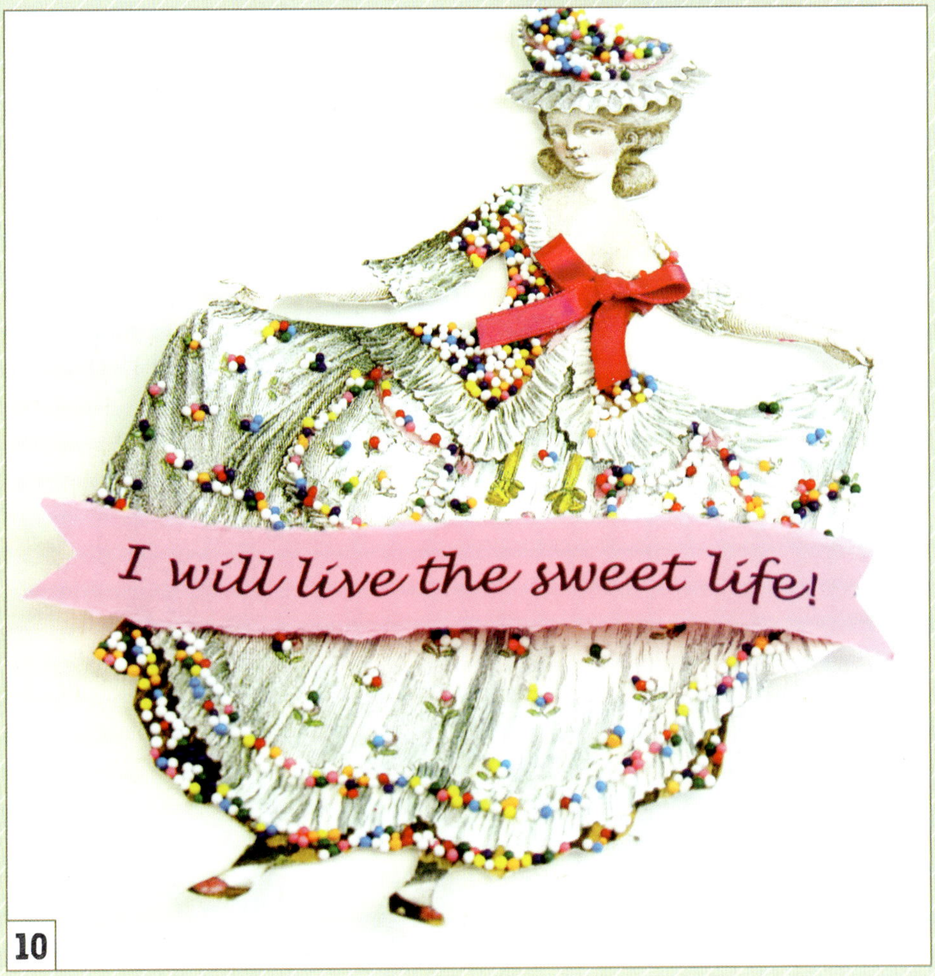

10

1. Cut your cardboard topper and bottom piece using the patterns on pages 75 and 76 and a piece to fit the back of the Vision Box.
2. Glue the topper on the box and spray paint the entire box and back cardboard piece in the pink spray paint and let dry.
3. Copy your eighteenth century woman (page 71) on cardstock and cut out.
4. Dabble some glue on your lady and sprinkle with the colorful sprinkles and allow to dry.
5. Dabble glue on the back piece of cardboard and sprinkle the colorful sprinkles on and let dry.
6. Paint the twigs with the florescent pink paint and let dry.
7. Glue the candies all over the entire box. Cover the sides, the topper, the bottom piece, and the face of the box using hot glue.
8. Paint the candies with glitter glue so they sparkle.
9. Add more glue and fill in some spaces with the colorful sprinkles.
10. Print out your Sweet Life saying on pink paper and glue in place.
11. Hot glue in the twigs and then glue in the candy-covered lady.

LIVE!

I saw the movie *Auntie Mame* with Rosalind Russell when I was a kid, and there is one line in the movie that has always stuck with me:

"YES! LIVE! Life is a banquet and most poor suckers are starving to death!"

It's true.

Life is a banquet, and you just have to get out there and take part, because if you don't, you're missing out. This little Vision Box is portable and is kept in my backpack to remind me I have to make the most of every day...and LIVE!

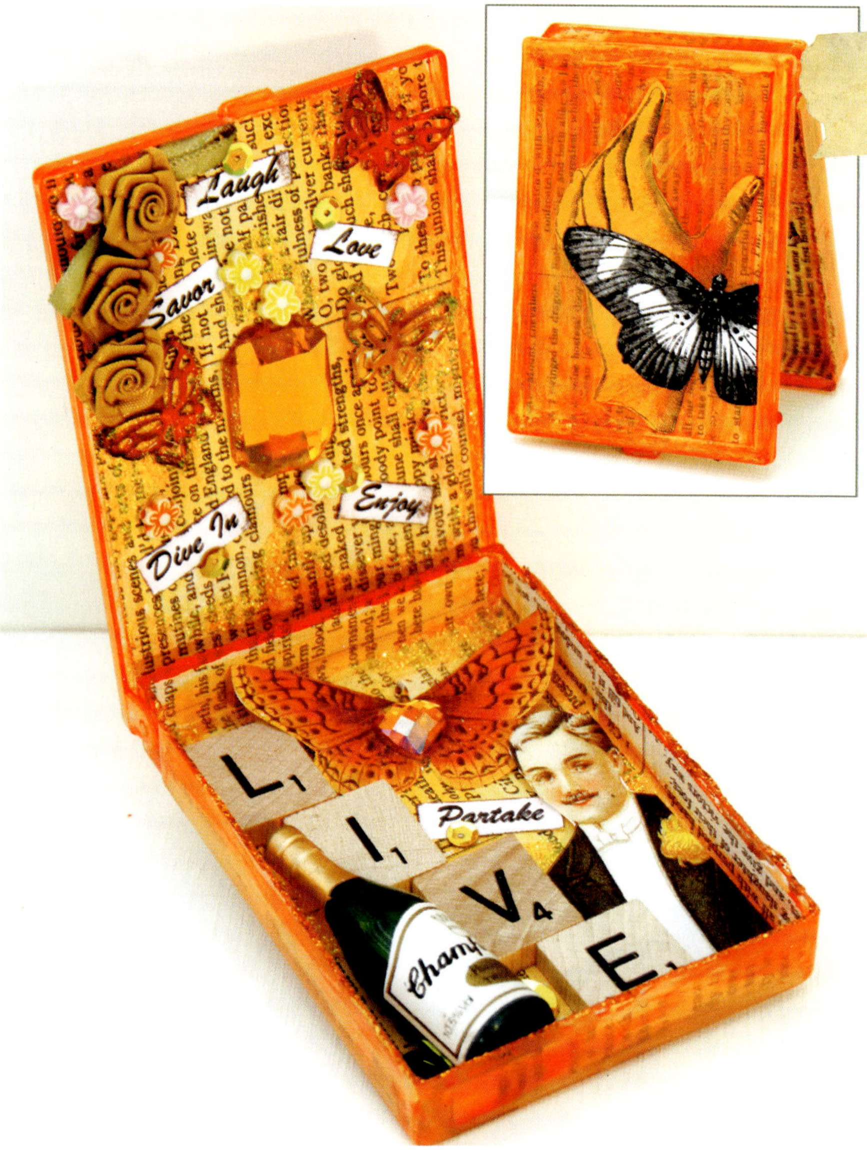

You'll need:

- Small clear plastic box (sold holding tacks and paperclips)
- Orange and gold acrylic paint
- Book pages
- Scissors
- Watercolor paint set
- Paintbrushes
- Letter tiles
- Jewelry pieces
- Ribbon flowers
- Small champagne bottle
- Printout of butterflies, hands, a dapper man, and your words to LIVE! by (I've provided this art on pages 66, 68, 69, and 77).
- Gems, beads, and sequins
- E-6000 Craft Adhesive
- Elmer's glue
- Glitter glue

The author used these products for the project. Substitute your choice of brands, tools, and materials as desired.

Life really is a banquet and you just have to get out there and take part because if you don't, you're missing out!

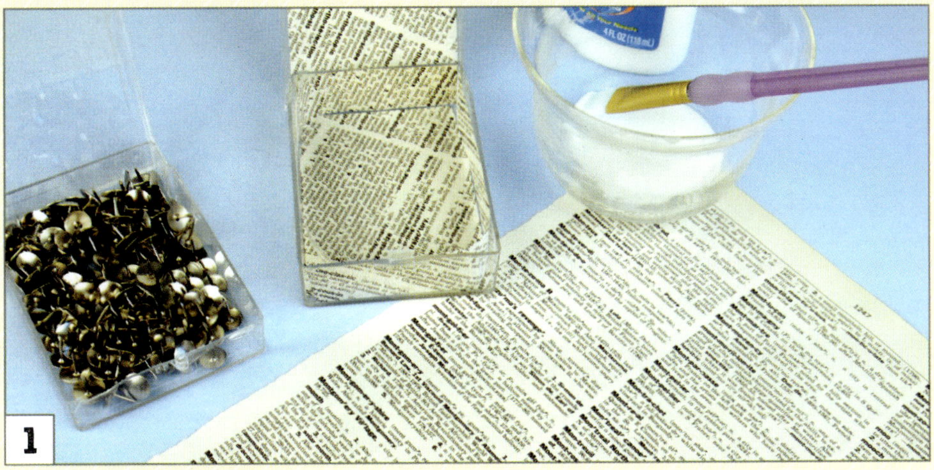

1

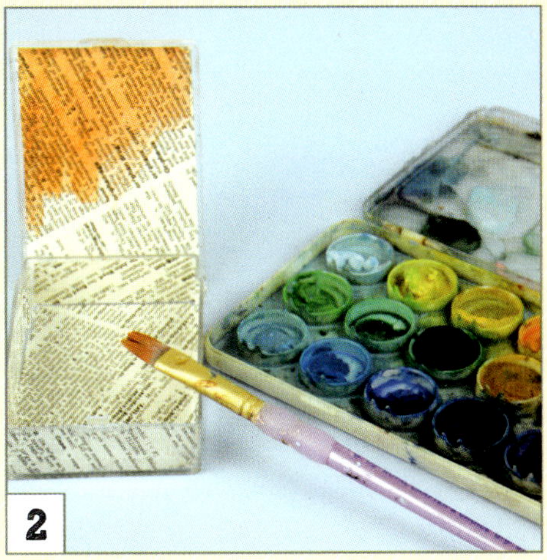

2

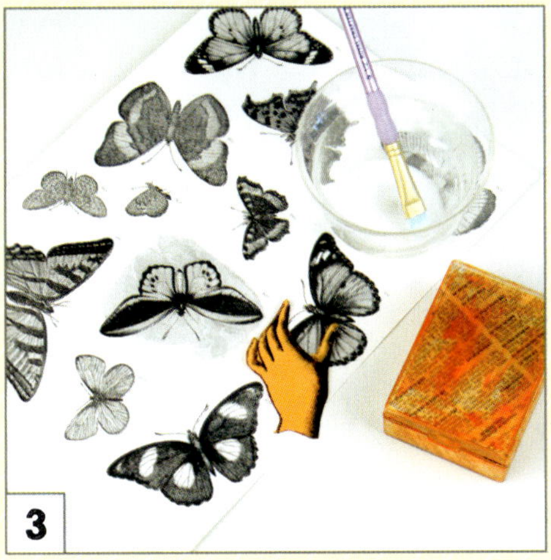

3

1. Cover the inside of your box with book pages using Elmer's glue and let dry.

2. Lightly paint the book pages with your orange watercolor and let dry.

3. Figure out the placement of your items before you glue them.

4. Glue in the images, words, tiles and then the gems, flowers, and jewelry pieces using small dabs of E-6000.

5. Paint some glitter glue in the corners and on the book pages to give them some sparkle.

6. Close the box and paint with the orange acrylic paint and let dry.

7. Add your hand and butterfly to the lid using Elmer's glue and lightly paint over the images and box with the gold paint and let dry.

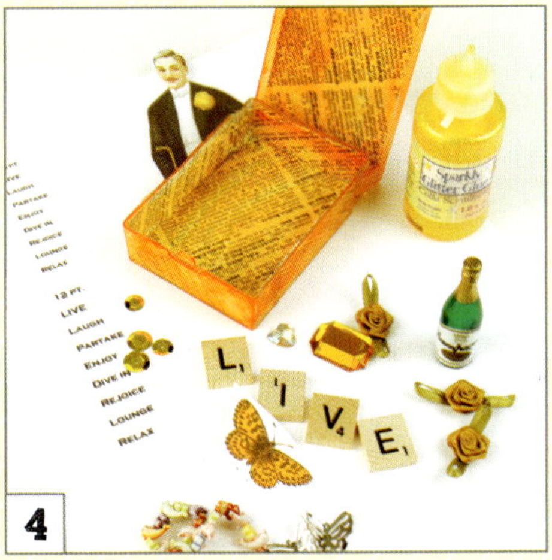

4

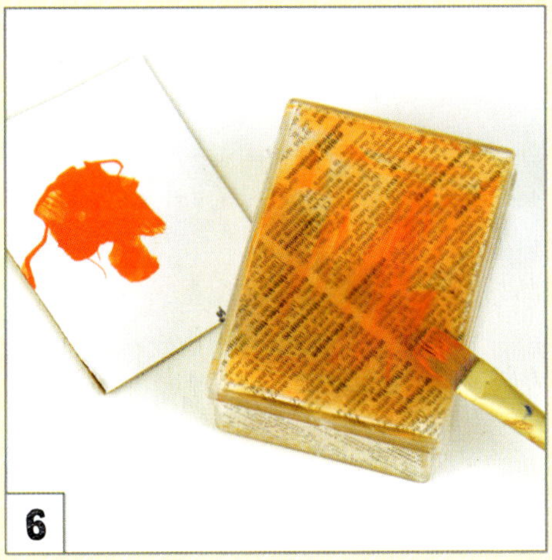

6

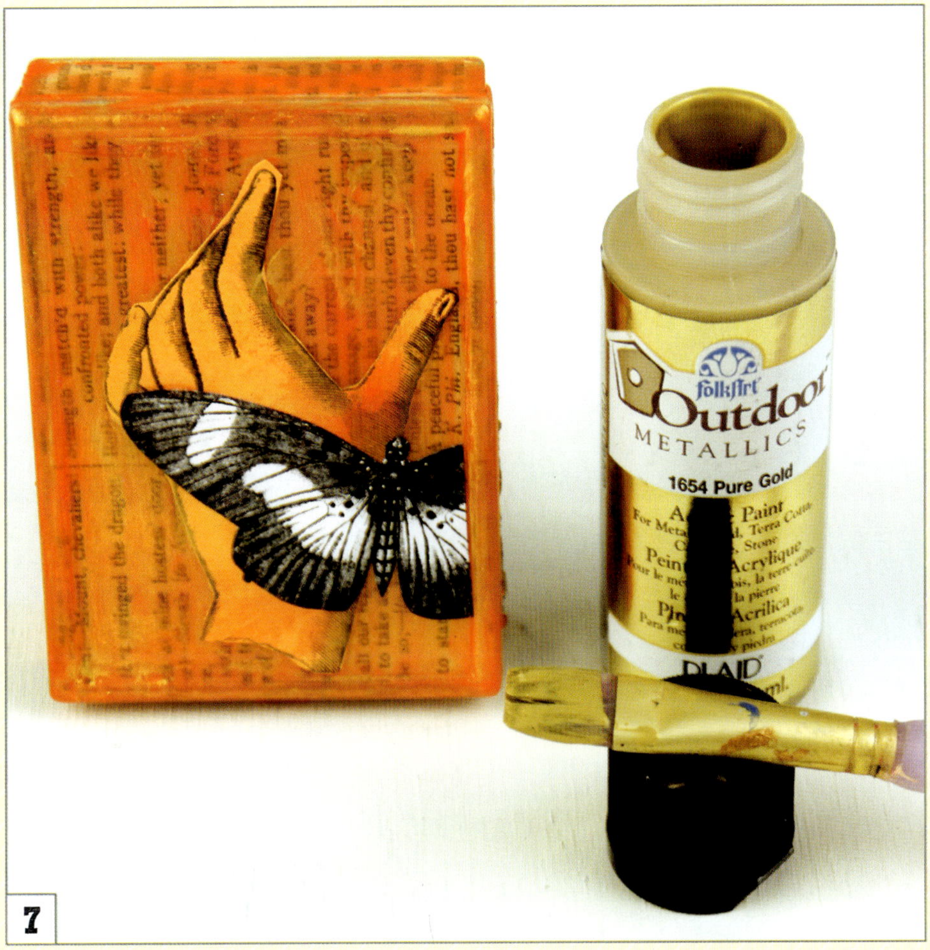

7

Love Nest

The Love Nest Vision Box is the perfect thing to make when you want to focus on creating your own love nest with someone. I imagined a cozy nest for two, complete with a baby on the way—it's in the egg. You can always put more photos and more eggs in this if you want.

Oh, and just a little hint, all the things you want for your love nest can be written down and put inside the egg before you seal it with the book pages.

That's where I put the magic.

Love Nest is the perfect Vision Box to make when you want to focus on creating your own love nest with someone.

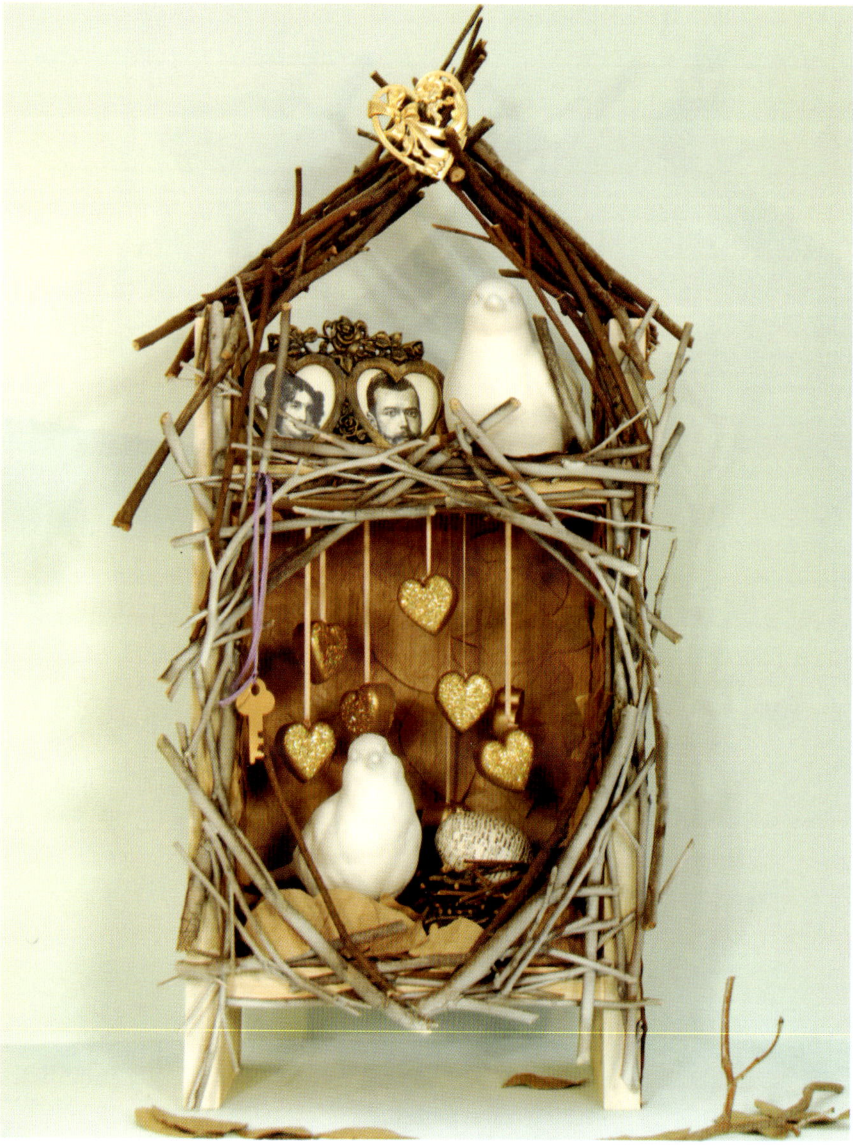

You'll need:

- Vision Box #3 instructions on page 13
- Half of a grocery bag filled with twigs that are 5" to 7" (127 to 178mm) long
- 30 small twigs to create the nest
- 2 yards (183cm) of brown craft paper or some brown paper bags
- Cardboard to cover back
- Paintbrushes
- Scissors
- 1 plastic Easter egg
- Book pages
- 2 ceramic birds (check 99 Cent store or thrift stores)
- Krylon spray paint (white primer and white)
- Hot glue gun
- Elmer's glue
- 1½ yards (137cm) of ¼" (6mm)-wide ribbon
- Plaster of Paris
- Heart-shaped rubber ice cube tray
- Krylon Gold Glitter Blast
- Small heart-shaped frame (I see these at every 99 Cent store I go to!)
- Small key
- Optional: Brass heart ornament (or ornament of your choice)

The author used these products for the project. Substitute your choice of brands, tools, and materials as desired.

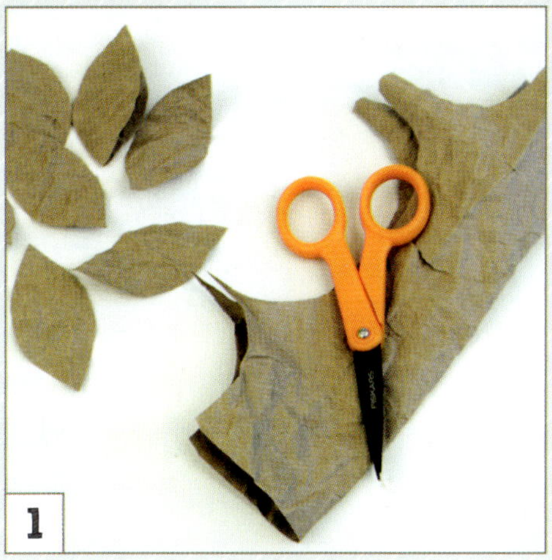
1

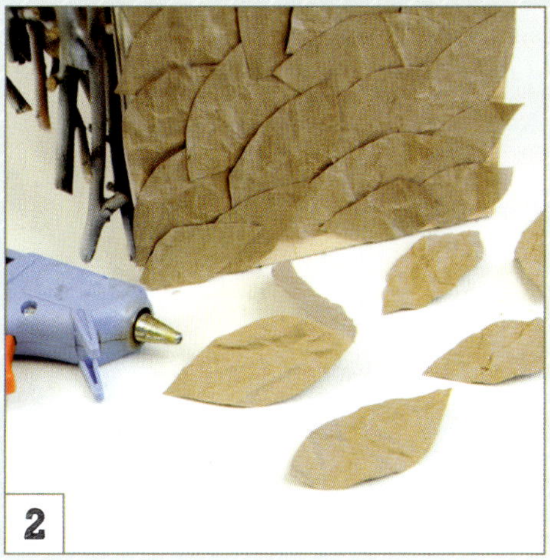
2

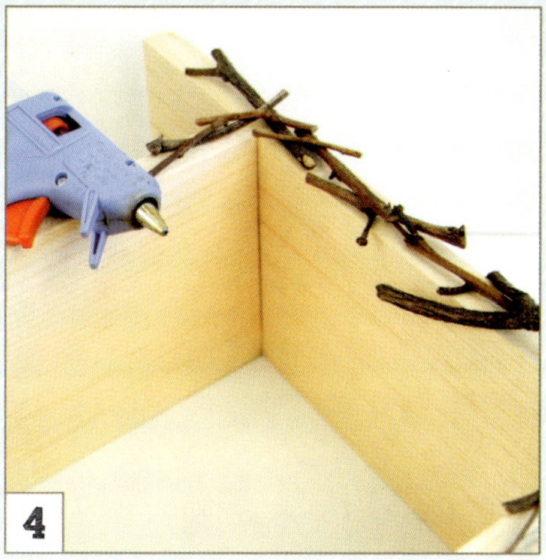
4

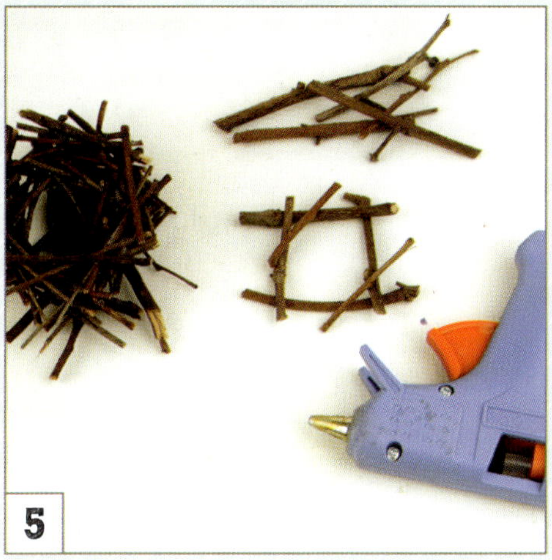
5

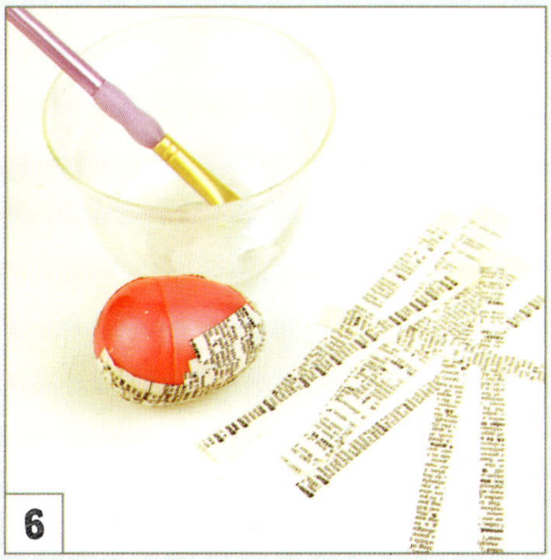
6

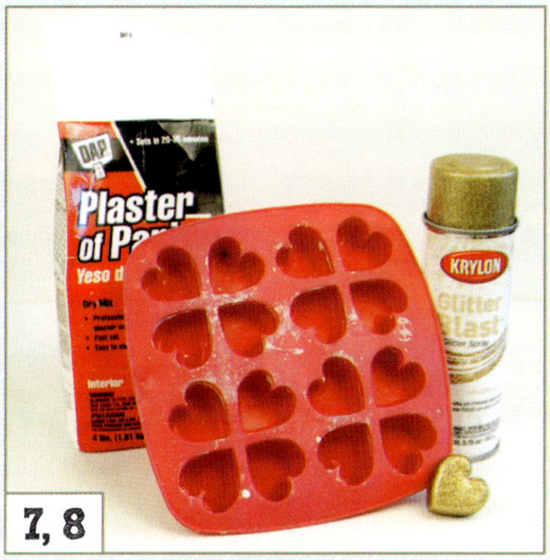

7, 8

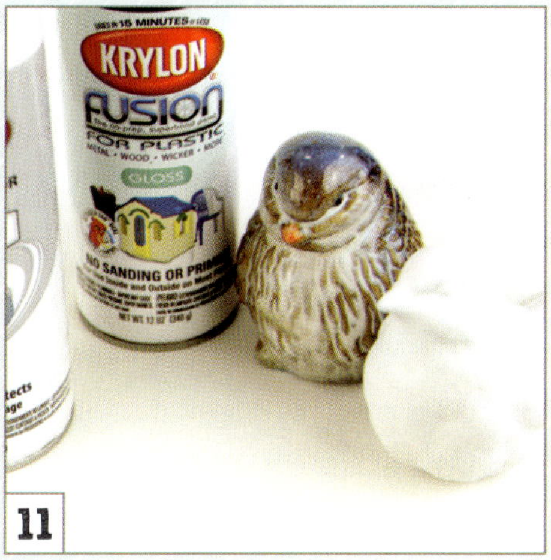

11

1. After your box is assembled, crumple up your craft paper or paper bags, flatten out, and cut out tons of leaves.

2. With your glue gun, cover the back piece of cardboard, and the inside and outside of your box with the craft paper leaves.

3. Hot glue twigs on the top of the Love Nest Vision Box at an angle, meeting in the middle to create the gable.

4. Hot glue more twigs on the face of the Love Nest until you get the effect you want.

5. Using the smaller twigs, build your nest using tiny dabs of the hot glue and building your nest upward by stacking the twigs one by one.

6. Fill your egg with written ideas of what you want in your love nest, coat with Elmer's glue, and adhere book page strips to it until it's completely covered.

7. Fill your rubber heart ice cube tray with plaster of Paris and let dry.

8. Remove your hearts and spray with Glitter Blast

9. Hot glue the hearts on small pieces of the ¼" (6mm)-wide ribbon and attach the ribbons to the inside top of the box with some more hot glue.

10. Fill your photo frame with you and your family or the person with whom you want to share your Love Nest.

11. Spray your ceramic birds with the Krylon white primer and then with the white spray paint and let dry.

12. Fill your box with the birds, nest, frames, and more loose leaves.

13. Glue on the leaf-covered cardboard back.

14. Add a charm at the top of the gable.

15. Use ribbon to tie the key to one of the branches on the outside of the box.

Lady Luck

There are lots of people out there who don't believe in luck but I say, "Why not believe in it?"

I mean, it doesn't hurt!

For the past 10 years, I've saved every coin and bill I've found on the street, and my lucky coin box has more than $200 in it. When I need some good luck, I shake the box and put my wish out there. I made this Lady Luck Vision Box for my friend, Josh, who seems to be with me every time I find a big bill on the street. He always screams out how unlucky he is and I decided it was time to change his way of thinking. I'm sure with all of these charms and found pennies that his luck is about to change.

I bet yours will, too if you make this Lady Luck Vision Box.

It can't hurt right?

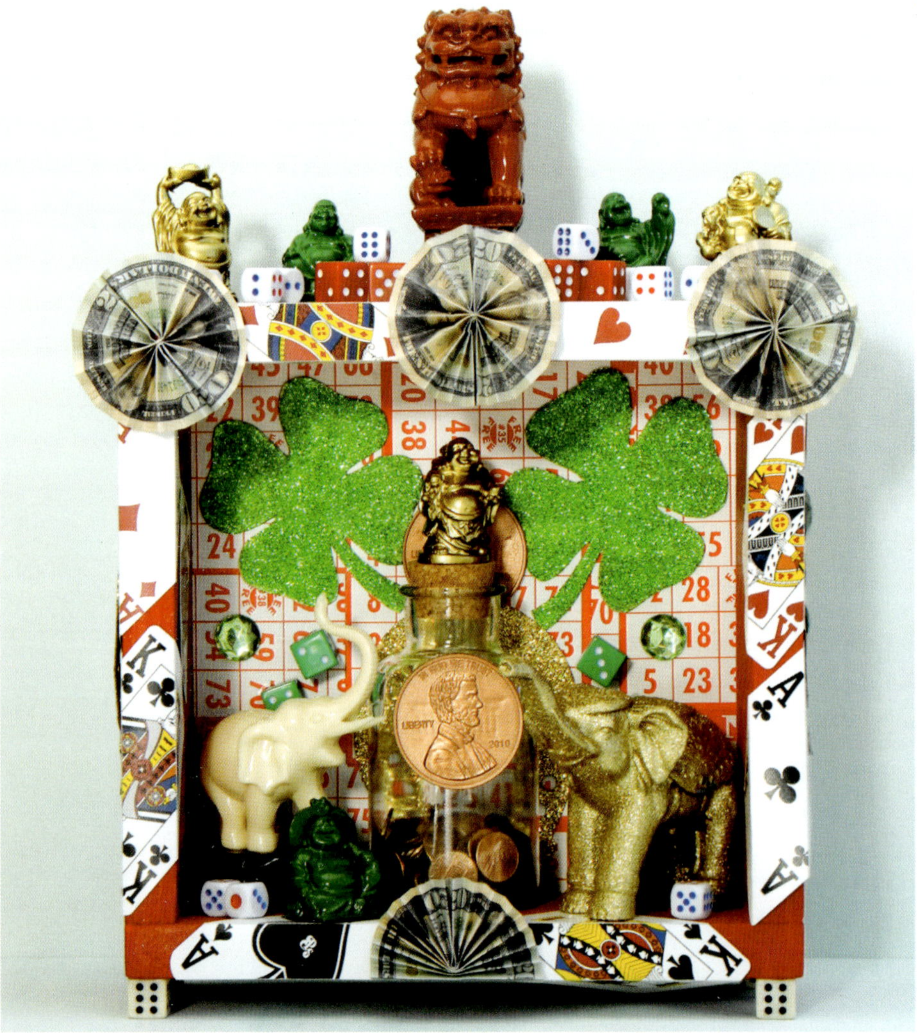

You'll need:

- ✦ Vision Box #2 on page 12
- ✦ Red, green, and gold Krylon Fusion spray paint
- ✦ Cardboard the size of the box
- ✦ Thin cardboard (I like cereal box cardboard)
- ✦ Bingo cards
- ✦ Playing cards
- ✦ Dice
- ✦ Gems
- ✦ Small Buddha figures
- ✦ Elephants with their trunks in the air
- ✦ Jar with cork top
- ✦ Lucky pennies
- ✦ Big fake money
- ✦ Color copies of money
- ✦ Hot glue gun
- ✦ Craft knife
- ✦ Elmer's glue
- ✦ E-6000 Craft Adhesive
- ✦ Krylon Glitter Blast in Lucky Green and Golden Glow

The author used these products for the project. Substitute your choice of brands, tools, and materials as desired.

When I need some good luck, I shake my Lady Luck Vision Box and put my wish out there.

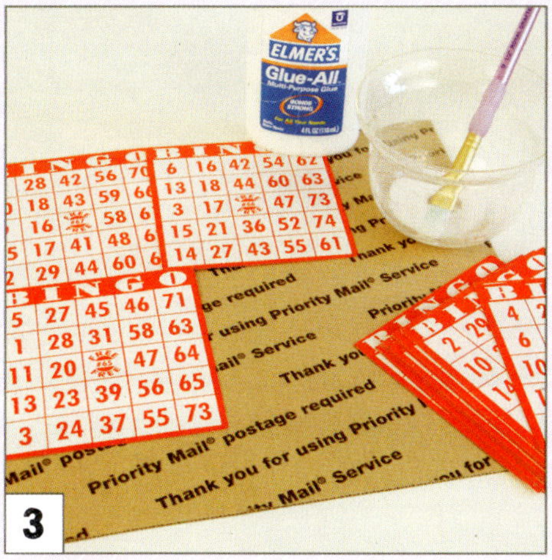

3

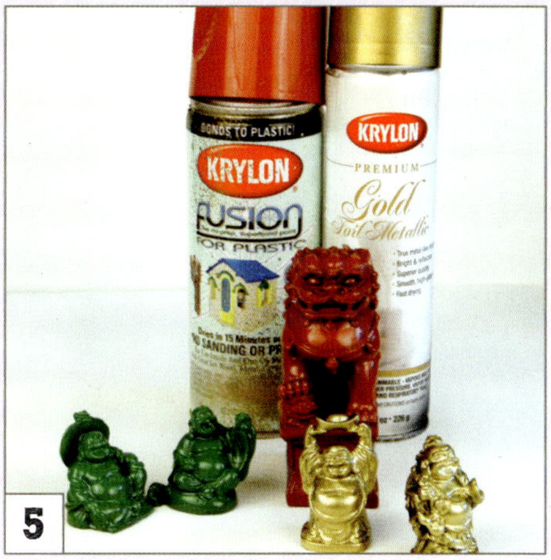

5

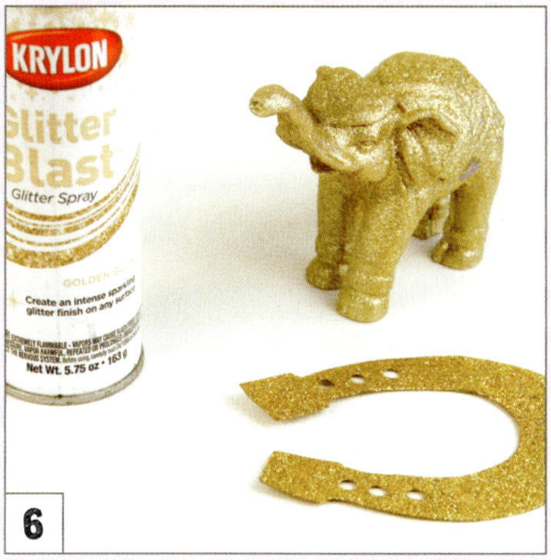

6

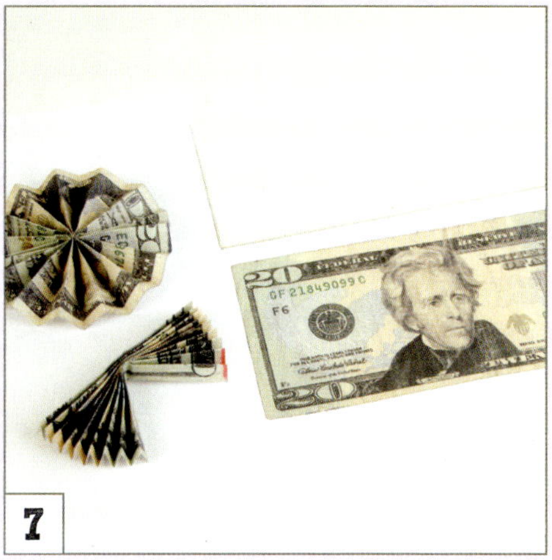
7

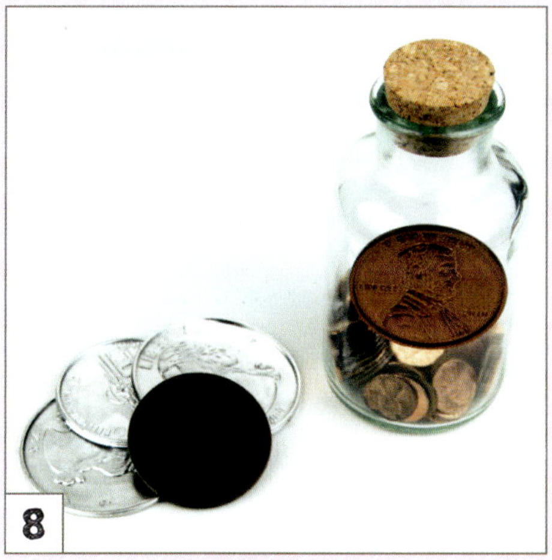
8

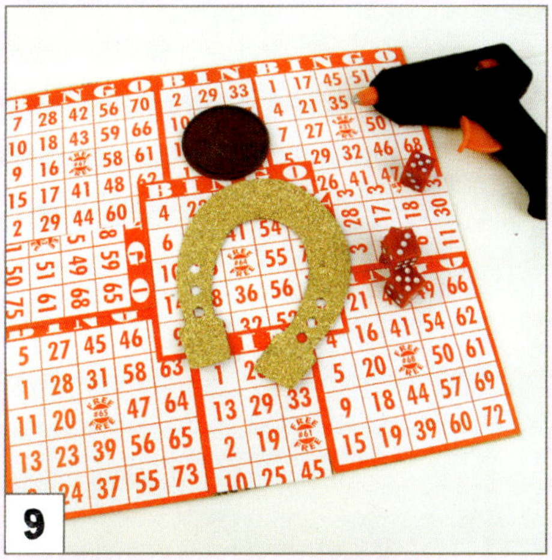
9

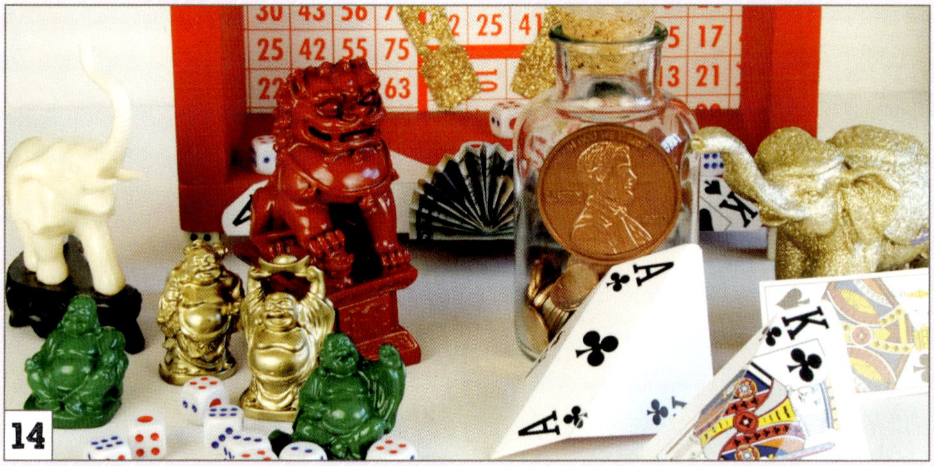
14

1. Cut your cardboard to fit on the back of your Vision Box.

2. Spray paint your box red and let dry.

3. Cover your cardboard back with bingo cards using the Elmer's glue and let dry.

4. Cut out your cereal box cardboard in four-leaf clover and horseshoe shapes using the patterns provided on page 76 and then spray them with the Glitter Blast.

5. Spray paint the Buddha figures with the green, gold, and red spray paint.

6. Glitter blast the elephants in Golden Glow

7. Copy your bills four times and fold like an accordion. Make three pinwheel shapes and one half-pinwheel shape like you see in the photo.

8. Glue a big fake penny on the jar and fill with pennies. (Use lucky found pennies if you have them!)

9. Glue a big fake penny, horseshoe, and two 4-leaf clover shapes, dice, and a couple of gems to the back cardboard piece and then glue on the back of the box with hot glue.

10. Fold your playing cards around the edges of the box and glue them on with the hot glue.

11. Glue the Buddhas, dice, and elephants in place with E-6000.

12. Glue the pinwheels on with hot glue.

13. Glue four dice for legs on the bottom of the box using E-6000 and let dry.

14. Add more dice, cards, fake money, and horseshoes to the sides of the box.

My Super Powers

Every once in a while, I feel like I need a reminder of what makes me special. (Somehow when my mom calls me "special," I don't always feel it's a compliment!) On those days, I work on my Super Powers Vision Box. It's a reminder of the things I like about myself and the ways I excel.

When you create your Super Powers Vision Box, write things like BEST COOK! And SUPER MOM! Or WONDERFUL FRIEND! These powers are what truly make someone super. Consider making this project for a child to help boost his self-esteem.

That is one of the true powers of a Super Powers Vision Box!

My Super Powers Vision Box is a reminder of the things I like about myself and the ways I excel.

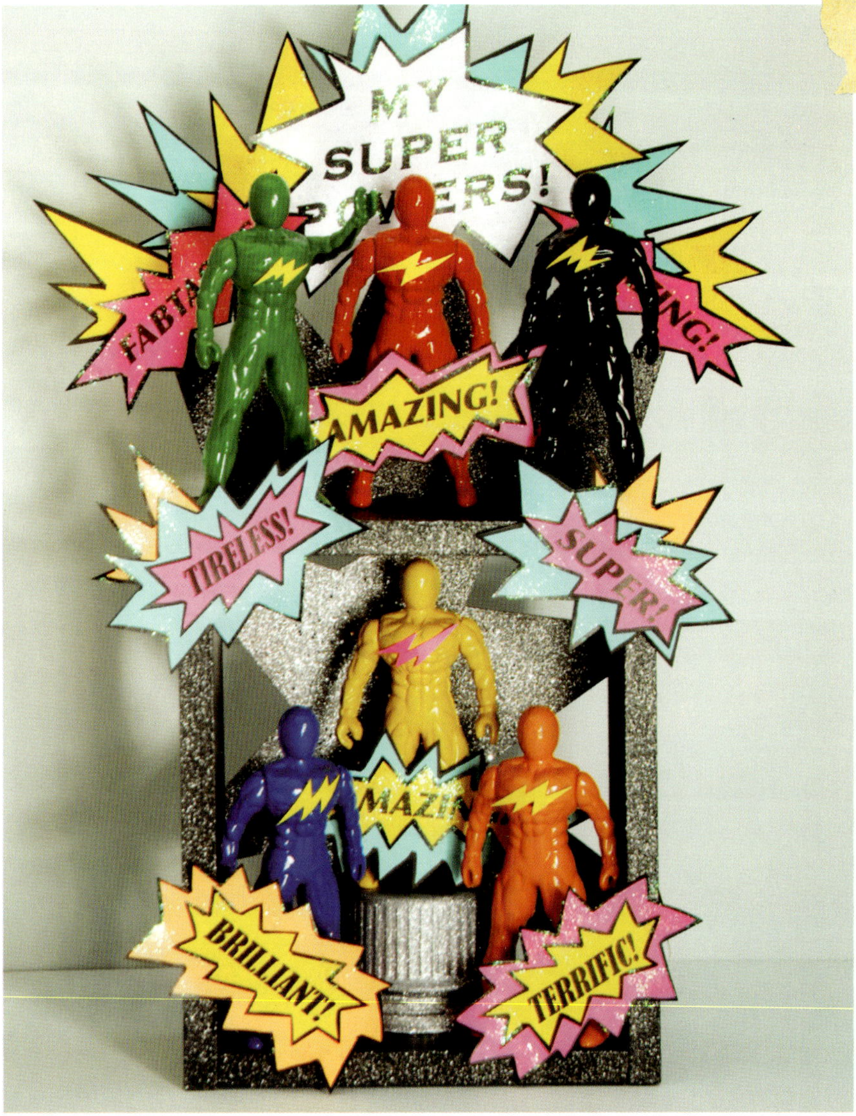

You'll need:

- Vision Box #1 on page 12
- 6 superhero toys (I got mine at the 99 Cent store)
- 5 bright colors of cardstock, including white
- Copy machine
- Elmer's glue
- Hot glue gun
- Scissors
- Glitter glue
- Krylon Fusion spray paint in six colors
- Laundry detergent cap
- Krylon Glitter Blast in Silver Flash and Starry Night
- Cardboard
- Craft knife
- E-6000 Craft Adhesive
- Elmer's Paint Pen in black
- Paintbrushes

The author used these products for the project. Substitute your choice of brands, tools, and materials as desired.

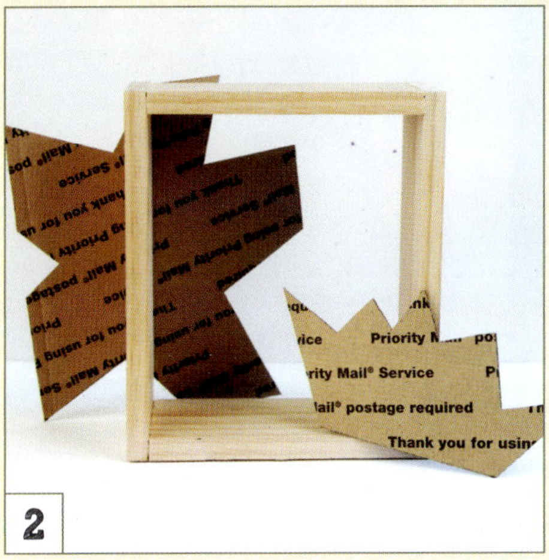

2

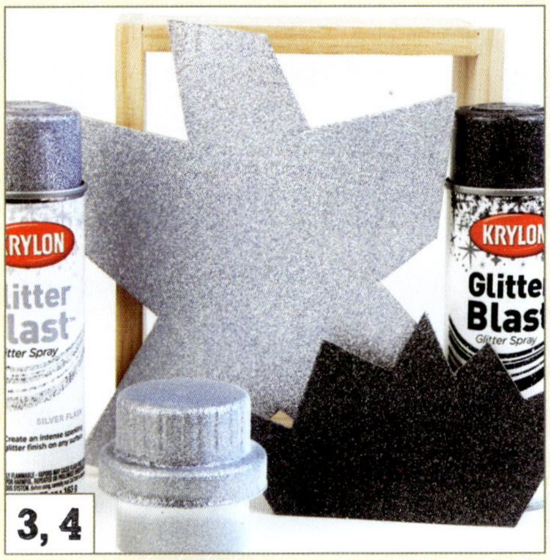

3, 4

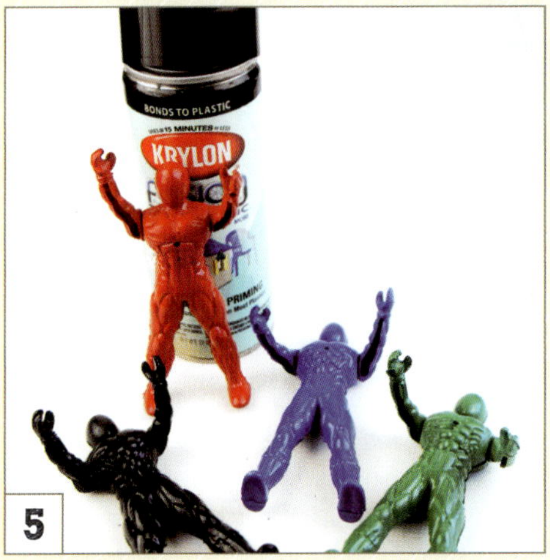

5

1. Prepare your box with the instructions on page 12.
2. Cut your cardboard back and topper.
3. Spray the box and topper with the Starry Night Glitter Blast and let dry.
4. Spray the cardboard back and laundry cap with the Silver Flash Glitter Blast and let dry.
5. Spray paint your super heroes in different colors and let dry.
6. Print out your super power words on 2 different colors of cardstock so that they are about 1½" to 2" (38 to 51mm) long. Use your own special words that reflect your own super powers.
7. Draw a starburst around each word with your black Elmer's Paint Pen or a Sharpie.
8. Cut them out with your scissors.
9. Draw starbursts on more cardstock just a bit bigger than your word starbusts in contrasting colors.
10. Cut them out and glue on the starburst words.
11. Paint the starbursts with a little bit of glitter glue and let dry.
12. Cut small lightning bolts from your cardstock scraps and glue them to the chests of the super heroes with the Elmer's and allow to dry.
13. Hot glue the topper to the top of the box.
14. Using E-6000, glue one superhero on the laundry lid and the other five on the box as seen in the photo.
15. Use E-6000 to glue the laundry lid to the inside of the bottom of the box.
16. With hot glue, add your superhero words around the box and on the topper.

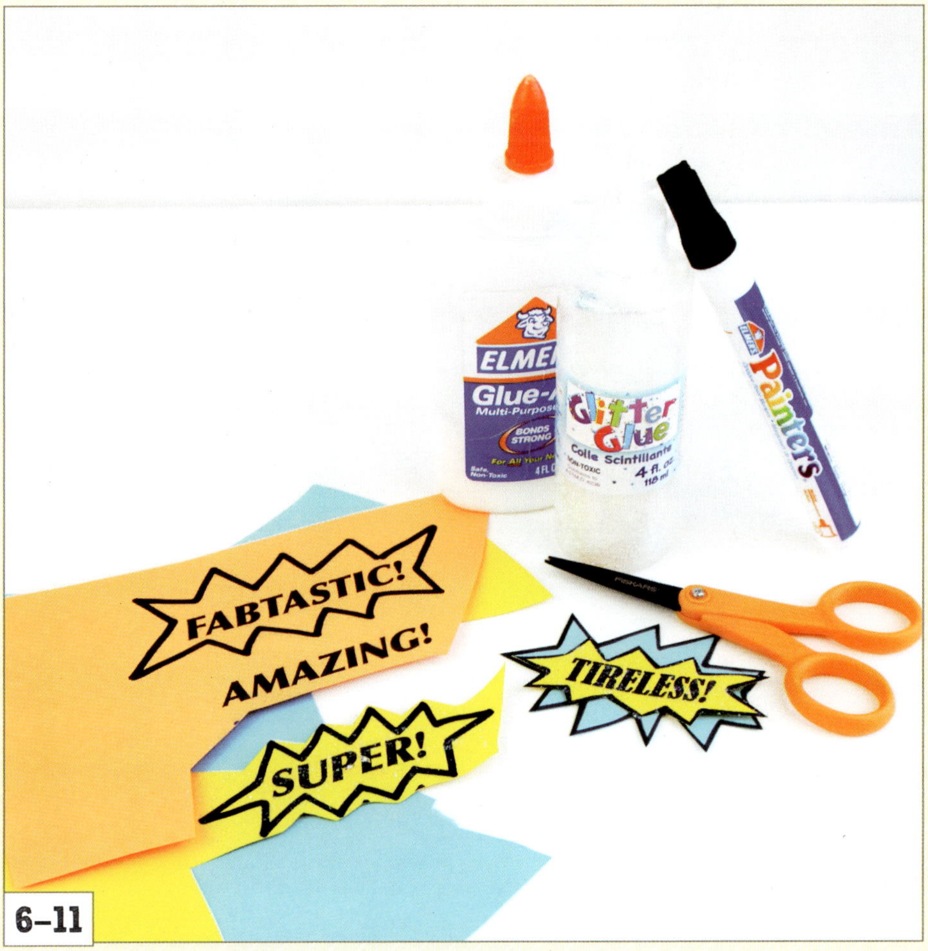

6–11

Overcoming Obstacles

I read somewhere that if a meteor were heading toward earth we would only have to move it a few inches to alter its course enough so it would miss us. That is a pretty cool thought. If we change the way we approach things just a little, we have the ability to make a big impact on our lives over time.

Hey, we all have obstacles and those things that make us feel tied down and unable to move. I say, break free of those restrictions. Leap over those obstacles and rise above it.

Get your mojo to go-go and change your course!

Leap over those tall buildings in a single bound.

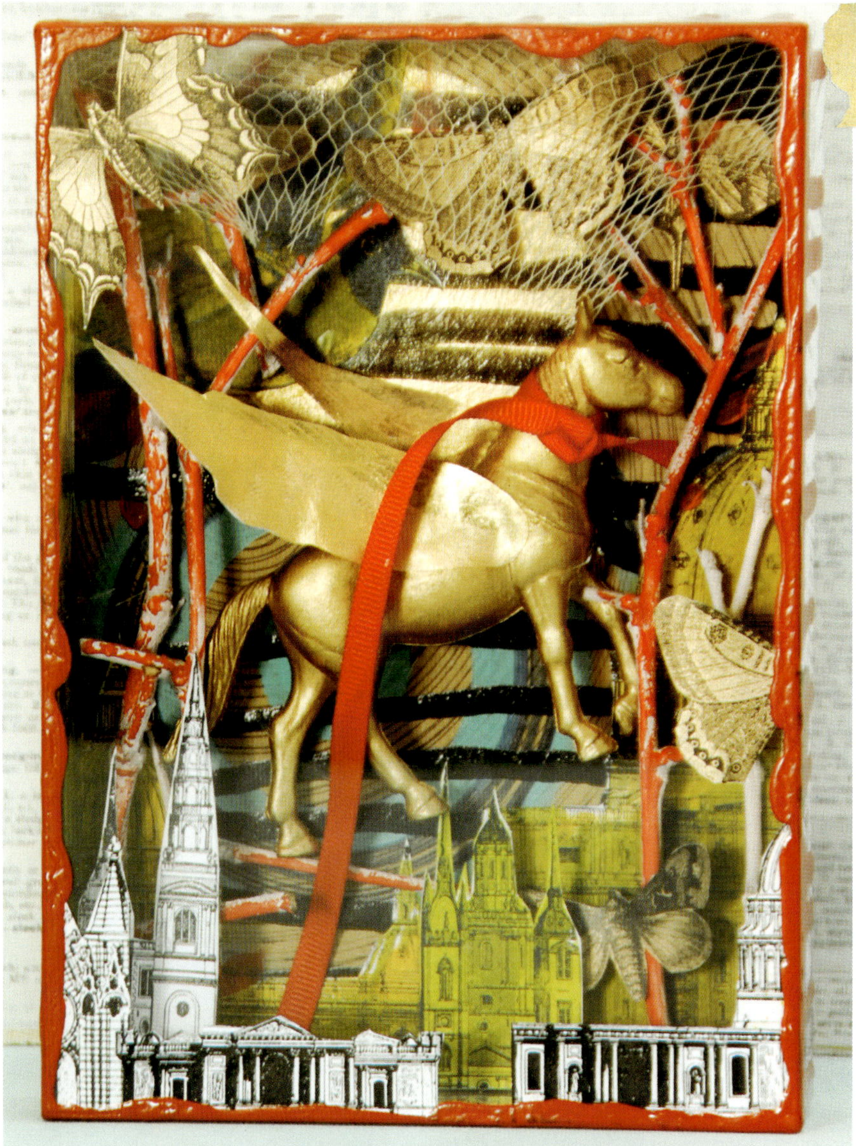

You'll need:

- 5" x 7" (127 x 178mm) clear plastic box frame
- Cardboard for the back
- Book pages
- Toy horse
- 10" (254mm) of ¼" (6mm)-wide ribbon
- Twigs
- Krylon spray paint (metallic gold color)
- Gold, black, blue, red, white, and yellow acrylic paint
- Watercolor set
- Paintbrushes
- Netting from a bath scrubber
- Images of birds, butterflies, and buildings (pages 65–66 and 73–74)
- Craft knife
- Scissors
- Ball-point pen
- Copy machine
- Elmer's glue
- Hot glue gun

The author used these products for the project. Substitute your choice of brands, tools, and materials as desired.

Get your mojo to go-go and change your course! Leap over those tall buildings in a single bound!

1. Cut your cardboard to fit the back of the box frame.
2. Paint the cardboard with your various acrylic paints. Use a ball-point pen to get some interest going and let some paint drip. Go crazy (that's the fun of it) and then let the paint dry.
3. Copy one of the birds on page 65, cut out the wings, and glue them on the toy horse. Then, spray paint the horse metallic gold and let the paint dry.
4. Tie a ribbon around the neck of the horse.
5. Copy and cut out the buildings on pages 73–74.
6. Paint some of the buildings with the watercolor set. I used yellows and oranges.
7. Copy and cut out the butterflies on page 66 and color wash with your gold acrylic paint and let them dry.
8. With your acrylics, paint the twigs red and pink and let dry.
9. Glue the book pages around the edge of the box frame on the outside.
10. Glue some of the buildings on the cardboard back.
11. Hot glue on the horse and the twigs.
12. OPTIONAL: I was tossing a bath scrubber and thought I would cut it apart and add it to the top. I thought it looked pretty neat! Glue it on with small dabs of hot glue.
13. Glue on more buildings and butterflies with the Elmer's so you have a 3-D effect.
14. Glue more buildings and butterflies onto the outside of the frame.
15. Glue the back on the frame with the hot glue.
16. Drip red paint around the edges, letting it drip down the sides and let the paint dry.

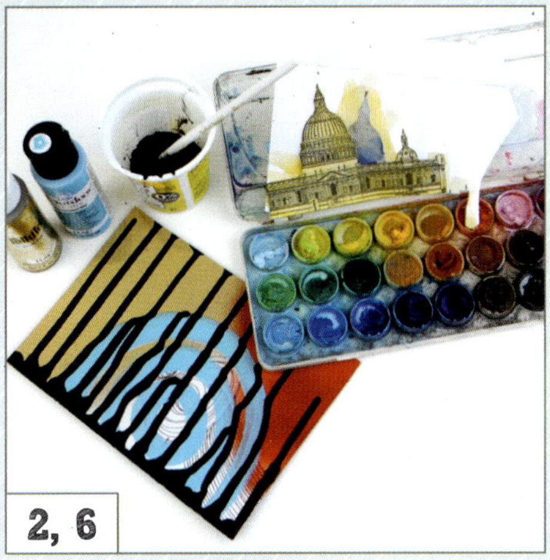
2, 6

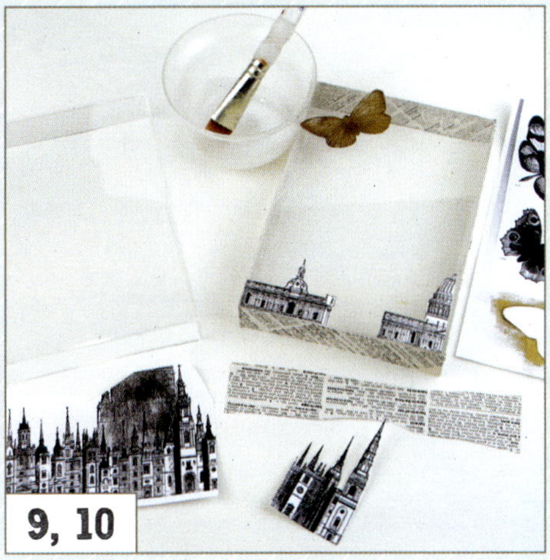
9, 10

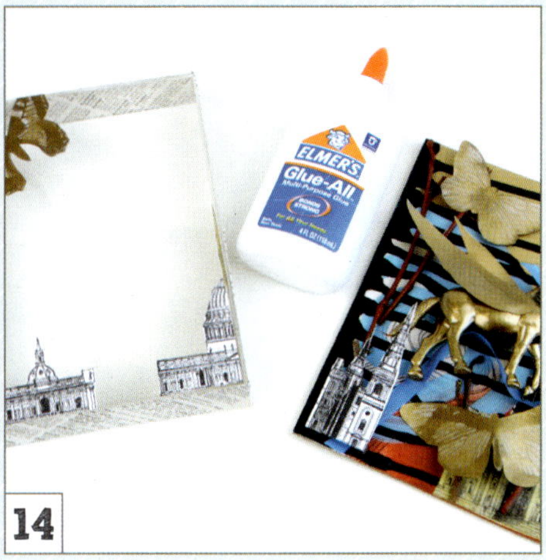

14

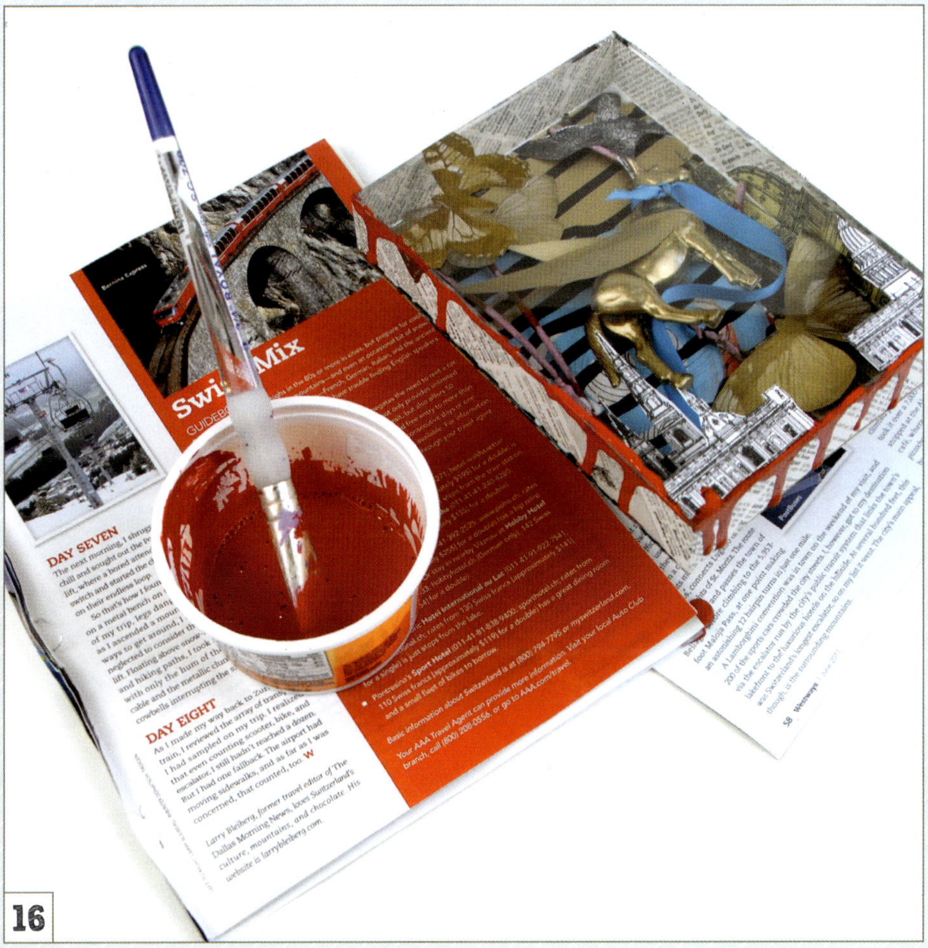
16

Pocket Angel

Altoids boxes are perfect for projects like this because they're portable and you can take your Vision Box with you wherever you go. Toss your own personal angel in your bag and I guarantee you'll feel wonderful having it with you.

This box would be a charming gift or the perfect mini box to keep on your desk at work. The beauty of it is it will remind you that even when you don't believe in yourself, there are those out there who do.

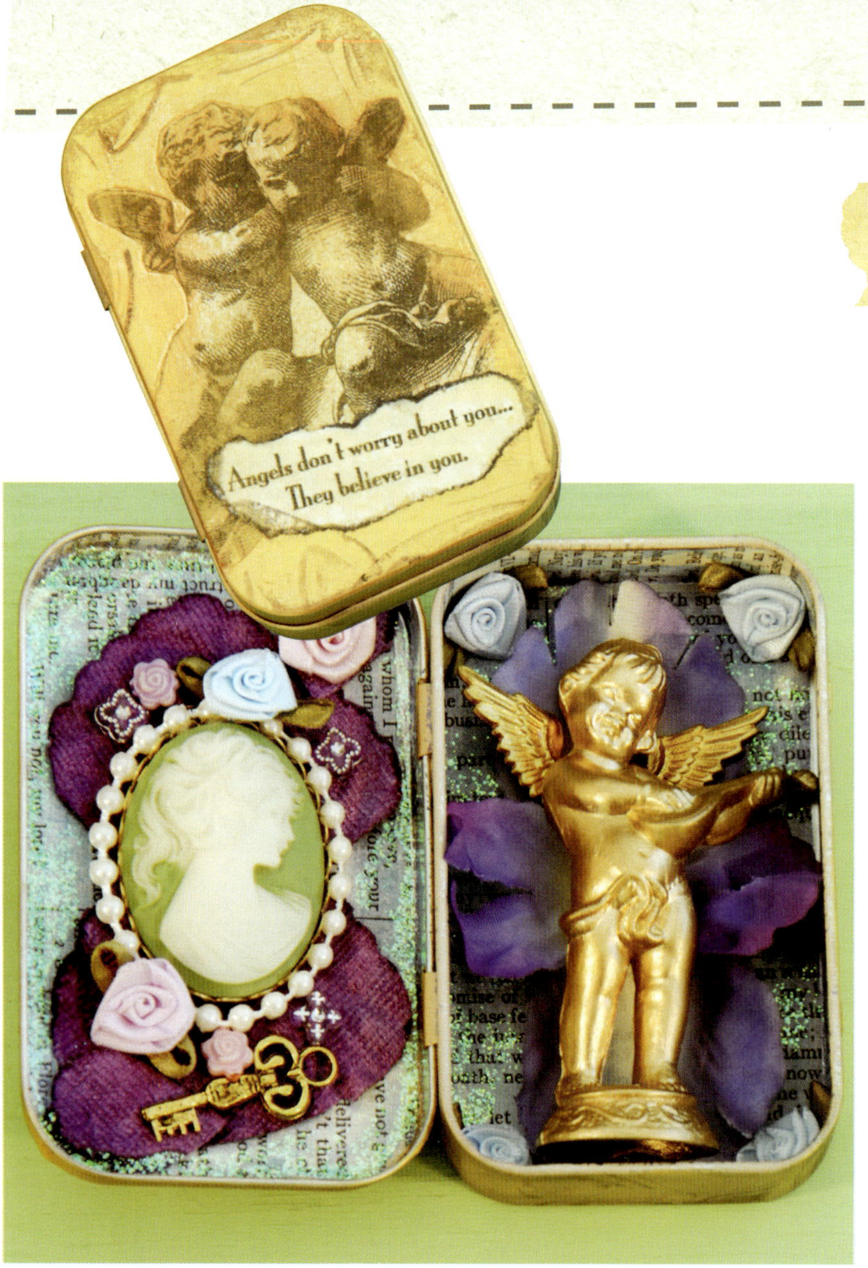

You'll need:

- Altoids tin
- Krylon spray paint (gold metallic color)
- Gold acrylic paint
- Watercolor set
- Paintbrushes
- Image of angels (page 63)
- Printout of your Vision Box saying
- Book pages
- Rubber stamps and permanent ink stamp pad
- Rag
- Small angel
- Cameo or piece of jewelry
- Pearls, ribbon flowers, a small key, faux flower petals
- Elmer's glue
- Hot glue gun
- E-6000 Craft Adhesive
- Glitter glue
- Scissors

The author used these products for the project. Substitute your choice of brands, tools, and materials as desired.

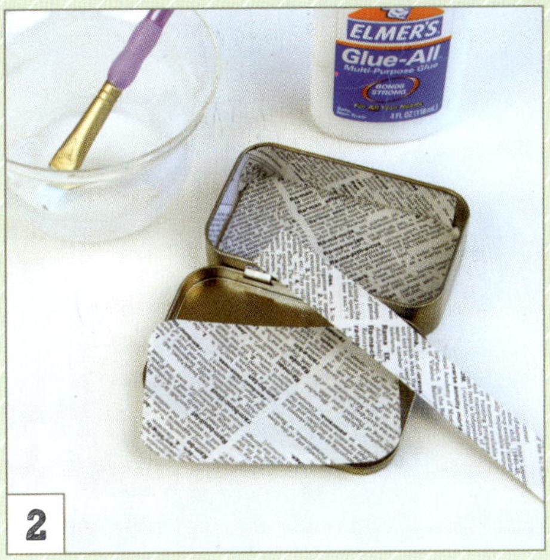

2

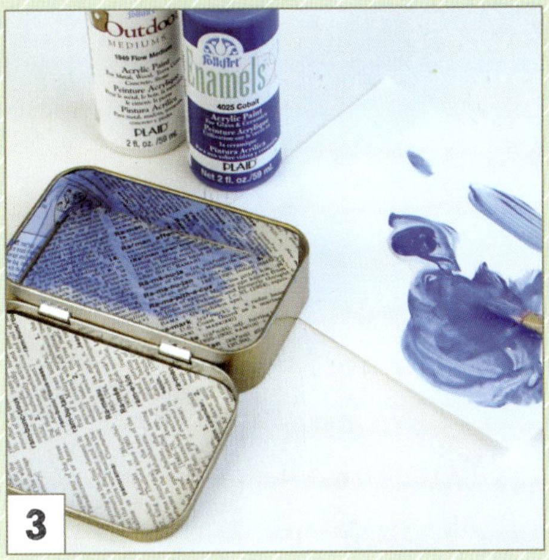

3

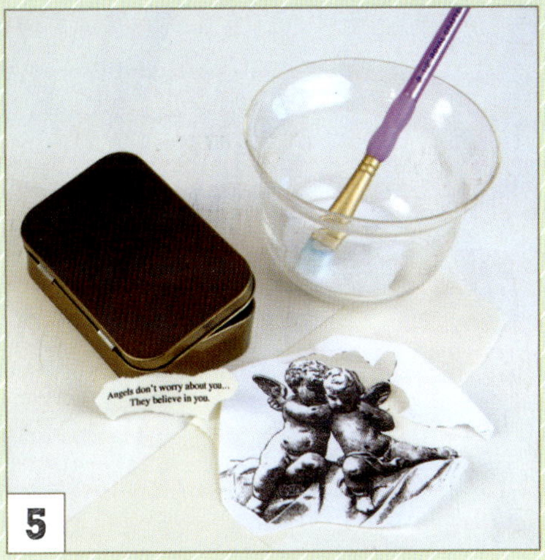

5

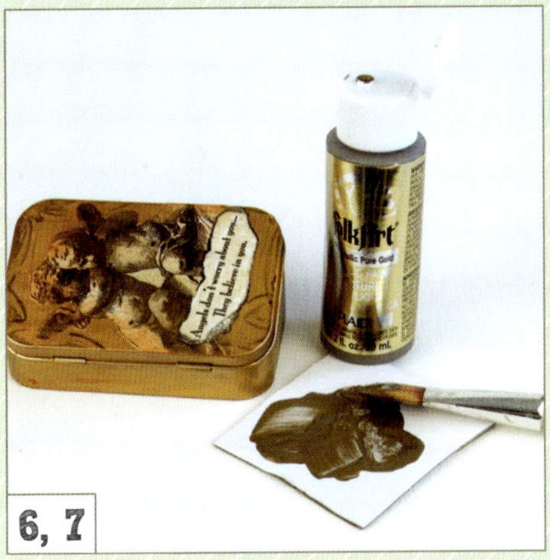

6, 7

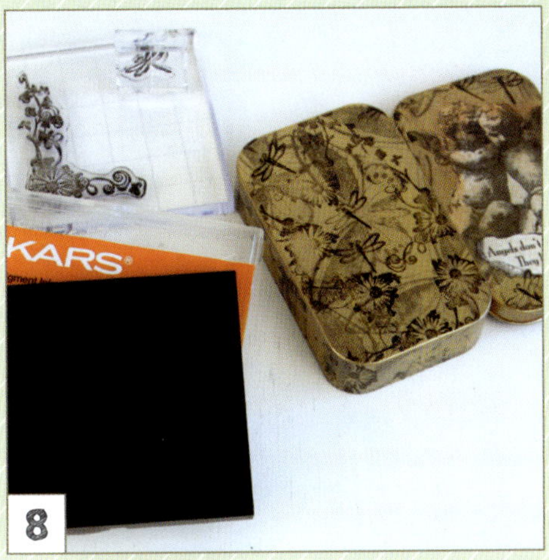

8

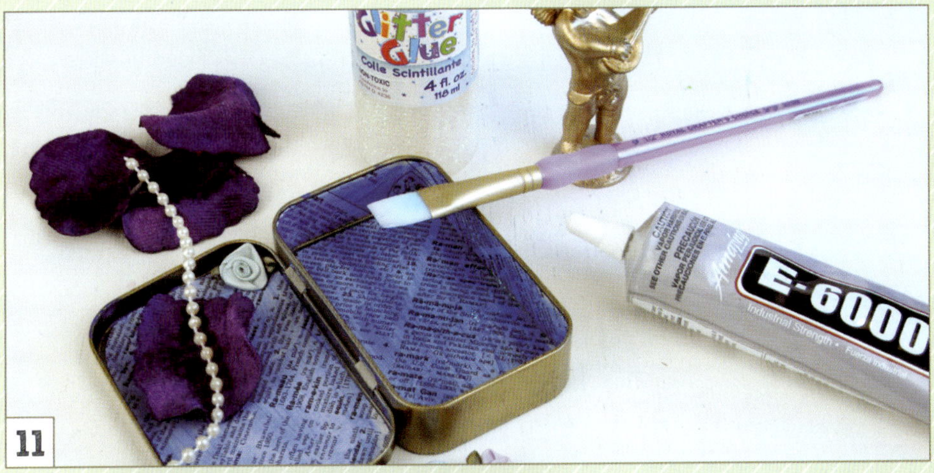

11

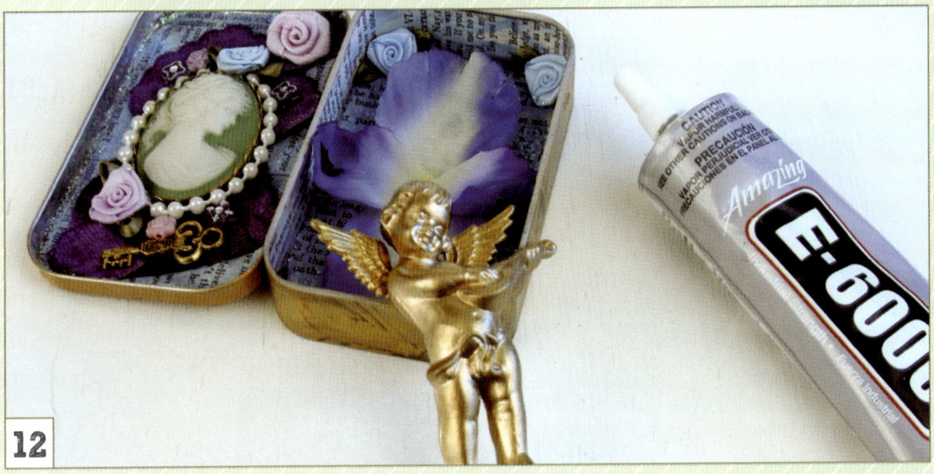

12

1. Spray paint your Altoids tin gold and let dry.
2. Cover the inside of the tin with your book pages and Elmer's glue and let dry.
3. Paint the book pages with some blue watercolor to give them some color. This doesn't have to be perfect.
4. Paint some glitter glue around the edges and over the book pages and let dry.
5. Cut out your angels and glue on the outer lid of the box.
6. Tear around your saying and with some black watercolor, paint around the edges to distress it.
7. Glue your saying over the angels toward the bottom of the lid.
8. Lightly stamp the box with your rubber stamp and permanent ink stamp pad.
9. Rub it off a little with a rag to distress it.
10. Rub some gold paint over the entire box to give it some texture and dimension.
11. Glue your faux flower petals on the inside of the lid and box.
12. Glue in your angel, cameo, pearls, beads, key, and faux flowers with small dabs of E-6000 and let dry.

Time Machine

The best way to ensure an amazing future is to pay attention to the present and take with you the lessons from the past. Well, at least that's what I try to do. Sometimes, just for kicks, I turn on this Time Machine Vision Box in hopes of changing my future.

The magic of a Time Machine Vision Box is that we get to create our future. Maybe not as quickly as we'd like, but we all have the power to do it. Pretty powerful stuff, don't you think?

Now turn this on and see where it takes you!

We all have the power to create our future. Pretty powerful stuff, don't you think?

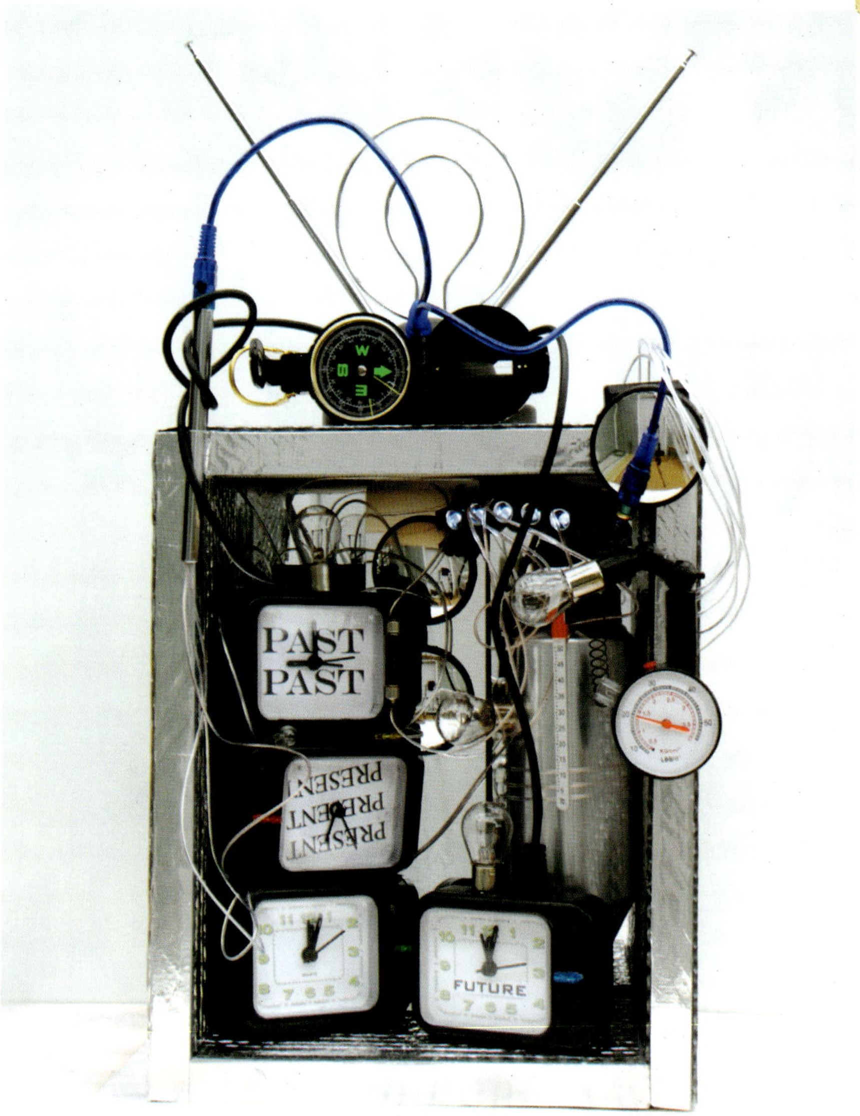

You'll need:

- Basic Vision Box #2 on page 12
- Cardboard to fit the back
- Plain aluminum can
- Scissors
- E-6000 Craft Adhesive
- Elmer's glue
- Hot glue gun
- Craft knife

The following items were all purchased at a 99 Cent store or found under my sink:

- Mirror that fits inside the back of the box
- Silver windshield cover
- Foil tape
- 4 clocks
- TV antennae
- Compass
- Several small light bulbs
- Speaker wire
- Tire pressure kit
- Hat clip light
- Rearview mirrors

The author used these products for the project. Substitute your choice of brands, tools, and materials as desired.

1. Cut your cardboard to fit on the back of your box.

2. Cut the silver windshield cover the size of every side of the box, including the back cover. Hot glue the pieces in place.

3. Tape around the edges with the silver foil tape.

4. With the E-6000, glue the mirror to the back piece of silver covered cardboard.

5. Take off the faces of your clocks, remove the hands, and glue in printouts of the words PAST, PRESENT, and FUTURE on the faces of the clocks.

6. Replace the clocks and glue 3 together, one on top of the other.

7. Poke a hole in the aluminum can and push in a light bulb.

8. Wrap the can in the speaker wire.

9. Glue in the small rearview mirrors and place in your clocks and aluminum can.

10. Glue on the extra pieces, the antennae, and the compass like you see in the photo (or any way you want).

11. Connect the extra wire from one spot to another. No rhyme or reason here, we just want it to look like a machine.

12. Add a light source on the top inside part of the box.

13. Turn on the light and get ready to travel.

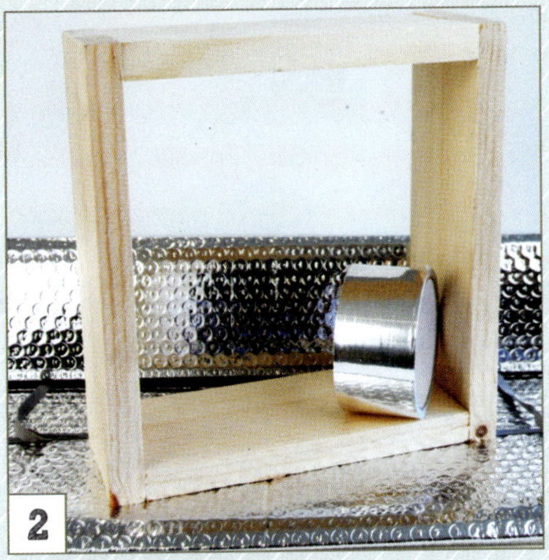
2

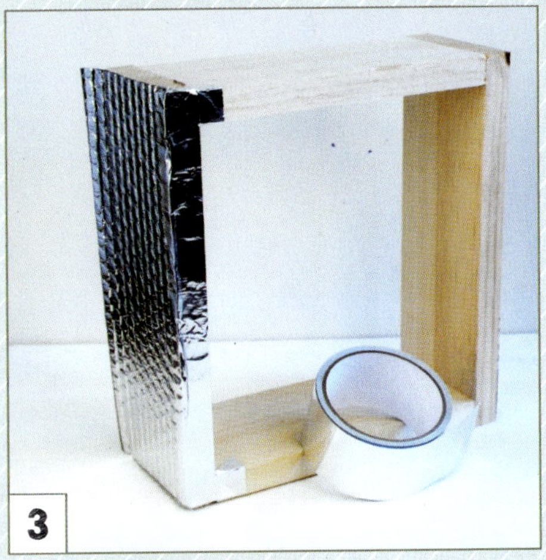
3

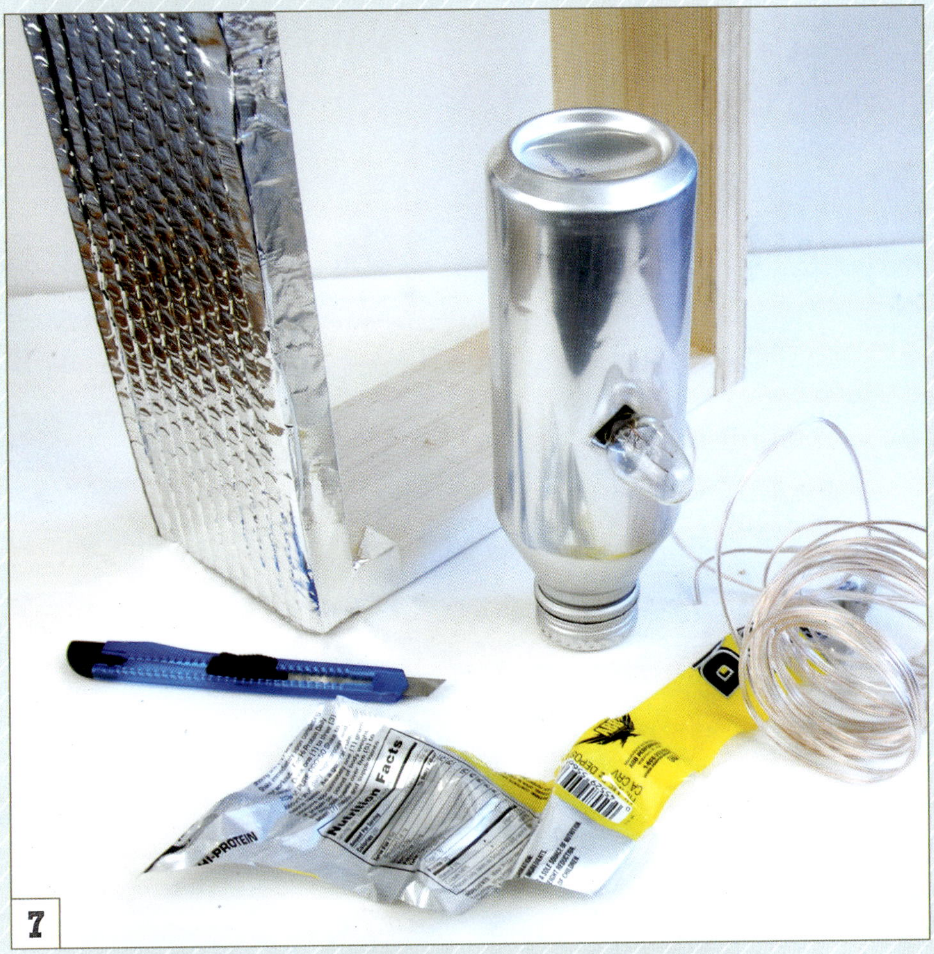

7

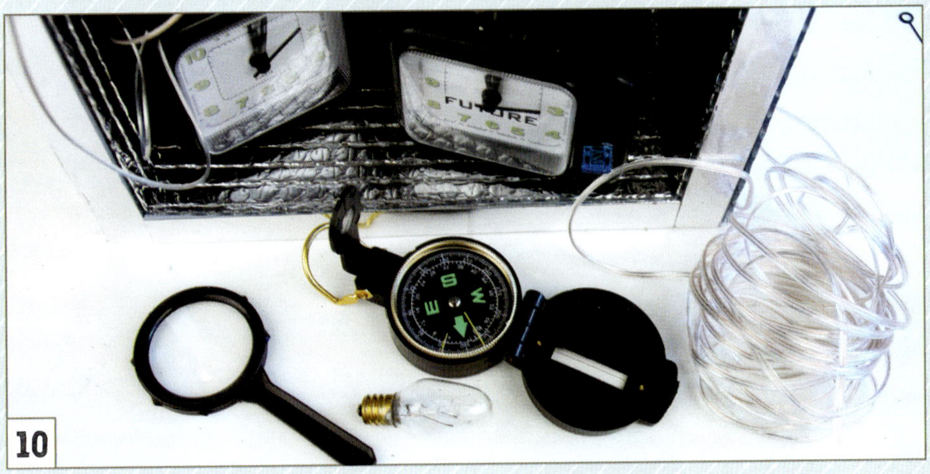

10

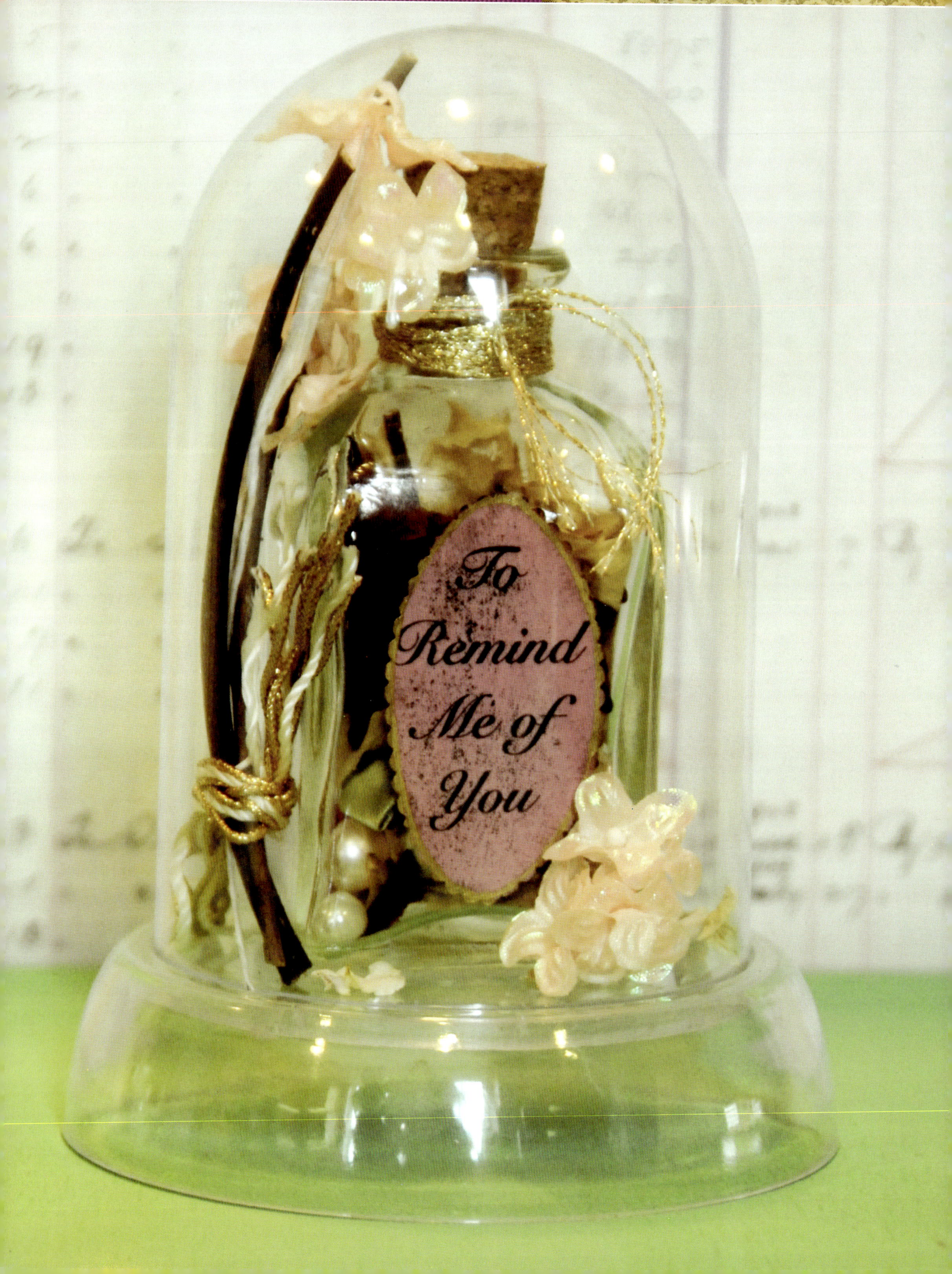
To
Remind
Me of
You

To Remind Me of You

The magic of memories is what we're creating here. Whether it is a special time you shared with someone, a trip you took, a romance, or a loved one, we all have small mementos in a box somewhere. Gathered all together I'm pretty sure they can start you on a magical trip down memory lane. This Vision Box is your ticket for that trip.

You may not have everything you want to put in this box right now, but in time, I'm sure it will be filled with wonderful things to help spark those memories.

You'll see.

You'll need:

- 7" (178mm)-tall plastic cake topper dome
- Bottle with cork top
- Gold thread
- Printout of your Vision Box saying
- Gold pen
- Stamp pad
- Twigs, flower petals, charms, pearls, faux flowers
- 6" (152mm) of cord or ribbon
- Scissors
- Elmer's glue

The author used these products for the project. Substitute your choice of brands, tools, and materials as desired.

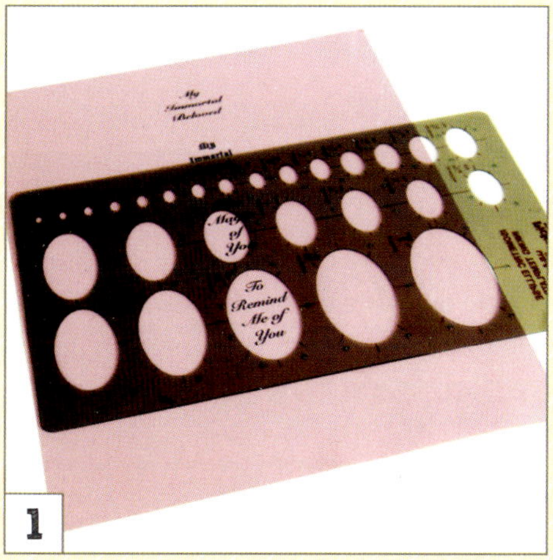

1

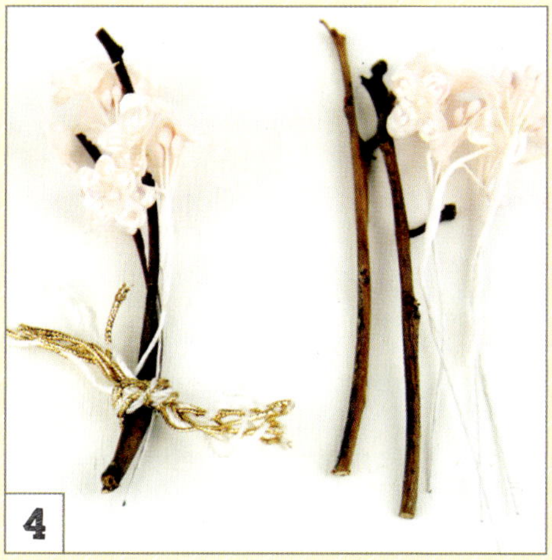

4

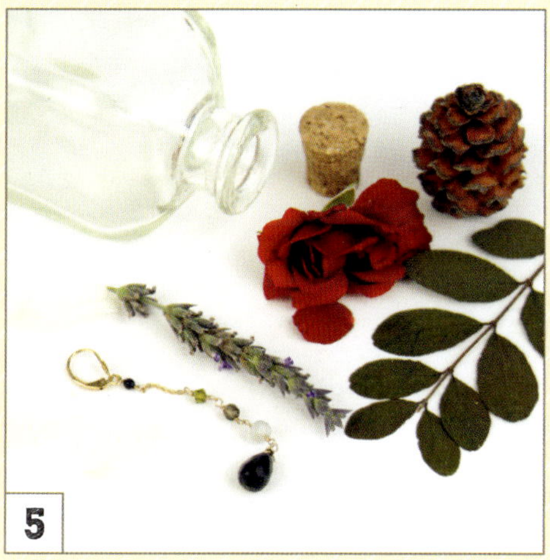

5

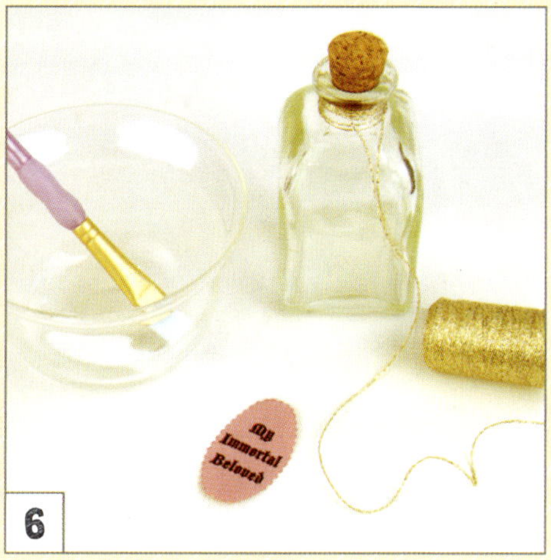

6

1. Print out your saying and cut out in an oval to fit on the front of your cork topped jar.
2. Go over the edge with a gold pen.
3. Press the words onto a stamp pad to distress them and then glue them in place with the Elmer's.
4. Tie up some twigs and faux flowers with your cord or ribbon.
5. Fill your jar with flower petals, charms, and pearls—anything that reminds you of that special person. You could even put photos in there.
6. Wrap the neck of your jar with gold thread.
7. Place the jar on the base of the dome and place the twigs and more flowers next to it and close the dome.

Untie My Heart

I made this box for a friend who got dumped! Yep, it's happened to all of us at one time or another and it's rough. For a while it seemed like she never wanted to date again, and I finally had to tell her to let go and untie her heart so she could open herself up to meeting someone else. She's married now and happier than I've ever seen her.

I believe that sometimes we have to remind ourselves to be open, vulnerable, and untie our hearts. It's the only way to really let someone or something in.

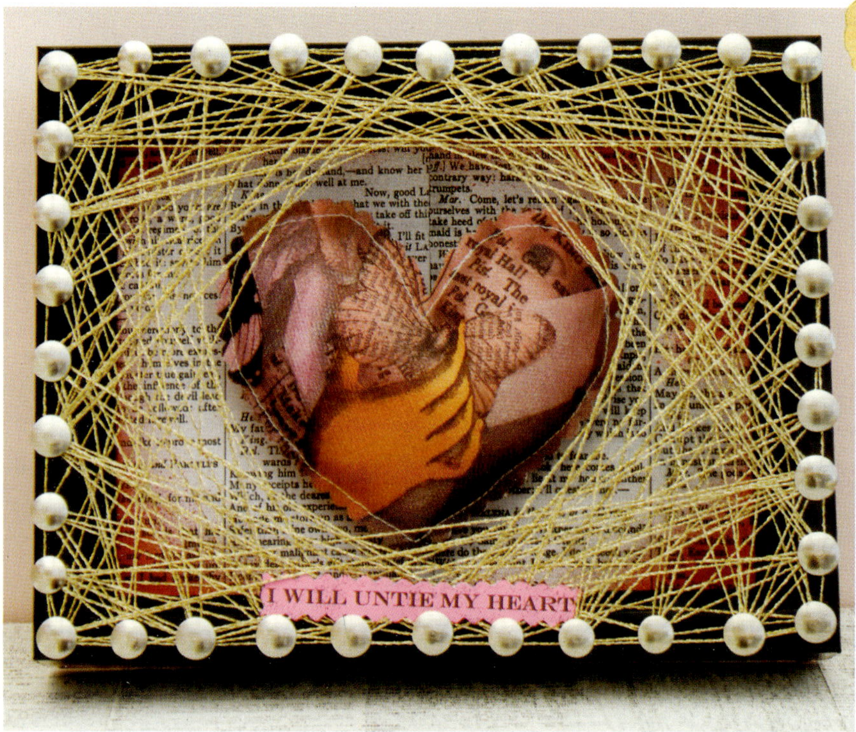

You'll need:

- 1 deep 5" x 7" (127 x 178mm) frame
- Cardboard for the back
- Book pages
- Krylon spray paint (red and black colors)
- Elmer's glue
- 1" (25mm)-wide paintbrush
- 1 sheet of Transfer Artist Paper (TAP)
- Small scrap of white cotton fabric
- Small bit of pillow stuffing
- Sewing machine
- Gold thread
- Thumbtacks
- Small hammer
- Craft knife
- Scissors
- Copy machine
- Small printout of your Vision Box saying

The author used these products for the project. Substitute your choice of brands, tools, and materials as desired.

We have to be open, vulnerable, and untie our hearts. It's the only way to really let someone in.

1. Remove the glass and backing from your frame.
2. Spray paint the frame black and let dry.
3. Cut out cardboard the size of the frame.
4. Cover your cardboard with book pages using very slightly watered down Elmer's glue and your 1" (25mm)-wide paintbrush and let dry.
5. Lightly spray the edges of the cardboard with the red spray paint.
6. Create a collage on your copy machine or use the art I've provided on page 68. Print it on your TAP and iron it on your white cotton fabric.
7. Cut your two identical hearts that are 3½" (89mm) wide at the widest part from your printed TAP fabric.
8. Sew the hearts together, leaving a 1" (25mm)-wide hole. Stuff the heart with the pillow stuffing and sew the hole closed.
9. Glue the heart in the center of the book page covered cardboard backing.
10. Lightly tack the thumbtacks all the way around the face of the frame.
11. Tie the gold thread around one of the tacks and start looping the thread from one tack to another leaving a hole so that your heart is exposed.
12. Tie off the gold thread when you're done and glue on the cardboard back.
13. Add your saying by weaving it in the threads or gluing it on.
14. Put this Vision Box in a place where you can see it every day.

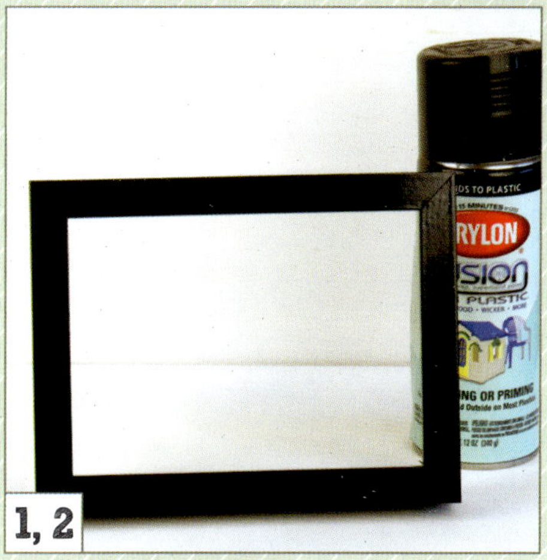

1, 2

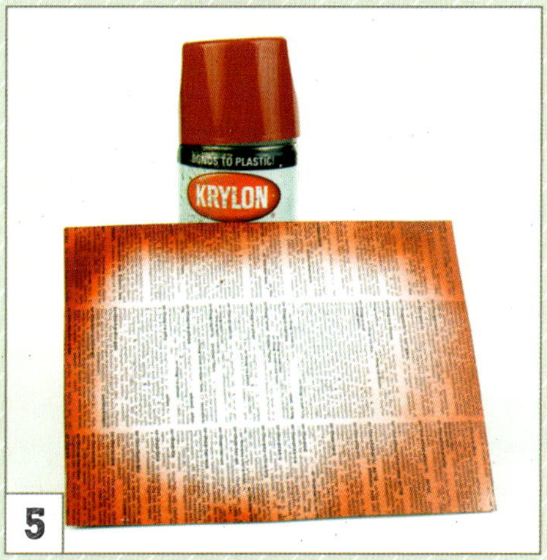

5

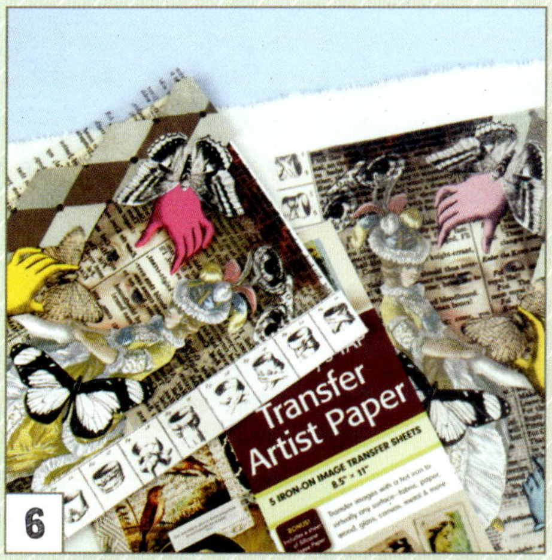

6

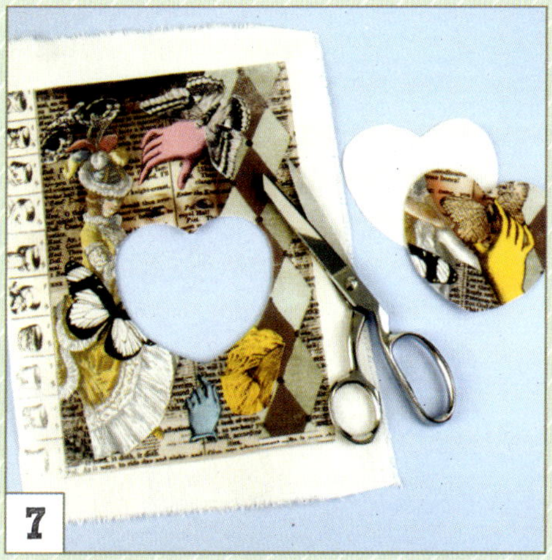
7

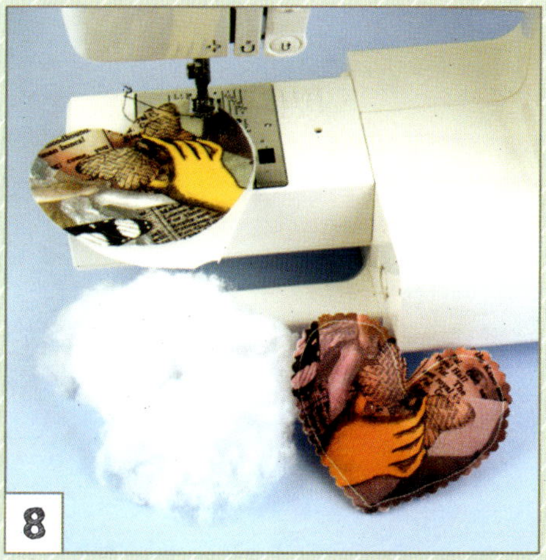
8

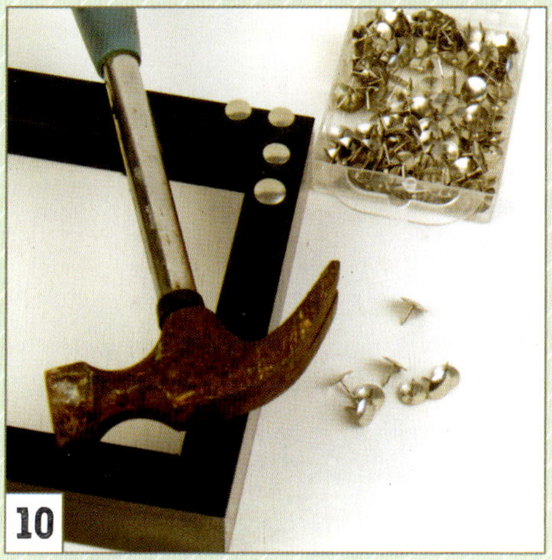
10

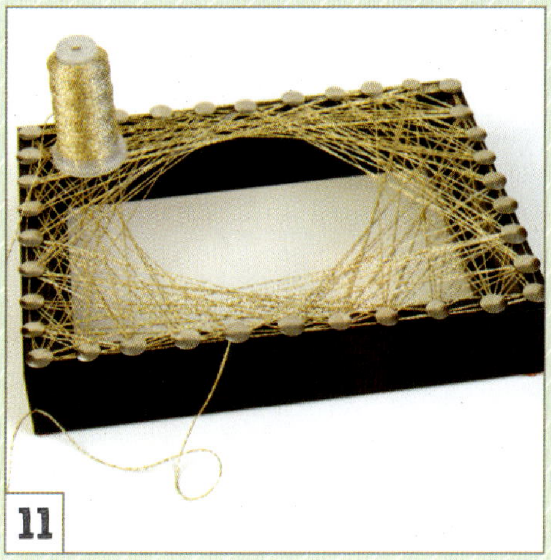
11

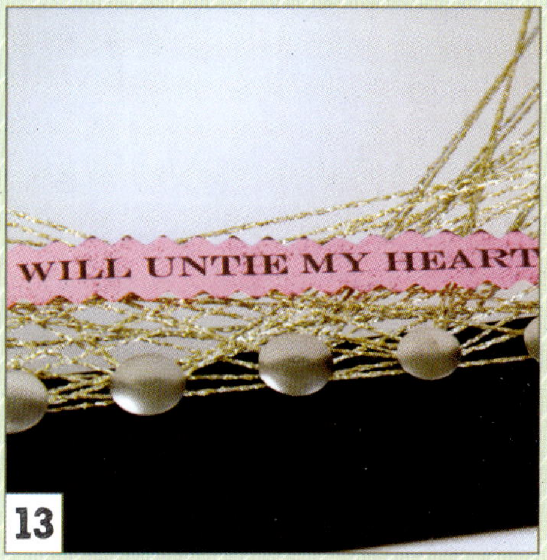

13

Wishing Box

It seems every day I wish for something. Mostly they are the same wishes repeatedly, but sometimes I toss in a new one for good measure. I really wish I was 5" taller, but that ship has sailed unless puberty strikes again. That is highly unlikely at my age.

For good measure, I like to write down my wishes and put them out in the universe. If you've been reading this book then you know I believe in putting things out there. I originally created this Vision Box for my nieces and nephews and they loved it. Their parents love it too because it ended up being the perfect list for birthdays and Christmas!

The magic of this Vision Box is that wishes are free and every once in a while one comes true and you get to pull it out of the jar and replace it with another one.

What could be more magical than that?

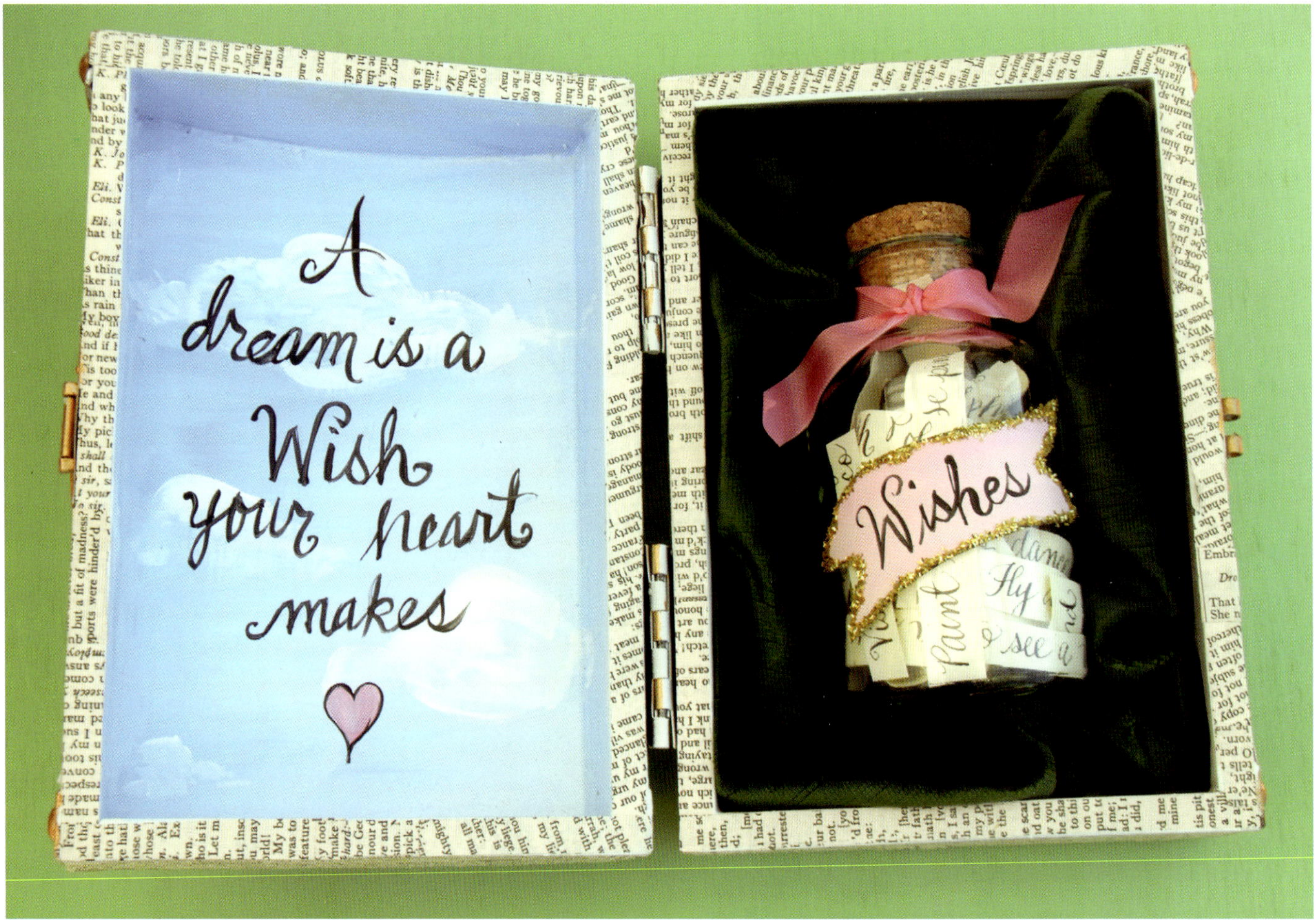

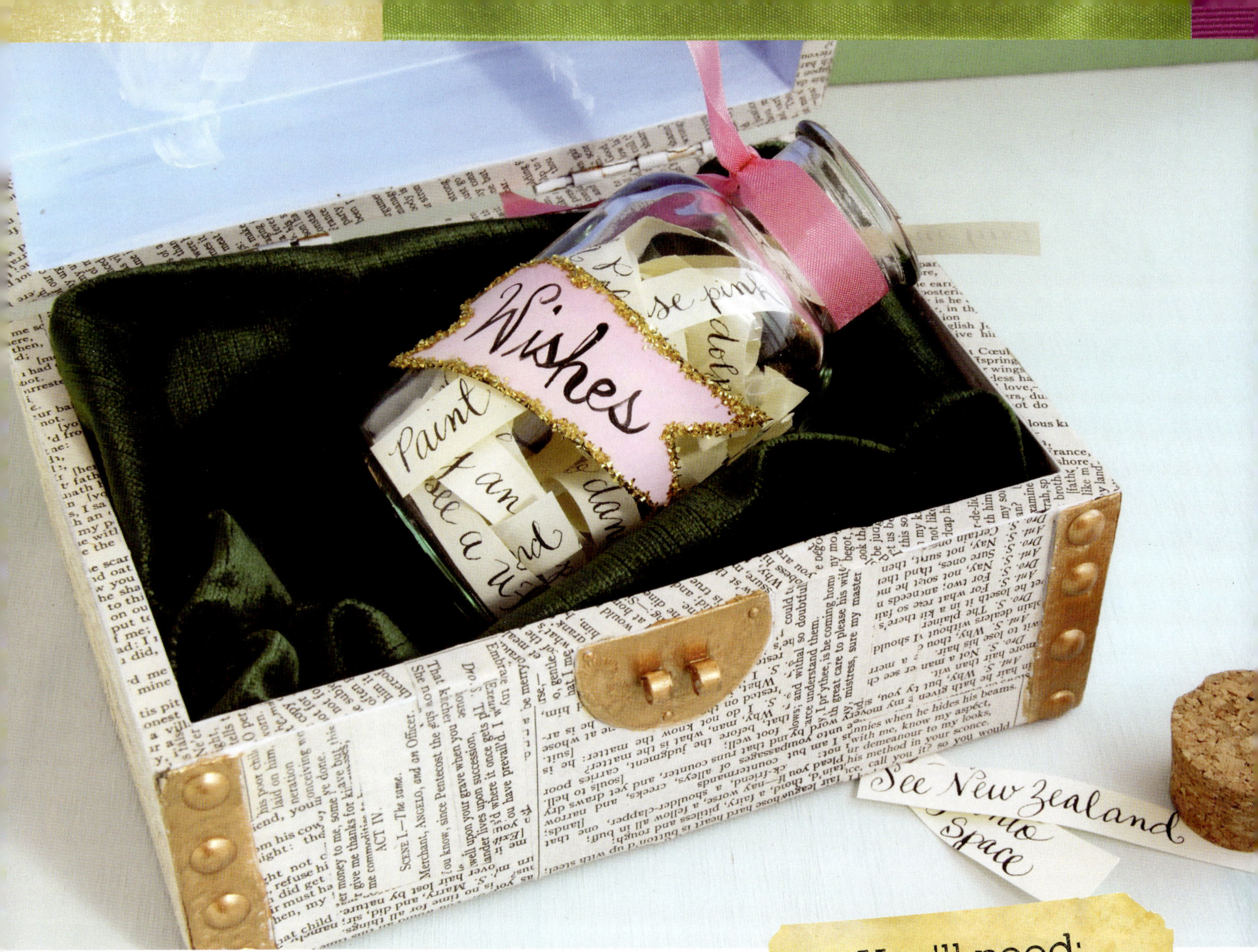

You'll need:

- Box with hinges (I found mine at a thrift store for $2)
- Jar with cork top
- Book pages
- Elmer's glue
- Set of artist brushes
- 8" (203mm) pink ribbon
- Pink copy paper
- Gold glitter
- Scissors
- Blue, white, and black acrylic paint
- 12" (305mm) square piece of velvet
- Enough pillow stuffing to fill the box

The author used these products for the project. Substitute your choice of brands, tools, and materials as desired.

Wishes are free and every once in a while, one comes true and you get to pull it out of the jar and replace it with another.

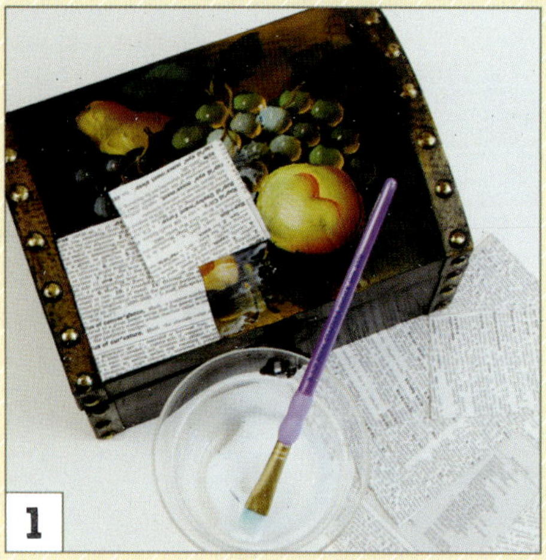

1

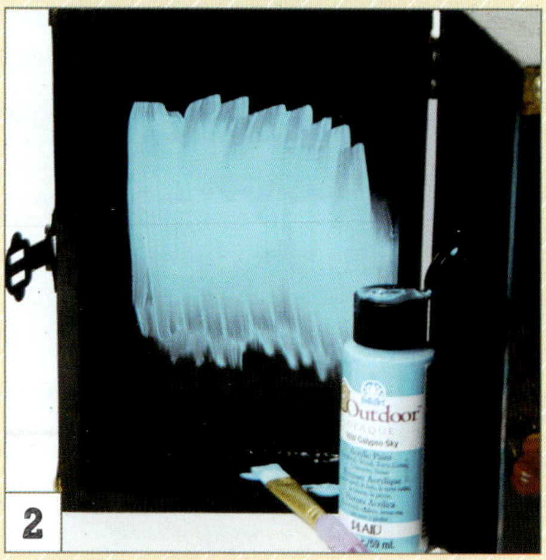

2

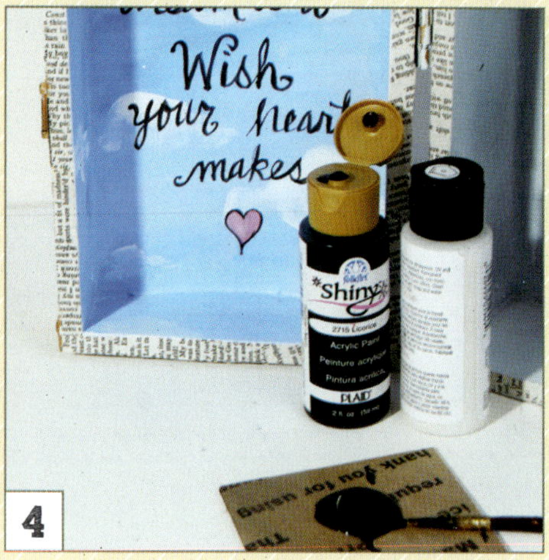

4

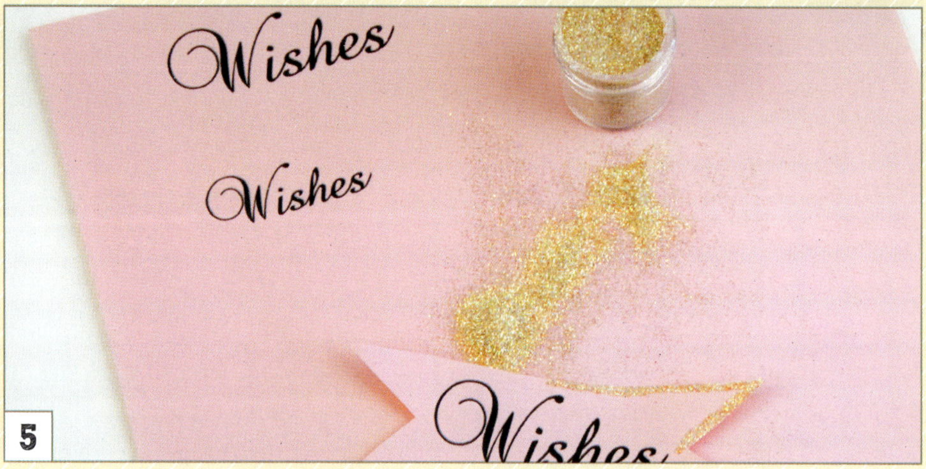

5

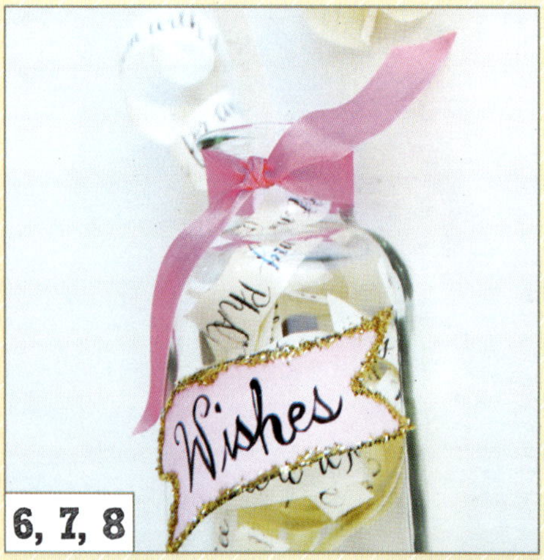

6, 7, 8

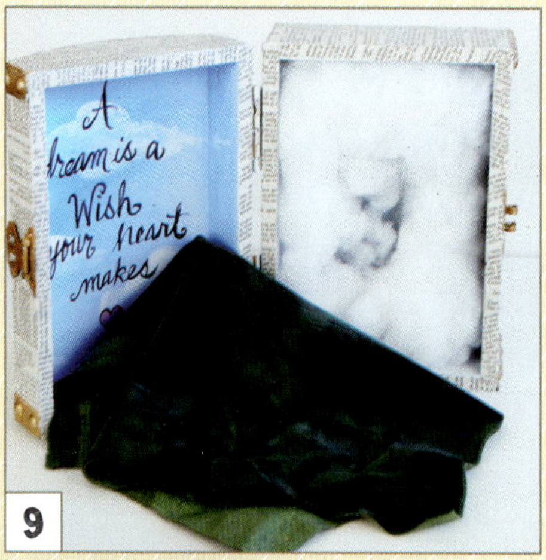

9

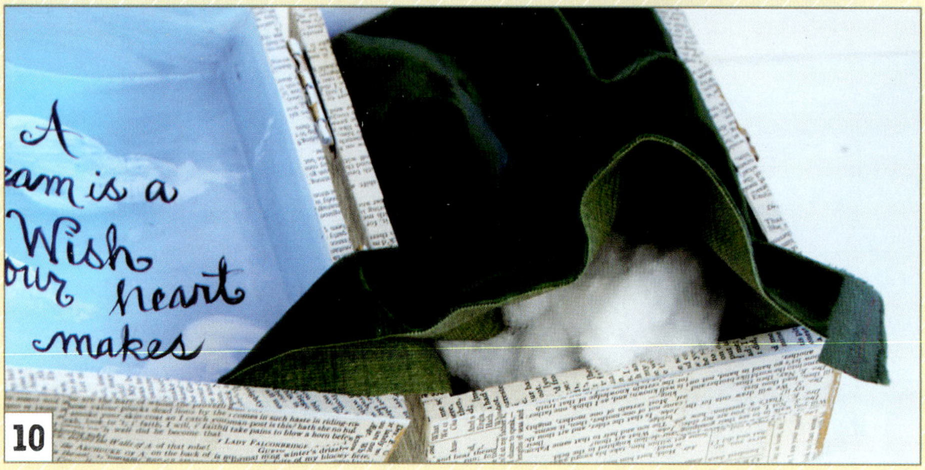

10

1. Cut your book pages in small squares and with some slightly watered down Elmer's glue, glue them to the entire outside of the box.
2. Paint the inside of the lid a light blue and let dry.
3. With the white, paint on some clouds and let dry.
4. With the black paint, paint your saying.
5. Print out the word WISHES on your pink copy paper, cut out, and glue gold glitter around the edges.
6. Write your wishes on plain paper and cut in strips and fill the bottle.
7. Glue the glitter edged wishes label on the bottle with the Elmer's.
8. Tie the ribbon around the neck of the bottle.
9. Fill the box with stuffing and press the bottle inside the stuffing so it takes shape around the bottle.
10. Place the velvet fabric over the stuffing and tuck the edges inside of the box.
11. Place the wish jar inside of the velvet and close the box.

Artwork & Patterns

These are the patterns I used for the projects in this book. You can photocopy them and use them to make your own Vision Boxes, or you can use other images that you find. It's up to you! You'll see some of the patterns repeated at different sizes. This is so you can use them for projects of any size. Have fun and let your creativity guide you!

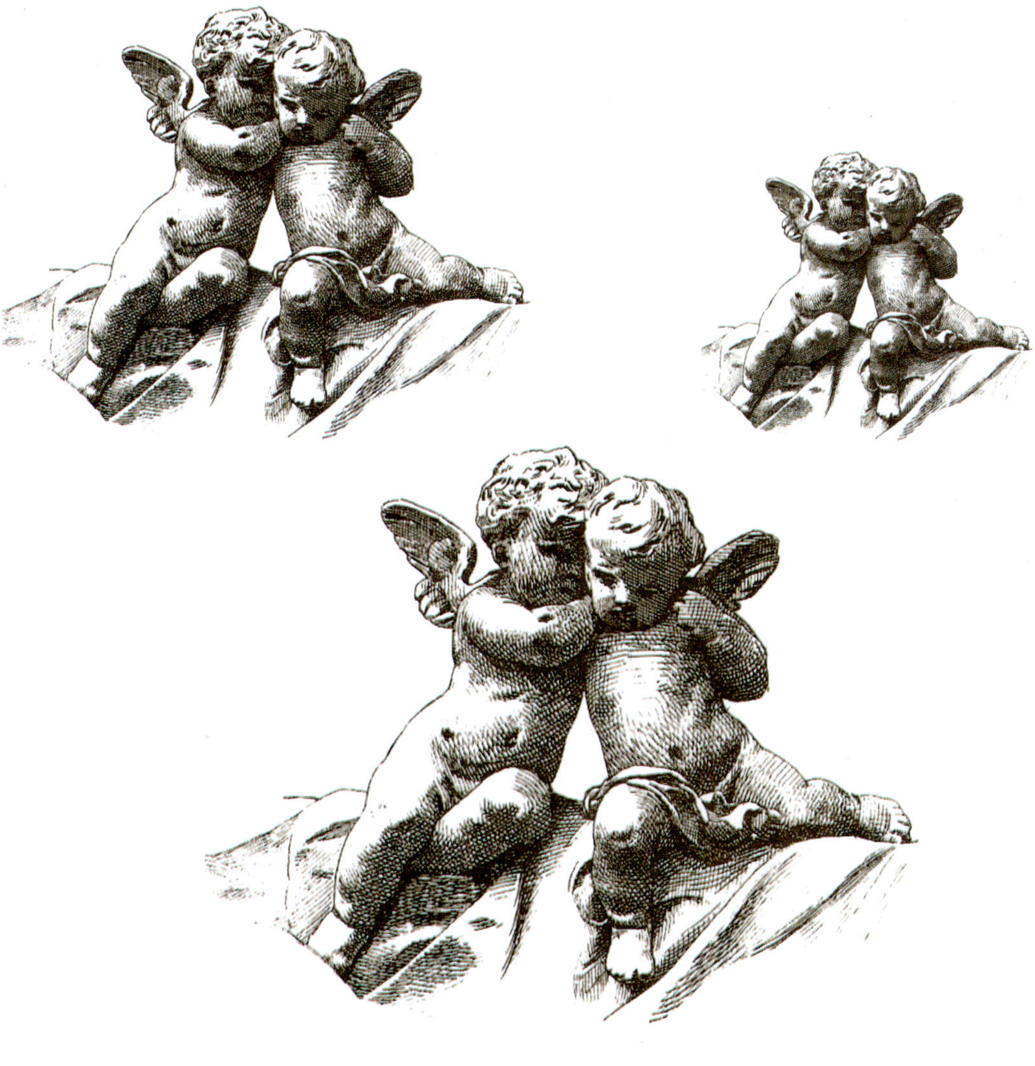

For *Pocket Angel Vision Box* pages 52–53

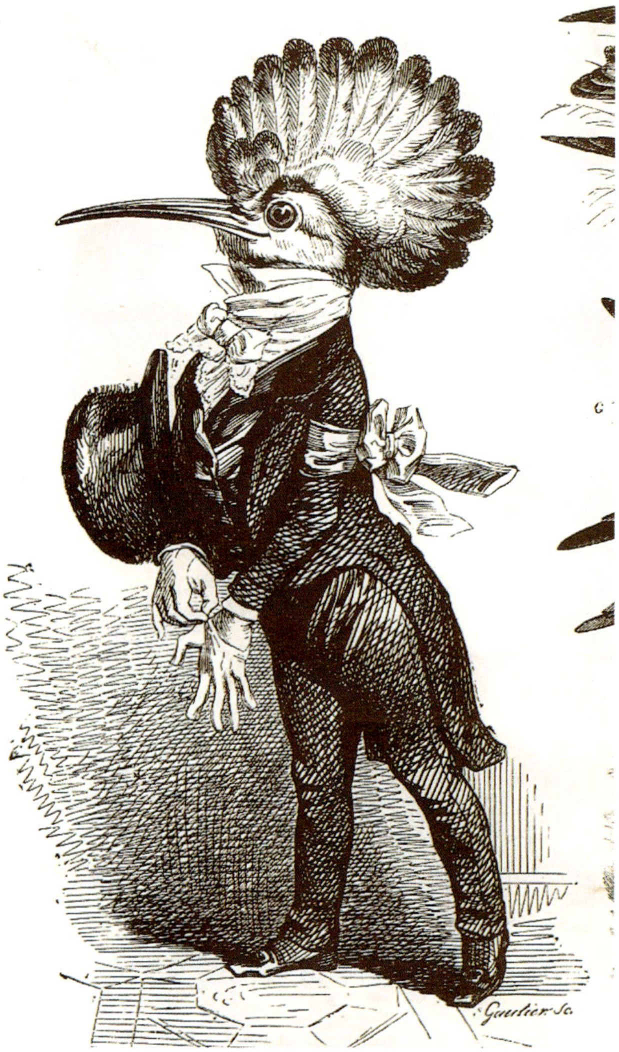

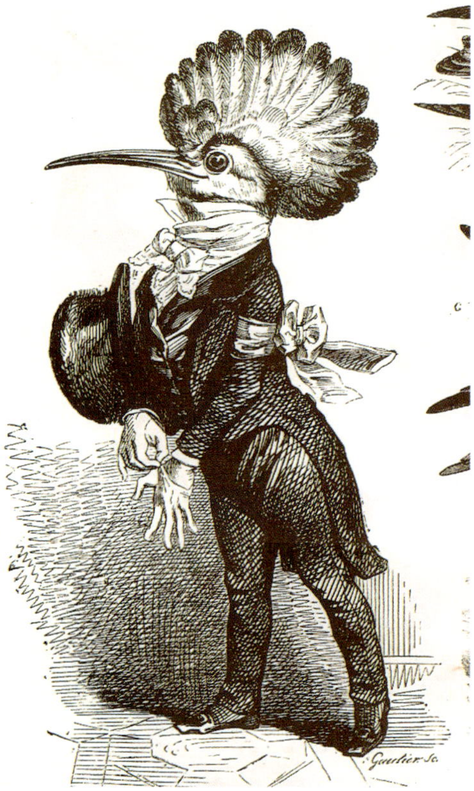

For *Flights of Fancy Vision Box* pages 24–25

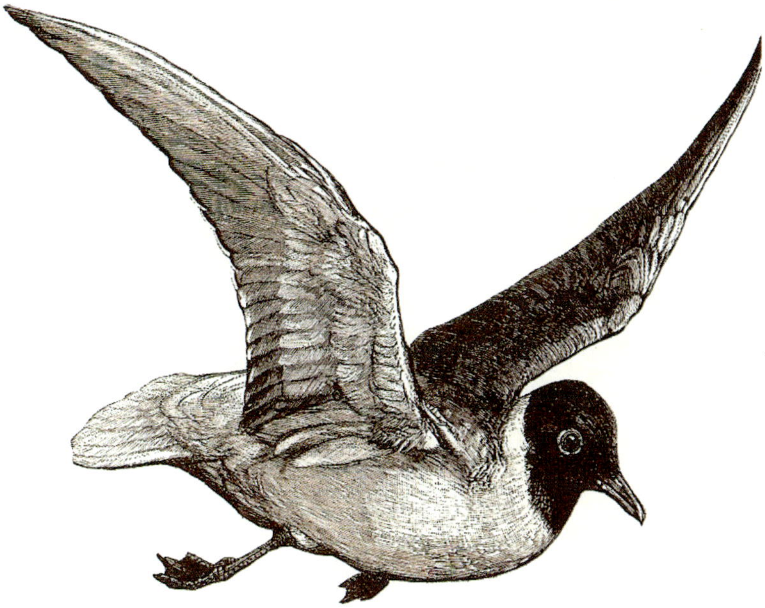

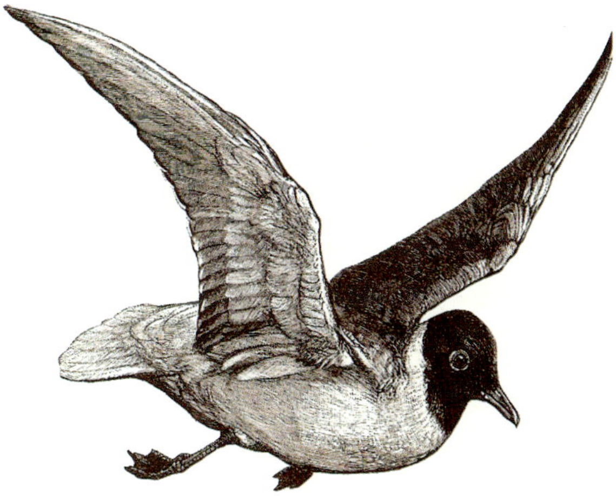

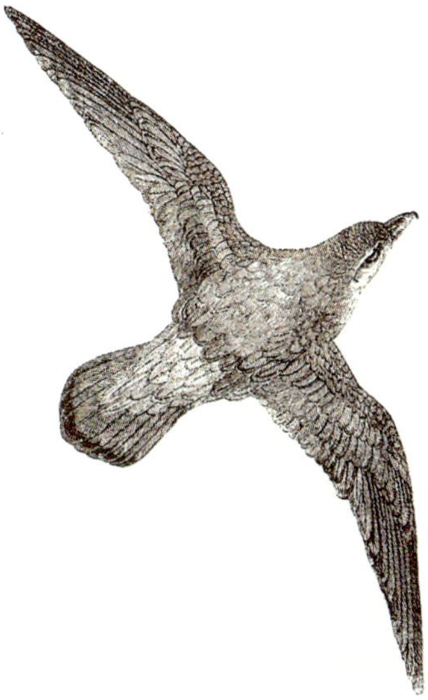

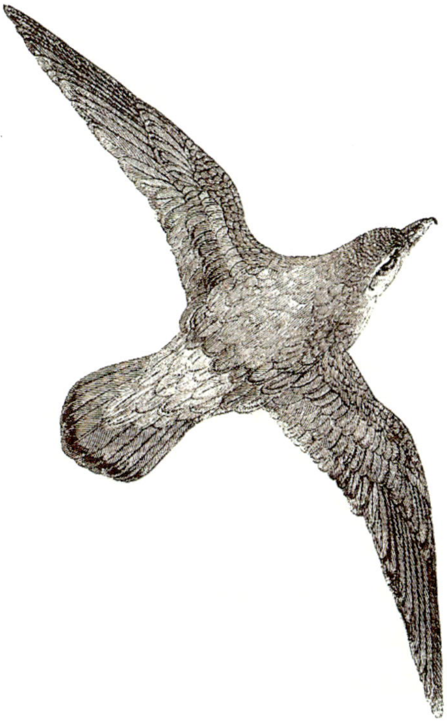

For *Flights of Fancy* and *Overcoming Obstacles Vision Boxes* pages 24–25 and 50–51

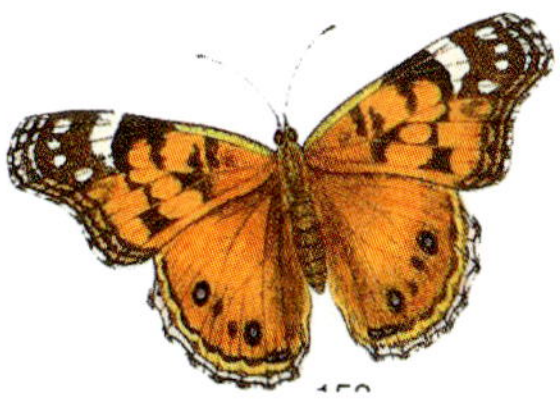

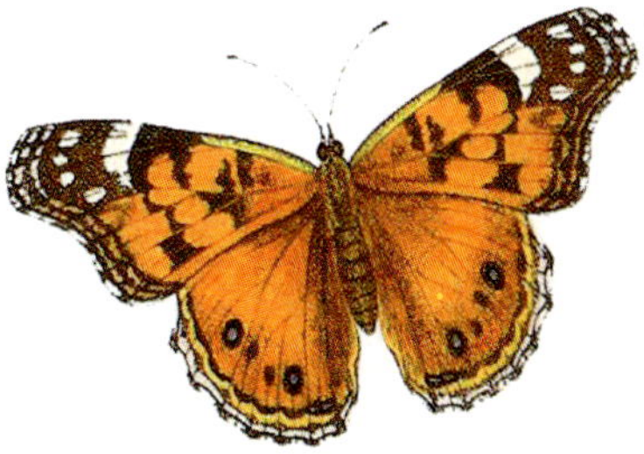

For *I AM Beautiful Vision Box* pages 32–33

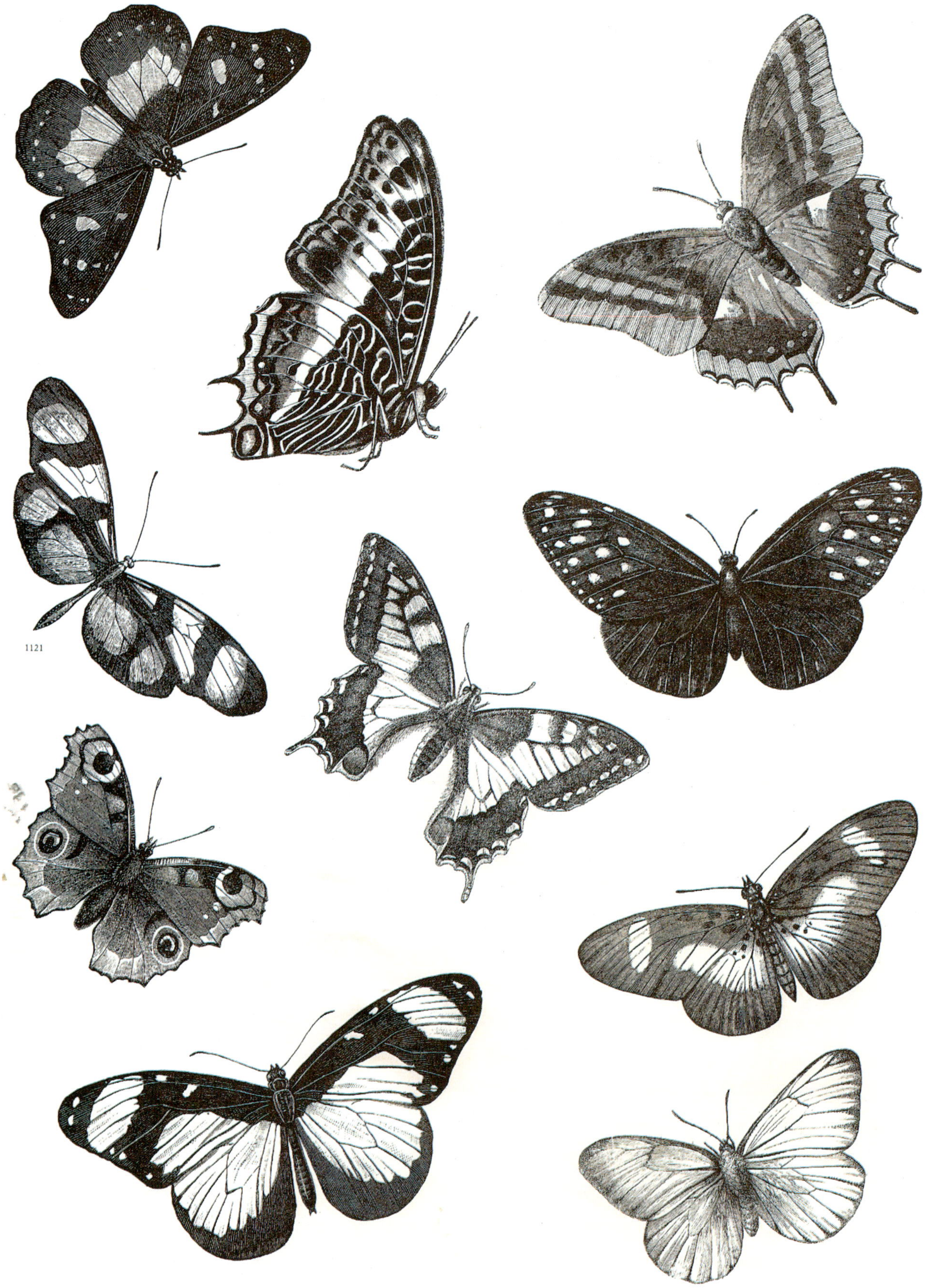

For *Flights of Fancy, Heart on My Sleeve, LIVE!, Overcoming Obstacles,* and *Untie My Heart Vision Boxes* pages 24–25, 28–29, 42–43, 50–51, and 58–59

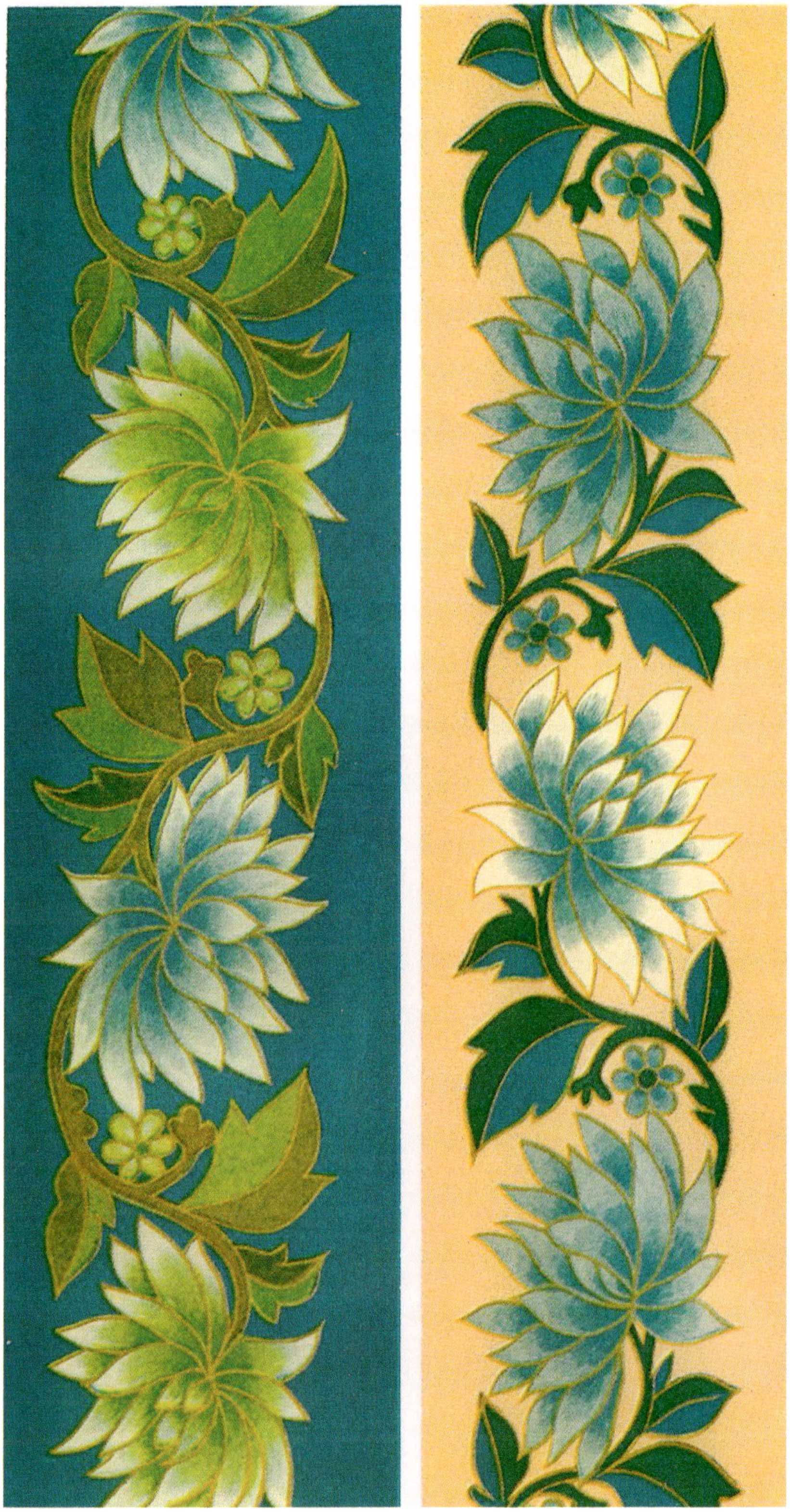

For *Flights of Fancy Vision Box* pages 24–25

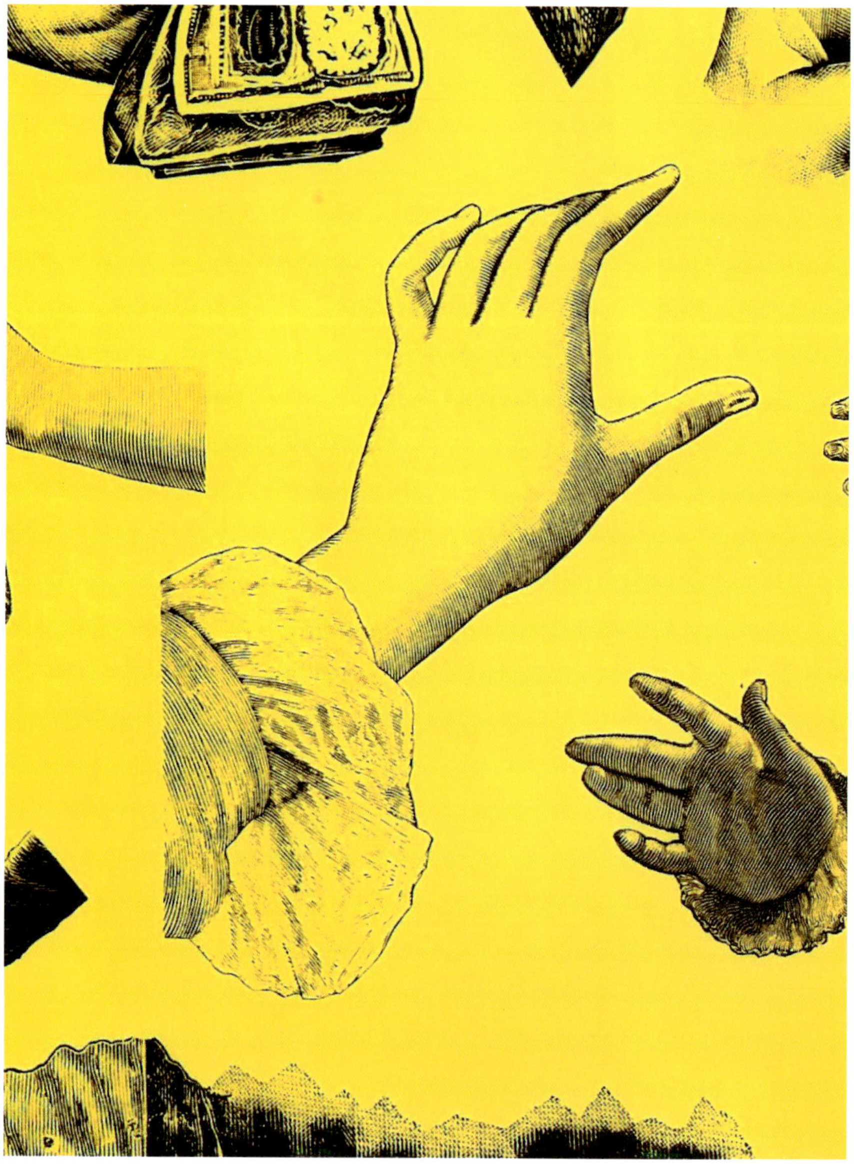

For *Live!* and *Untie My Heart Vision Boxes*
pages 42–43 and 58–59

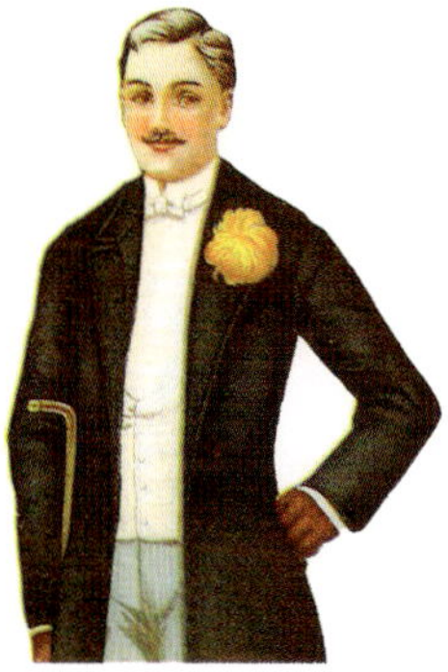

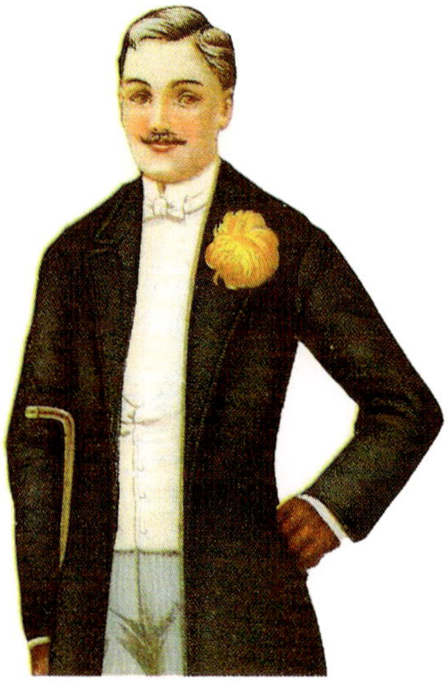

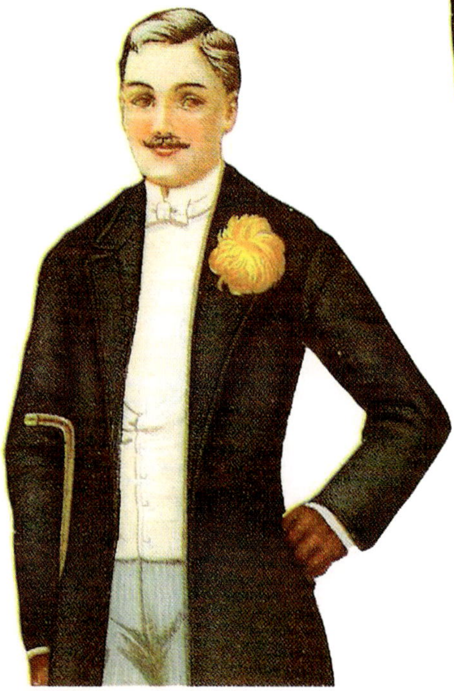

For *LIVE! Vision Box* pages 42–43

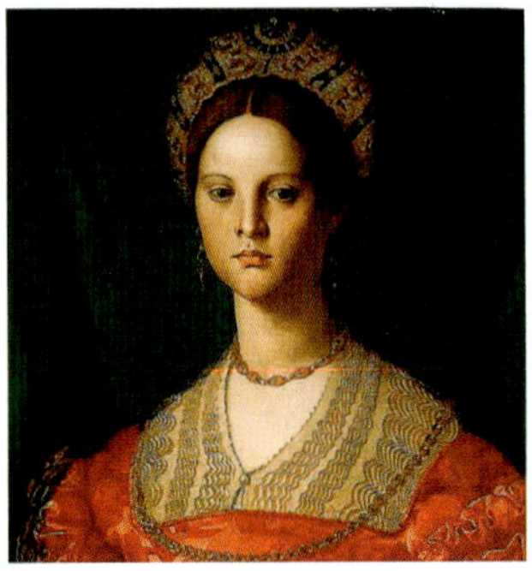

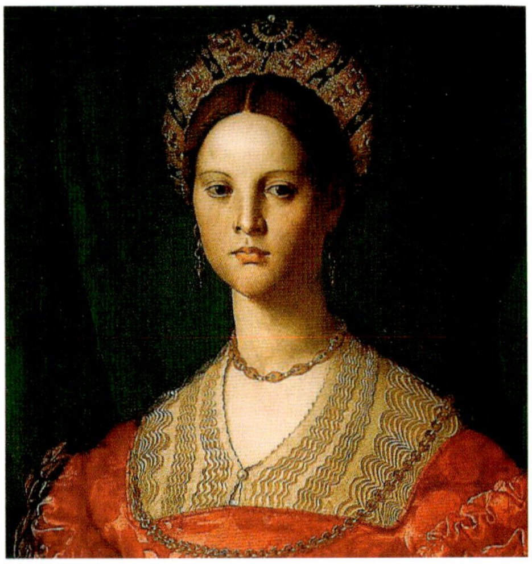

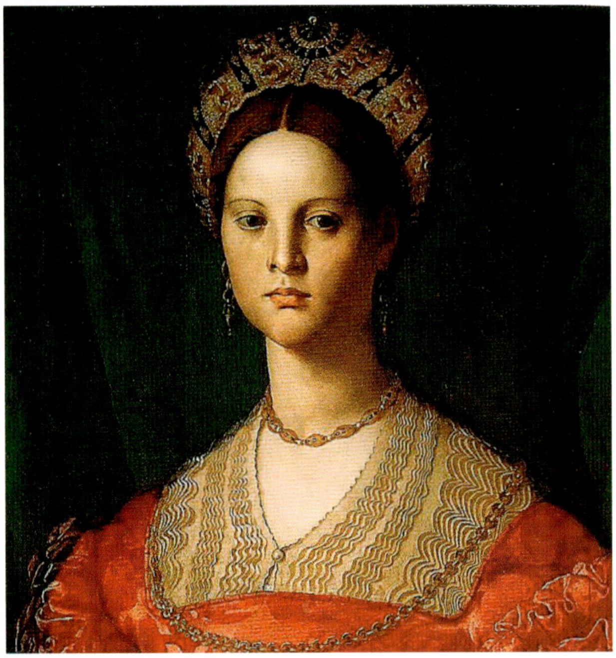

For *I AM Beautiful Vision Box* pages 32–33

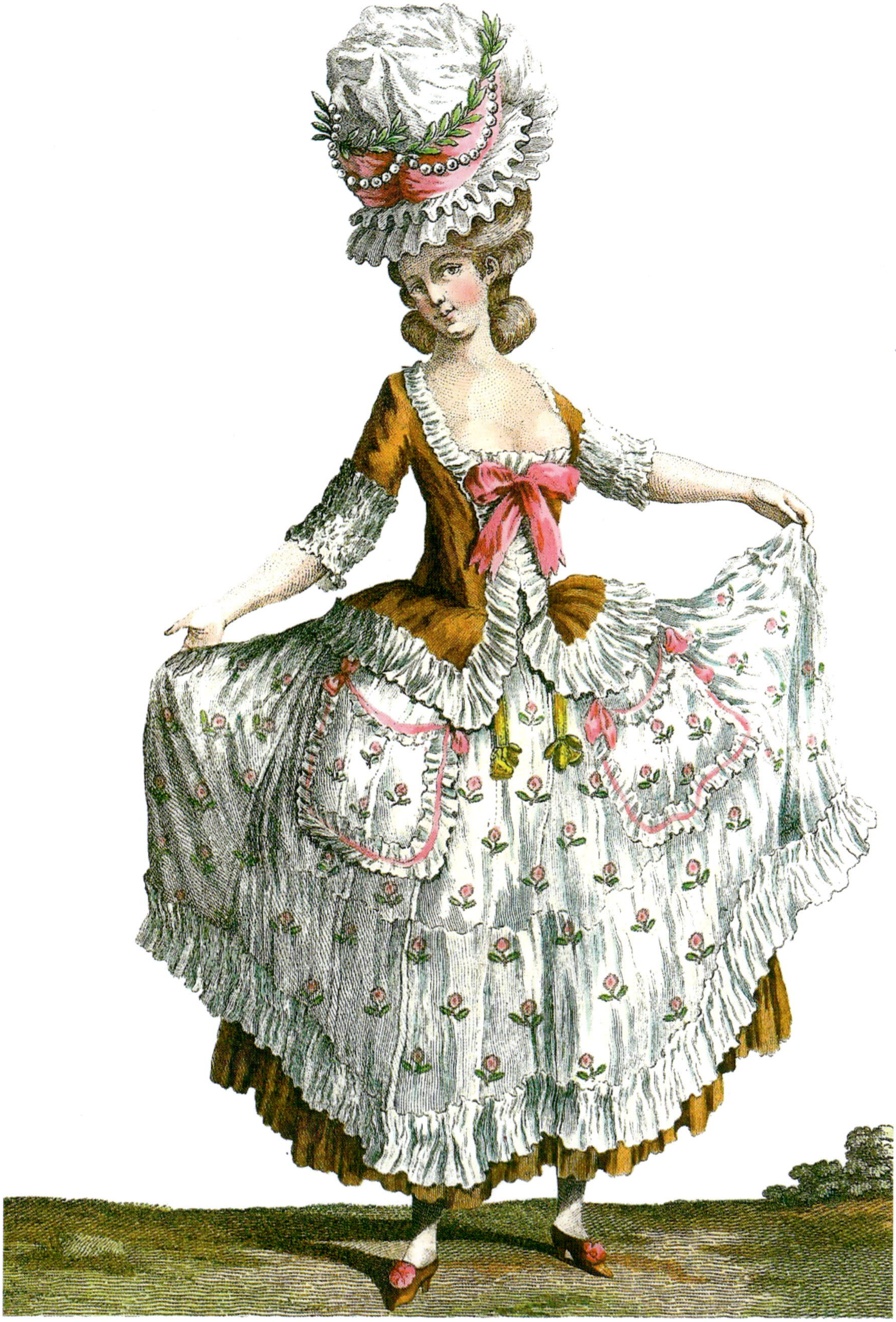

For *Live the Sweet Life Vision Box* pages 40–41

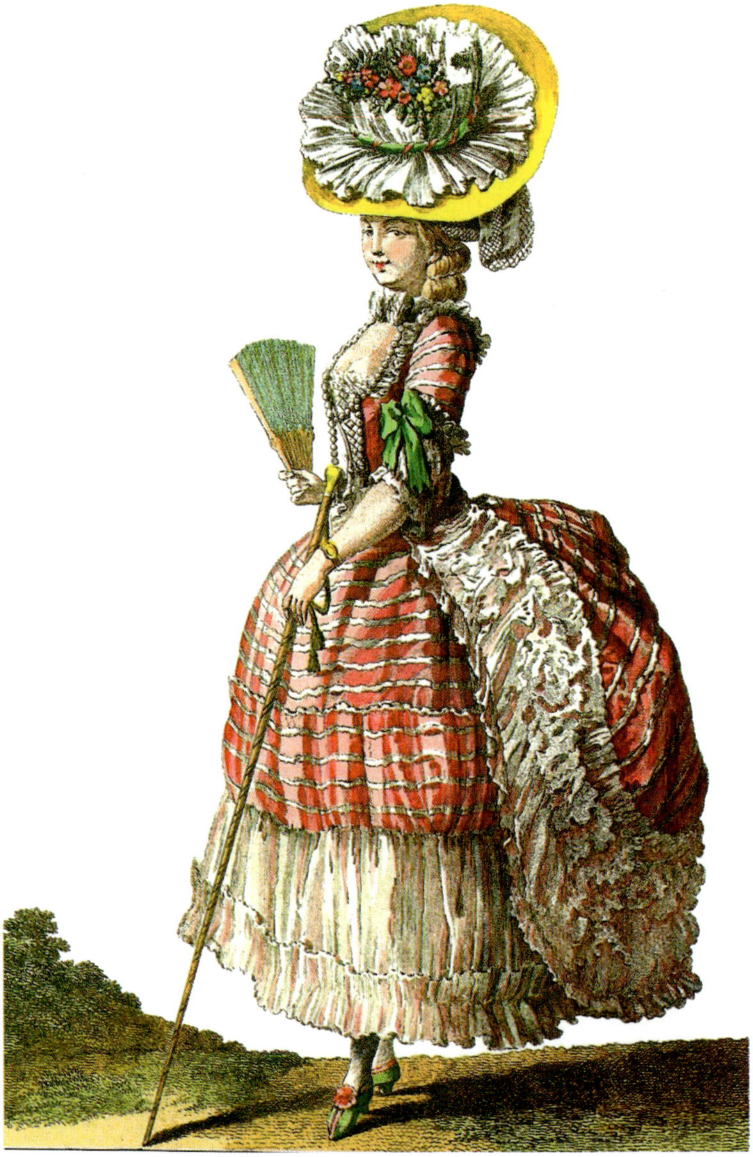

For *I WILL Stand Out Vision Box* pages 34–35

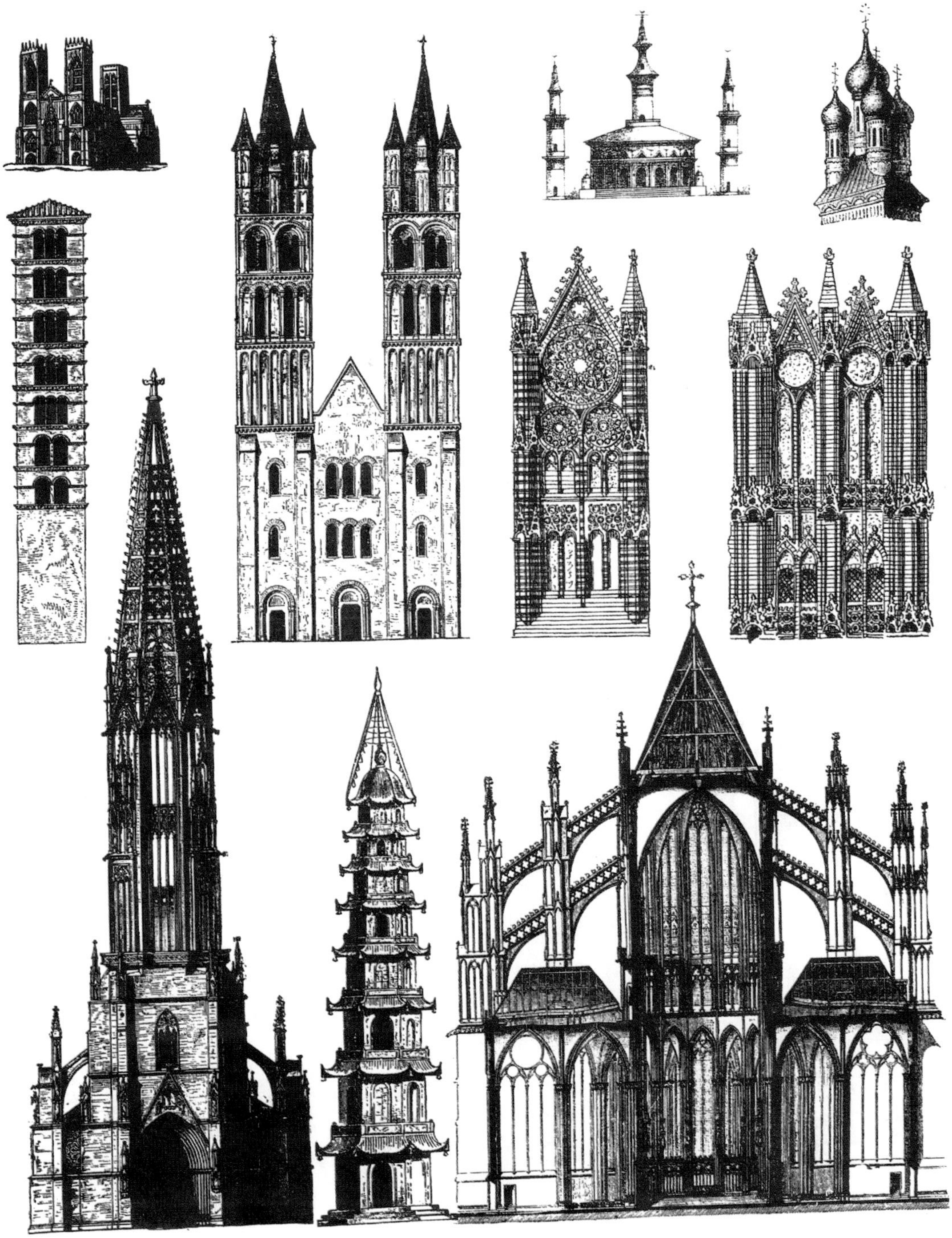

For *Overcoming Obstacles Vision Box* pages 50–51

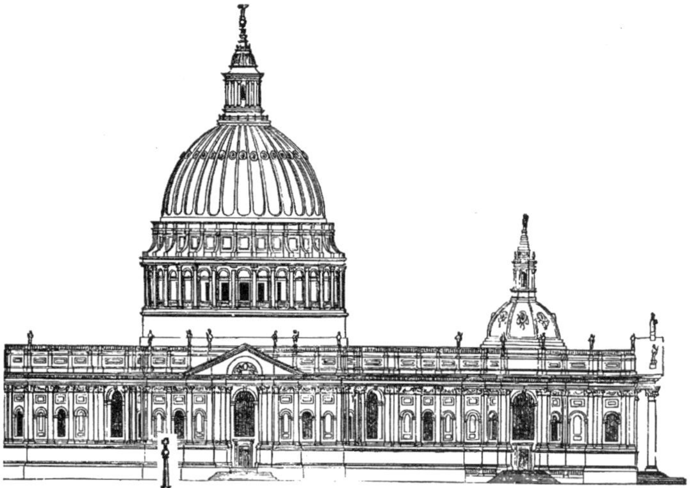

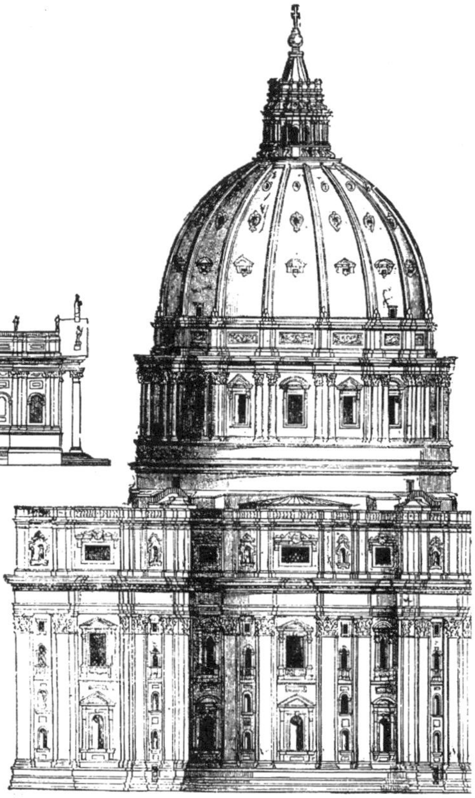

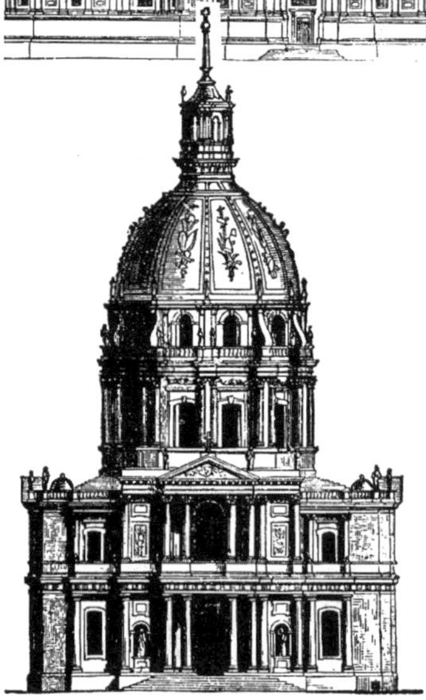

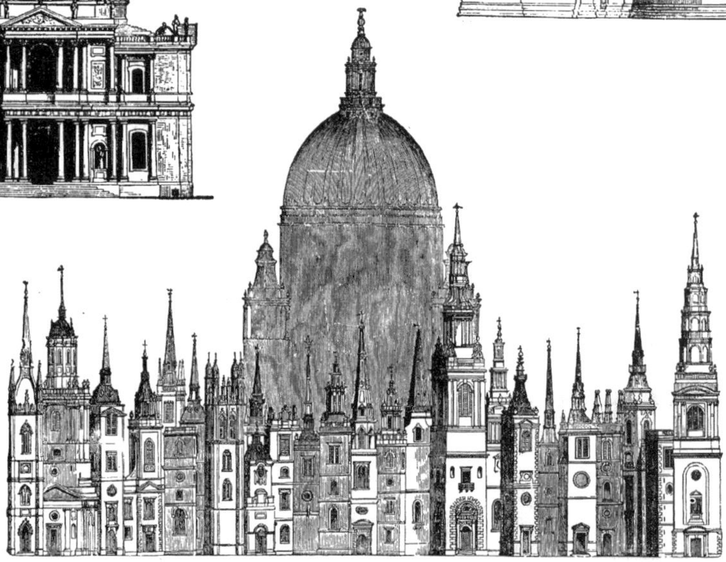

For *Overcoming Obstacles Vision Box* pages 50–51

For *My Super Powers Vision Box* pages 48–49

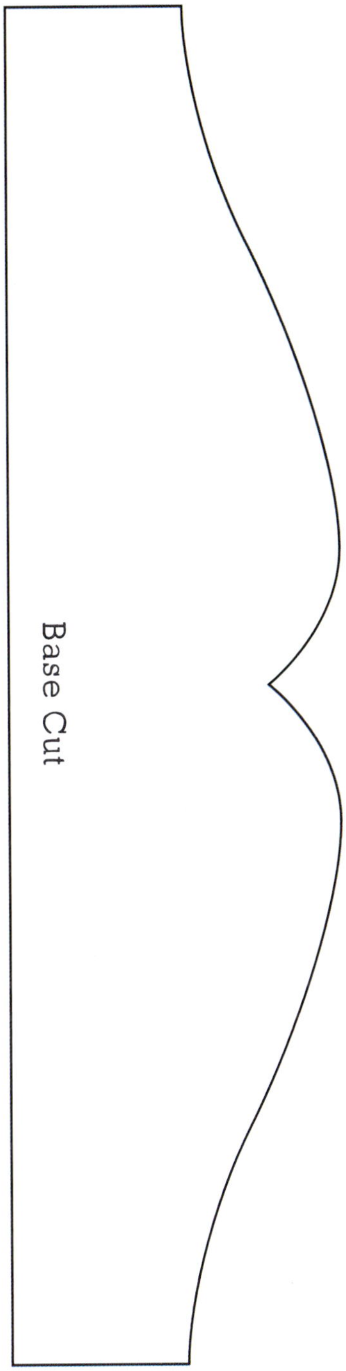

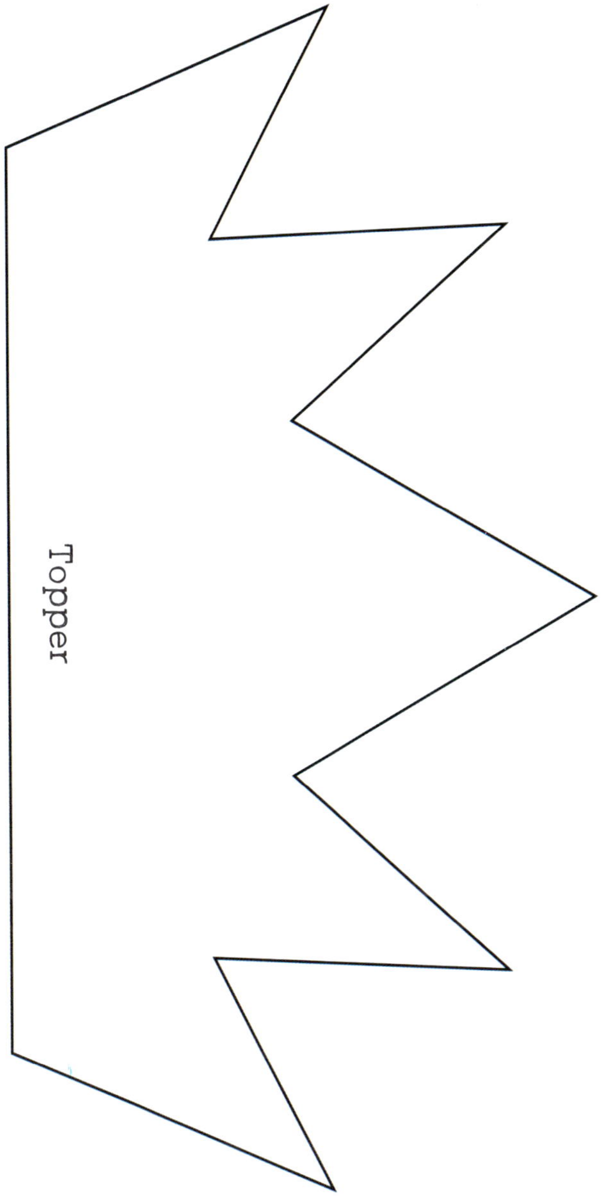

For *Live the Sweet Life! Vision Box* pages 40–41

For *Live the Sweet Life! Vision Box* pages 40–41

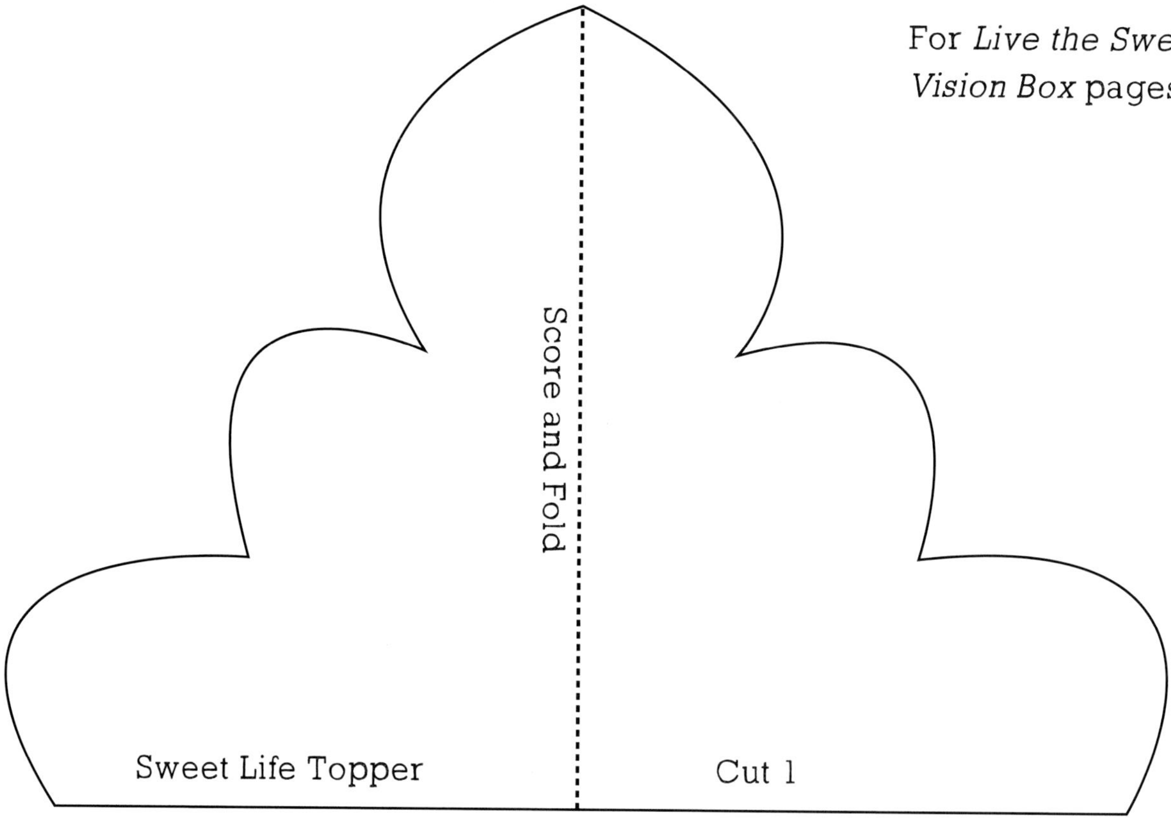

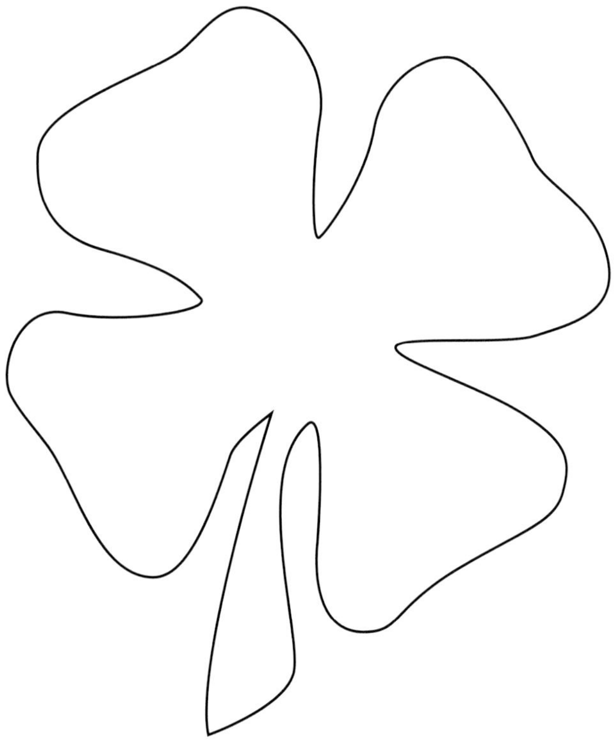

For *Lady Luck Vision Box* pages 46–47

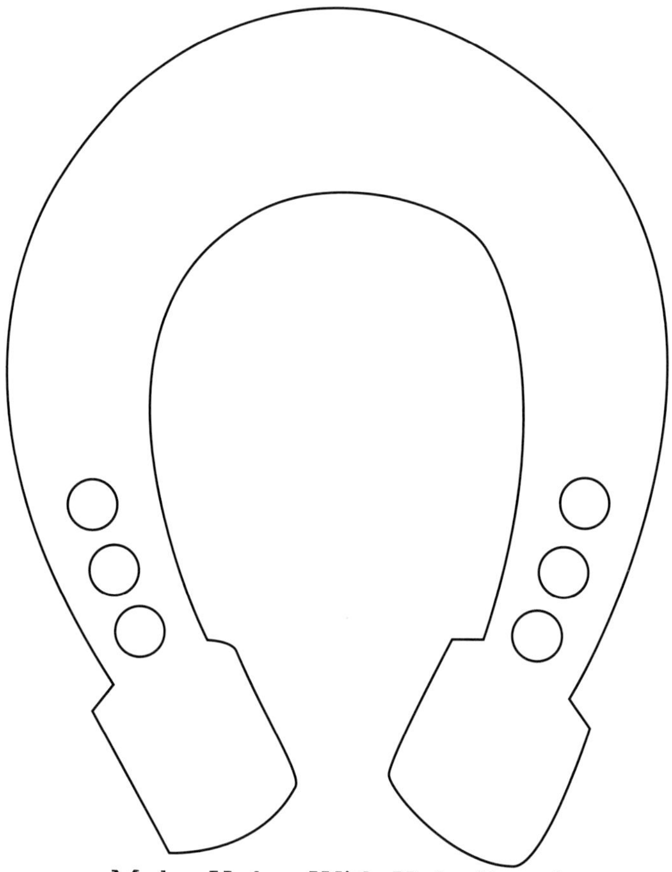

Make Holes With Hole Punch

I am beautiful * I am beautiful * I am beautiful

LIVE LAUGH PARTAKE ENJOY DIVE IN REJOICE LOUNGE RELAX

I will find love I will find love I will find love

I will find love I will find love I will find love

I will find love I will find love I will find love

I will find love I will find love I will find love

I will find love I will find love I will find love

I will find love I will find love I will find love

I will find love I will find love I will find love

Let Love happen.....
I'm right here Love.....
My heart is open.....
I'm ready when you are.....
I will find you Love....
Love is my destination....
I'm ready to share....
My other half is searching, too...
I will follow my heart....

For *Heart on My Sleeve, I AM Beautiful*, and *LIVE! Vision Boxes* pages 28–29, 32–33, and 42–43

Resource Guide

A.C. MOORE
www.acmoore.com
Wonderful craft store that's growing every year. Special items you can't find everywhere and great shopping atmosphere. I love it there and you will, too.

SILVER CROW CREATIONS
www.SilverCrowCreations.com
An amazing site with all kinds of terrific items for your Vision Boxes—truly special things that you won't be able to find anywhere else! Everything from baby dolls to tiny shoes and vintage charms. You'll love this site!

HOME DEPOT
www.homedepot.com
Great place to get the wood for your Vision Boxes and pick up your wood glue.

MICHAEL'S ARTS AND CRAFT STORES
www.michaels.com
Nationwide craft supply store that has everything. I used it like crazy for this book and you will, too.

FISKARS
www.fiskars.com
An amazing company that I couldn't get through my crafty day without. The best scissors ever. The razor edge scissors are my favorite and the Teflon scissors are a very close second.

JO-ANN FABRIC AND CRAFT STORES
www.joann.com
Terrific national fabric chain that just makes the world a better place. All of your fabric and sewing needs are here.

HOBBY LOBBY STORES, INC.
www.hobbylobby.com
Wonderful company with close to 500 stores nationwide! You'll definitely find some fun and special items and supplies here.

KRYLON SPRAY PAINT
www.krylon.com
Krylon products are available everywhere! Their new Glitter Blast spray paint is quickly becoming one of my favorite craft ingredients to use. Their Fusion spray paint can cover anything from a plastic chair to your neighbor's dog. It's amazing!

LOWE'S
www.lowes.com
It's a joy to shop at Lowe's. It's organized, the staff is knowledgeable, and you can find just about anything you need there for your projects.

ECLECTIC GLUE
(Makers of E-6000)
www.eclecticproducts.com
You cannot go wrong with these products because THEY WORK! Their line of adhesives is by far the best on the market.

STAPLES
www.staples.com
Get your copying done here! It's also a great place for things like stamp pads, envelopes, paper, photo paper, and cardstock.

99 CENT/DOLLAR STORES
What a great resource for just about anything you might need from ceramic birds for your *Love Nest Vision Box* to candy for your *Live The Sweet Life! Vision Box*. These stores should always be your first stop.

GOODWILL/SALVATION ARMY STORES
I found several boxes here to use for this book. I also found some terrific ceramic angels and birds. Right after hitting the 99¢ store, visit your neighborhood Goodwill or Salvation Army store. Save some money and help people out at the same time. Works for me!

PEARL RIVER
www.pearlriver.com
Amazing place for all of your Asian imports. If you are going for a Chinese theme, start by checking out this site. They ship, and the prices are great!

ELMER'S GLUE
www.elmers.com
You can find Elmer's everywhere, but just in case you want to see what else they carry, this is a good place to start. I like to buy the white glue by the gallon because I use so much. Their painters' pens are wonderful and X-Acto is also my go-to craft knife.

VINTAGEJEWELRYSUPPLIES.COM
Great place to get brass stampings like the crown seen on Frida Khalo on page 36. There are also tons of trinkets that would work well for your various Vision Box projects. I love this site. It's easy to use and the prices are fair.

YOUR TRASH BIN!
I believe we need to recycle as much as we can, so why not start by using what we discard for our projects? Cans, yogurt cups, plastic soda bottles...you name it—they are all perfect starts to many projects.

Index

Acquisition editor: Peg Couch

Copy editor: Heather Stauffer

Cover designer: Ashley Millhouse

Layout designers: Ashley Millhouse and Will Younger

Developmental editor: Paul Hambke

Assistant editor: Katie Weeber

Proofreader: Lynda Jo Runkle

Indexer: Jay Kreider

More Great Project Books from Design Originals

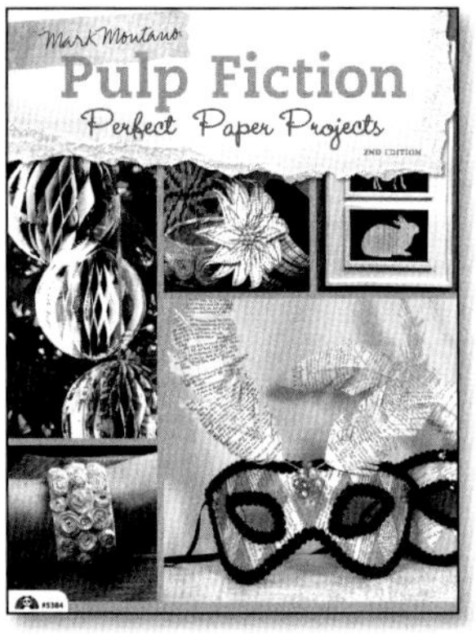

Pulp Fiction, 2nd Edition: Perfect Paper Projects

By Mark Montano

Breathe new life into found objects with these amazing and easy techniques presented by Mark Montano.

ISBN: 978-1-57421-413-0
$16.99 • 80 Pages

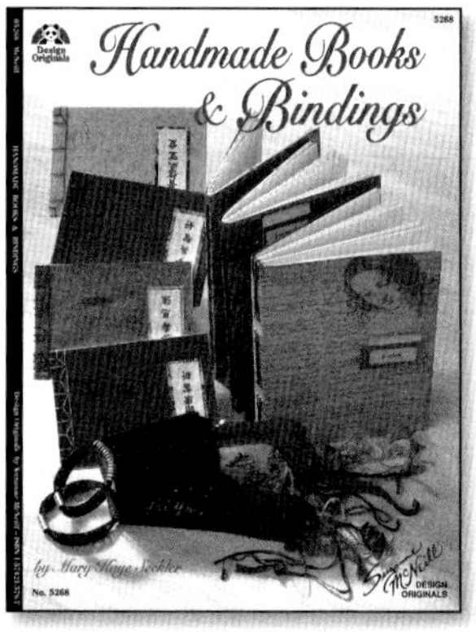

Handmade Books & Bindings

By Mary Kaye Seckler

Books & Bindings presents updated tools and techniques that make this ancient art form accessible.

ISBN: 978-1-57421-578-6
$16.99 • 52 Pages

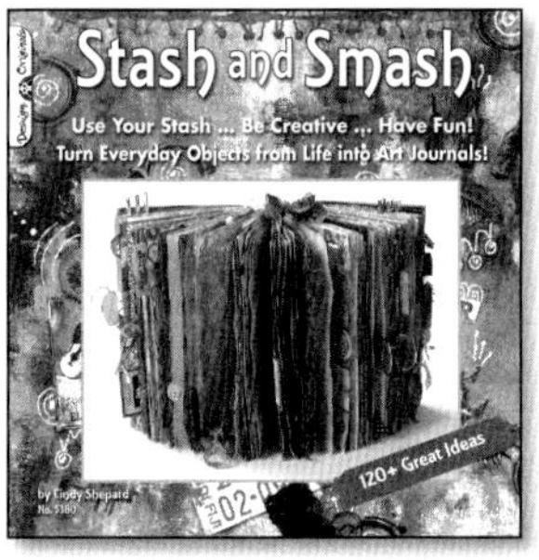

Stash & Smash: Art Journal Ideas

By Cindy Shepard

Be inspired to use your stash of papers, mementos and accents to create something wonderful! You'll find valuable tips, ideas, samples, and instructions for creating your very own 'Smash It In' journals.

ISBN: 978-1-57421-409-3
$16.99 • 48 Pages

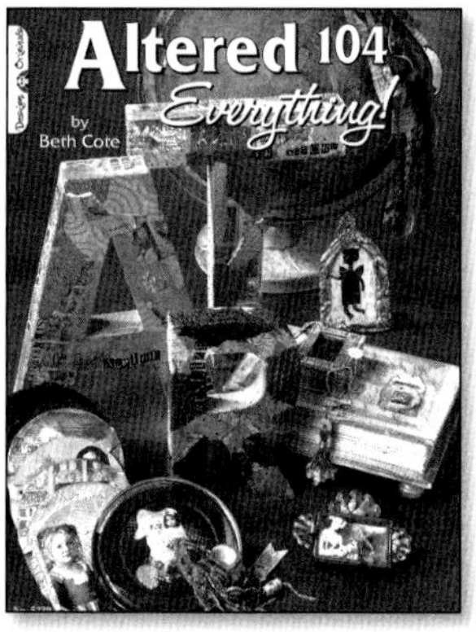

Altered 104

Everything

By Beth Cote

Alter your books, build shrines to memories, create tote bags, and reuse everything to make a personal work of art.

ISBN: 978-1-57421-549-6
$16.99 52 Pages

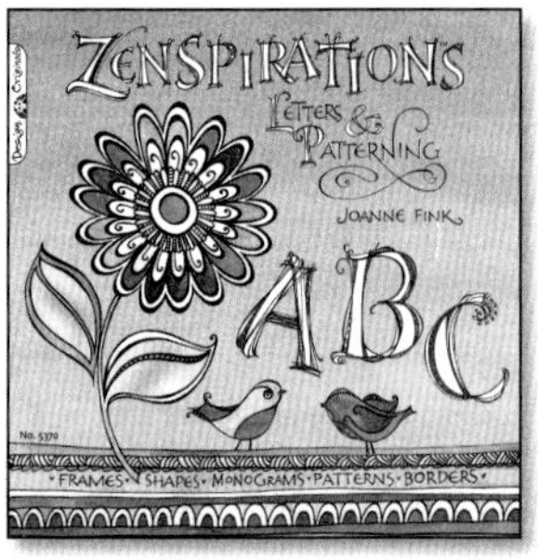

Zenspirations

Letters & Patterning

By Joanne Fink

Add interest and texture to any design using these decorative borders, frames, and shapes.

ISBN: 978-1-57421-699-8
$16.99 • 52 Pages

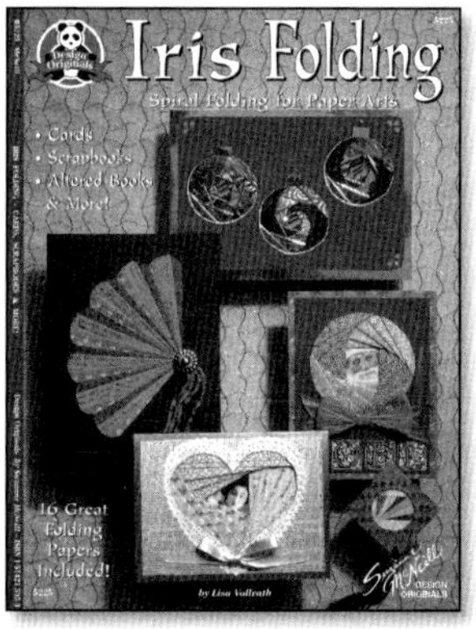

Iris Folding

Spiral Folding For Paper Arts

By Lisa Vollrath

Iris folding made easy—a great way to frame small photos, embellish bags and pages, and give focus to objects.

ISBN: 978-1-57421-535-9
$12.99 • 36 Pages

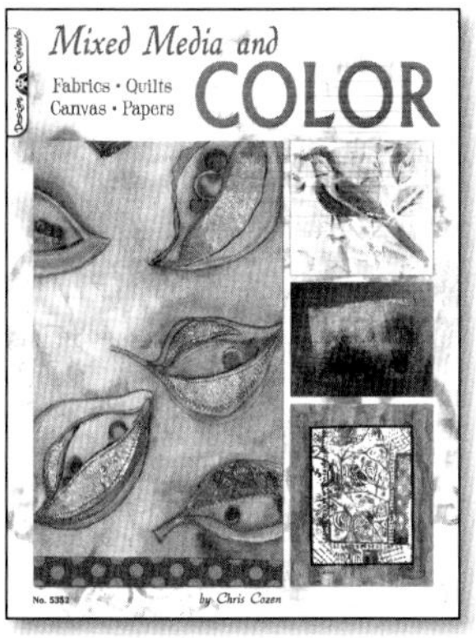

Mixed Media And Color

Fabrics, Quilts, Canvas, Papers

By Chris Cozen

Discover the unexpected and find yourself in a colorful fusion of exciting textures, paint and print.

ISBN: 978-1-57421-663-9
$18.99 • 52 Pages

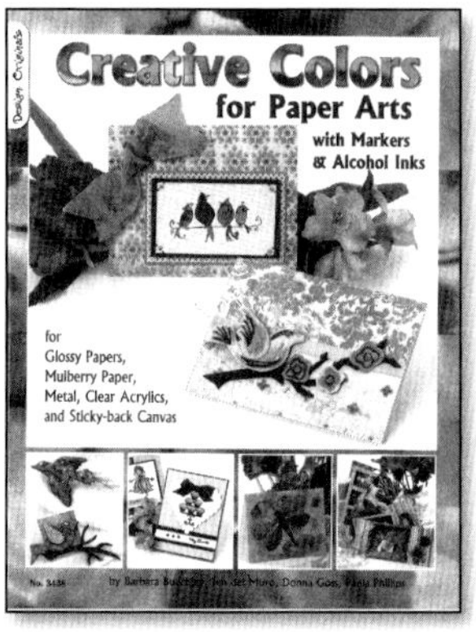

Creative Colors For Paper Arts

with Markers and Alcohol Inks

By Paula Philips, Jen De Muro, Donna Goss & Barbara Guechley

Add color with inexpensive markers and inks to colorize paper, acrylic, and canvas.

ISBN: 978-1-57421-290-7
$9.99 36 Pages

Look for These Books at Your Local Bookstore or Specialty Retailer

To order direct, call **800-457-9112** or visit *www.D-Originals.com*
By mail, please send check or money order + S&H to:
Fox Chapel Publishing, 1970 Broad Street, East Petersburg, PA 17520

# Item	US Shipping Rate
1 Item	$3.25
Each Additional	.25

Canadian & International Orders – please email d-originals.com@foxchapelpublishing.com or visit our website for actual shipping costs.